Critical Essays on
E. B. WHITE

CRITICAL ESSAYS
ON
AMERICAN LITERATURE

James Nagel, General Editor
University of Georgia, Athens

◆

Critical Essays on
E. B. WHITE

◆

edited by

ROBERT L. ROOT, JR.

G. K. Hall & Co. / New York
Maxwell Macmillan Canada / Toronto
Maxwell Macmillan International / New York Oxford Singapore Sydney

G. K. Hall & Co.
Macmillan Publishing Co.
866 Third Avenue
New York, New York 10022

Maxwell Macmillan Canada, Inc.
1200 Eglinton Avenue East
Suite 200
Don Mills, Ontario M3C 3N1

Library of Congress Cataloging-in-Publication Data

Critical essays on E.B. White / edited by Robert L. Root. Jr.
       p.   cm.—(Critical essays on American literature)
    Includes bibliographical references and index.
    ISBN 0-8161-7321-4
    1. White, E. B. (Elwyn Brooks), 1899– —Criticism and
interpretation.   I. Root, Robert L.   II. Series.
PR3545.H5187Z62   1994
818'.5209—dc20   93-38334
                                                                      CIP

The paper used in this publication meets the minimum requirements of American National Standard for Information Sciences—Permanence of Paper for Printed Library Materials. ANSI Z3948-1984.∞™

10   9   8   7   6   5   4   3   2   1

Printed in the United States of America

To my father,
Robert L. Root

Contents

♦

General Editor's Note

◆

This series seeks to anthologize the most important criticism on a wide variety of topics and writers in American literature. Our readers will find in various volumes not only a generous selection of reprinted articles and reviews, but original essays, bibliographies, manuscript sections, and other materials brought to public attention for the first time. This volume, *Critical Essays on E. B. White*, is the most comprehensive collection of essays ever published on one of the most important modern writers in the United States. It contains both a sizable gathering of early reviews and a broad selection of more modern scholarship as well. Among the authors of reprinted articles and reviews are Diana Trilling, James Thurber, John Updike, Joseph Wood Krutch, Malcolm Cowley, and Donald Hall. In addition to a substantial introduction by Robert L. Root, Jr., there are also two original essays commissioned specifically for publication in this volume, new studies by Ken Smith and Richard Nordquist on the rhetorical strategies in White's prose. We are confident that this book will make a permanent and significant contribution to the study of American literature.

JAMES NAGEL
University of Georgia, Athens

Publisher's Note

◆

Producing a volume that contains both newly commissioned and reprinted material presents the publisher with the challenge of balancing the desire to achieve stylistic consistency with the need to preserve the integrity of works first published elsewhere. In the Critical Essays series, essays commissioned especially for a particular volume are edited to be consistent with G. K. Hall's house style; reprinted essays appear in the style in which they were first published, with only typographical errors corrected. Consequently, shifts in style from one essay to another are the result of our efforts to be faithful to each text as it was originally published.

Critical Approaches to E. B. White: A Bibliographical Introduction

♦

ROBERT L. ROOT, JR.

E. B. White was a children's author, an essayist, a stylist, and a humorist. Readers tend to admire him primarily for one or more of those roles. He was also an indefatigable letter writer, a poet who wrote light verse, an editorialist, and the glib jokester of countless *New Yorker* "newsbreaks." His versatility as a writer makes measuring his accomplishment difficult. The task would be simplified if he had concentrated on a single genre, producing an oeuvre which might be compared to others of established literary merit. And yet, White's personality, and the intelligence, wit, and grace of his language, both unify his work, and make it singular. He is the standard against which others are measured, a major writer sui generis, in a field bounded only by his own achievements.

White began writing at an early age. Born 11 July 1899, in Mt. Vernon, New York, the youngest of six children, White's letters to his older siblings and parents give early evidence of his lively humor and casual grace. His early successes—a silver badge at age 11 and a gold badge at age 14 for stories published in *St. Nicholas*, a children's magazine—encouraged him to pursue writing. He wrote for his high school paper and was editor-in-chief of the *Cornell Daily Sun* as an undergraduate, contributing humor and poetry as well as editorials. In a sense his work for the *New Yorker* from 1926 through 1957 was merely an extension of his adolescent literary activity. Along the way he occasionally published "clipbooks" of his previously published poetry and prose; his only full-length books of previously unpublished material were three widely spaced children's novels. At the end of his career he was given more "gold badges"—honorary degrees from distinguished universities, awards such as the National Medal for Literature, a Pulitzer Special Citation, the Laura Ingalls Wilder Award, and the Presidential Medal of Freedom. He continued to write into his eighties and died on 30 October, 1985. Notices of his passing were reverent, often affectionate.

Shortly after White's death, essayist Joseph Epstein wrote that White's "was a career that strained after significance; but despite all the honors he won, he himself was never quite convinced he had achieved it." In Epstein's view his "obituarists and eulogists (they were one and the same)" had over-looked the darkness running through his writing, thus "obscuring . . . both the man he was and the writer he wished to be," leaving him "a writer vastly overrated and mostly misunderstood."[1] Similarly, essayist Phillip Lopate observed that while no one had "written more consistently graceful, thoughtful essays in twentieth-century American language," White had a "sedating influence on the form. White's Yankee gentleman-farmer persona is a complex balancing act between Whitmanian democratic and patrician values, best suited for the expression of mildness and tenderness with a resolute tug of elegaic depression underneath."[2] Both Epstein and Lopate respond to the persona of White's essays and have difficulty reconciling "elegaic depression" and "darkness" with the grace and humor so much admired in his prose. In essence, critical responses to White's writing depend upon interpretations of his persona in any given work. While this collection will give some sense of the range of those responses, it is at best only a representative sampling. This introduction will therefore provide both an overview of critical responses to White's various roles, as well as a context for the selected reviews and essays which follow.

HUMORIST AND POET

The earliest published critical responses to White focus on his work as a humorist and writer of light verse. His prose parodies, sketches, and parables had frequently appeared in the *New Yorker* before his first prose book, *Is Sex Necessary? Or, Why You Feel The Way You Do*, coauthored with James Thurber, was published in 1929. The reviews of *Is Sex Necessary?*, a parody of contemporary sex advice books, tended to be positive but also light, and even silly in keeping with the book's tone.[3] Thurber and White were acknowledged as accomplished humorists, ranked with such current and established figures as Stephen Leacock, Robert Benchley, Dorothy Parker, and Alexander Woolcott, all of whom wrote for the *New Yorker*.

White stayed closely involved with the magazine throughout the thirties. His only books were: two collections of "newbreaks," *Ho Hum* (1931) and *Another Ho Hum* (1932), both illustrated by O. Soglow; *Every Day is Saturday* (1934), a collection of "Notes and Comment" paragraphs; and *Farewell to Model T* (1936), a small book illustrated by Alain, reprinting an essay he had published under the name Lee Strout White. Though these volumes were slight, his weekly association with the *New Yorker* had already established him as a paragrapher and humorist by the time *Quo Vadimus?, or, The Case for the Bicycle* (1939), a collection of sketches, stories, and satires, appeared. Book reviewers took him more seriously, identifying him as "that penetrating observer of contemporary affairs"[4] and commenting admiringly on his prose style.[5] They also began to recognize the seriousness behind White's humor, observing that "he still considers being a humorist no laughing matter"[6] and pointing out a quality in his humor "strangely dreamlike . . . in a faintly nightmarish fashion."[7] Irwin Edman claimed that White's prose had always been "marked by a curious felicity, half anguish and half gaiety. It was edged fantasy, and at once whimsical and malign"; he credited White with being "an American humorist who is an American philosopher."[8]

This shift in critical attitude toward White may have been encouraged by James Thurber's affectionate profile in the *Saturday Review of Literature*, and Leonard Bacon's assessment of White, along with Thurber and Ogden Nash, in a subsequent article in that magazine.[9] Sounding a note that would resurface throughout critical considerations of White, Bacon objected to the "absurd prejudice in our minds which makes us believe that what is lightly said is probably trivial." In this he concurred with White's observation in his introduction to *A Subtreasury of American Humor* (1941) that "the world likes humor, but it treats it patronizingly. It decorates its serious artists with laurel and its wags with Brussels sprouts. It feels that if a thing is funny it can be presumed to be something less than great, because if it were truly great it would be serious."[10] Reviews of *A Subtreasury of American Humor*, coedited with his wife, Katharine S. White, singled out the introduction in particular for praise as "a major and most rewarding analysis of humor."[11] But by the time the book appeared, White's engagement with other genres would make his identification as a humorist less pronounced.

In "How to Tell a Major Poet from a Minor Poet" White observed that "any poem starting with 'And when' is a serious poem written by a major poet . . . Any poem, on the other hand, ending with 'And how' comes under the head of light verse, written by a minor poet"; moreover, "all poets whose work appears in 'The Conning Tower' of the *World*" [where White published much of his poetry] "are minor, because the *World* is printed on uncoated stock—which is offensive to major poets."[12] White had had occasion to observe the low critical regard for light verse in the reviews of his first collection of poetry, *The Lady is Cold* (1929); "How to Tell . . .", originally published in 1930, was undoubtedly a reaction to some of those reviews.

Edna May Walton's review, for example, patronizingly identified the "writer of light verse" as someone who "has a way of being just exactly where everyone else has been." Walton, who claimed that good light verse demands an ability to be "facile, subtle, amusing, and at the same time, obvious," acknowledged that White's "very deft psychological sonnets" are better than those of "many professing poetry," and attributed his failing to "probe very deeply into his own emotions" to his desire to please readers who would object to the "too-personal."[13] Walton's review implies a host of litmus tests for telling a major poet from a minor poet; another reviewer compared him favorably with Dorothy Parker and A. A. Milne, while acknowledging he was "a skilful versifier with a rare sensitiveness for words" who showed "flashes of poetic distinction."[14] Clearly light verse could be appreciated but not accepted as the work of one "professing poetry." Nearly ten years later, White's second collection, *The Fox of Peapack and Other Poems* (1938), was judged to be "a necessity to anyone who likes excellent light verse, nonsense verse, and parody."[15] Nevertheless, a critic who found White to be "more original" than Ogden Nash, with "a quality of wistfulness and true poetry," felt that American light verse had reached its limit.[16]

Although some verse appeared in *The Second Tree From the Corner* (1953), *The Fox of Peapack* was White's final collection of poetry. In 1981, as part of a continuing project to publish a uniform edition of his work, begun with *The Letters of E. B. White* (1977) and *The Essays of E. B. White* (1978), White compiled *The Poems and Sketches of E. B. White*. The poems were drawn from his published anthologies as well as uncollected and unpublished sources. Critical response to the collection varied widely: some critics concluded that White "was not a poet,"[17] that "the poems are not great literature,"[18] and that the poems "lack the wit we are accustomed to find in White's prose"[19]; others identified him as "one of the most charming writers of light verse around . . . capable on occasion of writing lyrics fully as affecting as the best of his essays"[20] and felt that "at his best White reaches past light verse to the territory of Housman, with simple and classic declarations that may outlast his weightier works."[21]

The prose in *Poems and Sketches* was generally more favorably received. It included no unpublished pieces; most had appeared in the *New Yorker* and had already been republished in *Quo Vadimus?* or *The Second Tree From the Corner*. Many were parables, short stories, and parodies; some were "Notes and Comment" paragraphs. Most reviewers found it far weaker than the earlier collection of essays; Edward Hoagland wrote that "the sketches which resemble short stories are nowhere near the caliber of those which amount to short essays."[22]

There are few extended analyses of White as a humorist. Edward Martin, in *H. L. Mencken and the Debunkers*, identifies White as a "satiric commentator on American culture," "less savage than Mencken or Marquis," and notes that "he tends toward the nonsensical and the fabulous as his most comfortable modes of expression"; Norris Yates connects White to the tradition of humor he drew upon at the start of his career and sees the influence permeating White's less obviously "humorous" later work.[23] Stephen L. Tanner examines White's theory of humor as expounded in his preface to the *Subtreasury*, interviews, and letters and illustrated in his own practice; Thomas Grant analyzes White's humor as it appears in his sketches, essays, and poems about New York City.[24]

Paragrapher and Essayist

Despite the amount of poetry and humor that White published, the chief focus of his writing during the late twenties and throughout the thirties was the *New Yorker*'s anonymous "Notes and Comment" page, several separate paragraphs per week for which White was the principal—and often the sole—contributor. *Every Day is Saturday* (1934) reprinted 229 "Notes and Comment" paragraphs and established White as the page's primary author. Reviewers of the collection were casual about identifying the form, calling them "short essays" or "editoral paragraphs" or nothing at all[26]—one reviewer eschewed labeling and quoted liberally from White to illustrate a comparison with Thoreau.[27] Morris Bishop later claimed that the pieces in *Every Day is Saturday* "represent the apotheosis of the paragraph. . . . It is the poetic substance in these paragraphs which makes them still radioactive in many memories."[28]

The success of the essay "Farewell, My Lovely" (later published in book form as *Farewell to Model T*) may have helped White to decide to give up the weekly grind of paragraphs in favor of more personal and serious literary work. In 1937 White took a sabbatical from the magazine and after moving with his wife and son to Maine in 1938, began writing a monthly column, "One Man's Meat," for *Harper's Magazine*. The column retained many of the features of the "Notes and Comment" page—White's wit, style, personality, and his habit of clustering several short pieces—and allowed more personal observation and serious reflection, of increasing importance to White as the world headed toward war.

When the columns were collected in *One Man's Meat*, published first in 1942 and then in an expanded version in 1944, reviewers treated White with a new seriousness. Rose Feld observed, "Blessed with a critical mind, a gift for simplicity of expression and a wry sense of humor he emerges as a man with something to say, not a self-conscious author."[29] Other critics connected him to the literary tradition of the essay. Irwin Edman in particular insisted that "White has hauntingly combined the poetry of observation and the philosophy of shrewd, usually gentle, sometimes biting moral insight" and concluded that "Mr. White is our finest essayist, perhaps our only one."[30] Henry Canby placed him "unhesitatingly, with our cracker-box tree-stump philosophers."[31] The chief reservations expressed by critics had to do with his supposed lightness; Diana Trilling found White's "powers on a minor scale" in comparison to Montaigne and accused him of "going around rather than over intellectual hurdles,"[32] while Edward Weeks felt that White had yet "to show us how deeply he feels."[33]

In the main the critical response to *One Man's Meat* established White as an essayist—indeed, Morris Bishop felt he had "done much toward preserving the essay from death. . . . chiefly because he has brought the poetic spirit as well as verbal felicity into popular journalism."[34] It also raised the issue of the seriousness of White's work, which Scott Elledge wrestled with prior to writing his biography of White.[35] The essay entitled "Once More to the Lake" has come to be regarded as perhaps the quintessential twentieth-century American essay, continually reprinted as a model for young writers and frequently subjected to critical analysis. Leonard G. Heldreth has examined its "cyclical images of three generations of men and images of masculine sexuality" and Roger S. Platisky has offered a "mythic interpretation" focusing on White's use of ritual and archetype.[36] Richard Cox has used the essay to model a paragraph by paragraph stylistic analysis.[37]

White gave up the *Harper's* column in 1943 and returned to writing the "Notes and Comment" page, moving it toward a more forthright editorial style. Over the next decade and a half, he used it as a platform for observations on such crucial issues as the progress of the war, the war's aftermath, the creation of the United Nations, the dangers of the atomic age, the deterioration of the environment, civil rights, and McCarthyism.

World government was among his most recurrent themes. His paragraphs on this topic were first collected in *World Government and Peace* (1945), an unbound pamphlet of twenty pages, then expanded in *The Wild Flag* (1946), a book he described nervously as "my debut as a THINKER."[38]

Reviewers of *The Wild Flag* responded not only to White's ideas about world government but also to his persona and supposed *New Yorker* worldview. *Time* accused him of "practiced glibness (Author White made his reputation as a humorist)" and whimsy;[39] *The Nation* charged that the *New Yorker's* values were "sacred to its own bourgeois sophistication," concealing a middle class "fear of dispossession";[40] *Partisan Review* credited White with "good will and intelligence" but objected that the purpose of the book was "only to arouse certain familiar responses in the liberal middle-class reader."[41] Other readers found White's observations pungent and accurate. Warren Beck wrote that White "speaks the luminous vernacular of common sense."[42] Irwin Edman was even more forceful in White's defense: "One could hardly find anywhere a more persuasive plea for not only the global mind but global citizenship and global government."[43] In general, reviews were favorable, though they often reflected the reviewer's political orientation. It was White's most sustained work of advocacy.

White's next "clipbook" of previously published writing was a wide-ranging anthology, *The Second Tree From the Corner* (1954), which included paragraphs written between 1935 and 1953, essays, poems, introductions from three books, sketches, and short fiction. It is the book most representative of the range of White's writing. Reviews were generally positive. Irwin Edman announced: "It is time to declare roundly . . . that E. B. White is the finest essayist in the United States. He says wise things gracefully; he is the master of an idiom at once exact and suggestive, distinguished yet familiar."[44] Other critics were equally laudatory, if more willing to point out the unevenness in the quality of the selections.[45] Robert E. Sherwood noted that "the sense of melancholy which has always been evident in his writings, even the funniest ones, increases as the world in which he lives becomes more and more exasperating," but he found "nothing passive about his melancholy" because of his "persistent and zestful capacity for indignation."[46]

The same year that *The Second Tree From the Corner* was published, White wrote an essay on Thoreau for *The Yale Review*, as well as a longer essay for the *New Yorker*, "Our Windswept Correspondents / The Eye of Edna." White had written longer essays only infrequently, but nearing retirement he began a series of longer pieces for the *New Yorker*, presented as domestic counterpoint to such exotic and sophisticated features as Janet Flanner's regular "Letter from Paris." In 1962, those pieces, together with the *Walden* essay, the Edna essay, and a long comic piece called "The Rock Dove," were collected and published as *The Points of My Compass*.

Once again, reviews were preponderantly favorable, with the usual caveats about White's whimsy or the fact that not all the pieces had held up over the years. The concern over whimsy led Herbert Gold to declare White the master of the "semisequitur," a turn from the seriousness of his conclusions to some homey remark about the back kitchen.[47] Wilfrid Sheed disdained this device as White's " 'the chipmunks are getting scarcer' approach."[48] But most reviewers tended to praise White as a stylist, identifying him as "one of the true American masters of style,"[49] "one of the great prose writers of our language,"[50] and "the most influential of living American prose writers."[51] Thus, the reviews of his final collection of new material treated White as an established, significant figure in contemporary letters.

After the publication of *The Points of My Compass* White continued to write essays intermittently, as well as editorials, paragraphs, and letters to the editor. In *The Essays of E. B. White* (1977), he included a few of these late essays along with previously collected pieces. The book at last provided an overview of White's work as an essayist. Richard Freedman called White "our finest living practitioner" of the essay and compared him to Montaigne, although he "lacks the Frenchman's ultimate profundity."[52] Eudora Welty focused more on the character of White himself. "What joins all these essays together is the love held by the author for what is transitory in life. . . . It is a love so deep that it includes, may well account for, the humor and the poetry and the melancholy *and* the dead accuracy filling the essays to the brim, the last respects and the celebrations together."[53] Nigel Dennis cited as one of White's achievements "the extent to which he manages to avoid being 'writer-conscious': his search is for the plain word and his concern is for the subject."[54] Spencer Brown identified White as "our preeminent essayist" whose work exemplified "the modern informal essay." "The structure of a White essay resembles the configurations of a corps de ballet, in its confusing and harmonious and interlacing whirls of snowy tutus, gliding long-legged on point . . . into the predestined arrangement. White's genius is in expatiation, in byways."[55] The publication of the essays was an occasion for summations and appreciations.

With the publication of both *The Letters of E. B. White* and *The Essays of E. B. White*, Harper & Row began a uniform edition of his works. Over the next few years White oversaw the preparation of *The Poems and Sketches of E. B. White* and wrote introductions to new editions of *One Man's Meat* and *The Second Tree From the Corner*. Since his death, however, the plan for a uniform edition seems to have been abandoned by HarperCollins, the new publishing megafirm; recently it published *Writings from the New Yorker 1927–1976*, edited by Rebecca M. Dale.[56] The book has received little critical attention to date and is problematic for several reasons.

Its format eschews the uniform edition approach of the most recent collections. More importantly, by selecting only previously uncollected paragraphs, editorials, and casuals (and ignoring all the pieces collected in *Every Day is Saturday*), its editor has compiled an anthology entirely composed of work that White himself had repeatedly rejected for his earlier collections. Moreover, its organization is vaguely thematic—paragraphs are grouped under headings like "Nature," "The Word," "Thoreau," "Curiosities and Inventions," "One World," "Whims," with paragraph titles supplied by the editor; thematic groupings are organized chronologically, rather than throughout the book as a whole. This makes it difficult to trace White's development as a paragrapher. Critics had often noted that, even in his strongest collections, some of White's material was dated or uneven; here the collection is almost entirely made up of the dated and the uneven.

LETTER WRITER AND STYLIST

Critics have constantly remarked upon White's distinctive prose style. While some have doubted the purposes to which he put it, most have admired it. As Benjamin DeMott, reviewing *The Essays*, observed, "what is beyond criticism in a White essay is the music. The man knows all the tunes, all the limited lovely music that a plain English sentence can play—the affordable balances ("It took an upheaval of the elements and a job at the lowest level to give me the relief I craved"), the affordable vowel songs ("the tonic smell of coon"), everything. On nearly every page, there are subtleties of rhythm and pace, interweavings of the sonorous and racy rare in most contemporary writing."[57] Two of White's books were chiefly reviewed in light of his accomplishment as a prose stylist.

The Letters of E. B. White (1977) was White's longest book and, in its comprehensiveness, served as a partial autobiography. Reviewers often focused more on White's life than on White the letter writer.[58] Others took the occasion to praise White's style as the exemplum of Swift's definition of style ("proper words in proper places"), or "the perfect illustration of Buffon's dictum that 'the style is the man.'"[59] Others noted that the persona and prose style of the letter writer were that of the essayist.[60] Wilfrid Sheed observed that "White's notes to the milkman achieve effects that the others sat up all night for."[61] Donald Hall identified White's style as "elegant and forceful, brief, idiomatic, rhythmic, particular, and pointed" and concluded that "if The Style is the man, the man's daily improvised exercises add up to E. B. White's best book."[62] Spencer Brown described the style as "speech rhythm with the cagey devices of classical rhetoric: repetition, understatement, hyberbole, anticlimax, climax, the withholding of information until the right word comes along to make the sentence and the information end like the fall of a hammer."[63]

Surely intense loyalty to White as a stylist has made so many critics and teachers admire his revision of William Strunk's *The Elements of Style*, a project begun when a publisher wanted to reissue the 1918 book with White's *New Yorker* "letter" on Strunk as introduction. The first edition of the Strunk and White *Elements of Style* was published in 1959; it has since been revised twice.

Critical reaction to White's revision of *The Elements of Style* was most favorable among journalists, who worried about the ways in which "language is always slipping into imprecision" and felt "a responsibility for resisting the process of attrition and decay."[64] They welcomed the prescriptiveness of the book as a way to resist permissiveness and slovenliness and to achieve "proper prose."[65] At least one precisionist, Hyman Enzer, felt that the value of the book was in Strunk's portion; he complained that White's "addition on 'Style' lacks the precision and tone so characteristic" of the original and that, in reminding writers about "readers, designs and attitudes, White alloys the purity of Strunk's detachment."[66]

By contrast, *The Elements of Style* was poorly received by scholars of composition and rhetoric, more for Strunk's original sections than for White's additions. Their objections focused on the narrowness and unreliability of the prescriptive rules and the limitations of the "plain" or "casual" style that the book advocates.[67] In the most extended attack, Monroe Beardsley examined the logic behind a number of rules from Strunk's portion of the book and found them contradicted by White's own final chapter.[68] Berel Lang objected that the rules in *The Elements of Style* are less concerned with effective style than with moral behavior: "To summarize the ideals of written style for Strunk and White, then, is to compose a model of human character: honest, plain, forthright, patient, simple."[69]

In a postscript to the "Will Strunk" essay in *The Points of My Compass* White himself admitted, "I felt uneasy at posing as an expert on rhetoric, when the truth is I write by ear, always with difficulty and seldom with any exact notion of what is taking place under the hood."[70] His role as a reluctant pedagogue placed him uncomfortably in the path of more dedicated grammarians and prescriptivists. As he wrote to a friend, "life as a textbook editor is not the rosy dream you laymen think it is. I get the gaa damndest letters every day from outraged precisionists and comma snatchers, complaining every inch of the way."[71]

White's stylistic and rhetorical devices have been the subject of two dissertations. His style has been examined thoroughly by John Wesley Fuller in "Prose Style in the Essays of E. B. White"; his use of ethos, pathos, and logos in his essays is the subject of Dale Everett Haskell's "The Rhetoric of the Familiar Essay: E. B. White and Personal Discourse."[72]

CHILDREN'S AUTHOR

White's children's books have been so popular and beloved that in many ways they have eclipsed the literary nonfiction to which he devoted most of his energy as a writer. All contain traces of autobiography. In *Stuart Little*, its hero's stature, family status, love of sailing, experiences in cross-country travel, and romanticism are all reminiscent of White himself. *Charlotte's Web* drew on White's life on his farm. The central plot of *The Trumpet of the Swan* was connected to a scandal involving White's own father, while its romantic plot may reflect White's marriage to Katharine (the "Serena" of his earlier love poems).

When *Stuart Little* was being considered for publication, Anne Carroll Moore, then Head of Work with Children at the New York Public Library, advised the publisher against it.[73] Some of the elements she objected to—the open-ended conclusion, the episodic nature of the plot—continually surface in criticism of the book. For example, Malcolm Cowley found it "very engaging" and "entertaining" but also "a little disappointing" because "the parts are greater than the whole, and the book doesn't hold to the same mood or move in a straight line."[74] More recently, Alice H. G. Phillips, while calling it a "modern classic," ranked it lower that *Charlotte's Web* because "it is a succession of picaresque incidents rather than an integrated story, and both its villains and supporting good guys, though interesting, are underdeveloped."[75] In contrast, some of those very features have led Peter Neumeyer to judge it "the most inspired, the most surprising, the freshest, the funniest of White's books."[76]

When White's second children's book, *Charlotte's Web* was published in 1952, *The Horn Book* published two reviews: Anne Carroll Moore didn't care for the animals and objected to Fern because her role wasn't central and her behavior "unrealistic";[77] Jennie D. Lindquist, on the other hand, found the book to be "just as original as *Stuart Little*" and praised White for getting "beauty and wisdom into the story along with the humor."[78] Other reviews agreed with Lindquist.[79] P. L. Travers, the author of the Mary Poppins books, praised its "sense of delight in daily things";[80] Eudora Welty noted that the book has "the liveliness and felicity, tenderness and unexpectedness, grace and humor and praise of life, and the good backbone of succinctness that only the most highly imaginative stories seem to grow."[81]

The reviews of *The Trumpet of the Swan* (1970) were also generally admiring. Michele Murray complained that "the novel is possibly too long to sustain the single tone of pastoral elegy in which it is written" but noted that "for any other writer, this would be enough."[82] Similarly, Margaret Hentoff commented that "even when imperfect, Mr. White leaves most other children's book writers far behind."[83] Most other reviewers were less critical and more welcoming. John Updike wrote that while it is less "sprightly than *Stuart Little* and less rich in personalities and incident than *Charlotte's Web*" nonetheless "it is the most spacious and serene of the three."[84]

In the period since White's last children's book appeared, critics have chiefly, but not exclusively, focused on *Charlotte's Web*. Although he confesses a fondness for the boy who looks like a mouse, Gerald Weales acknowledges that "*Charlotte's Web* is probably a better book than *Stuart Little*, a more complicated one, a deeper one."[85] Rebecca J. Lukens ranks *Charlotte* highest, *Stuart* second, *Trumpet* third; her highly successful *Critical Handbook of Children's Literature* uses *Charlotte's Web* as a touchstone throughout the entire work.[86] Roger Sale, focusing on *Charlotte's Web*, refers to the other two books as not "even good enough to be called a distinguished or considerable failure."[87] Certainly neither have inspired the same degree of interpretation and analysis as *Charlotte's Web*.

Such close readings have revealed the richness of the book and the density of its texture. Peter Neumeyer has taken the view that it is "a great book" because it sets forth "a historically and anthropologically basic and primal theme."[88] John Griffith has argued that the book is "the fantasy of a lonely, yearning imagination."[89] Perry Nodelman found it to have a two-part structure typical of many children's novels and asserts that, "in telling his story twice, once from the viewpoint of innocence and in terms of naive literary skills, and then from the viewpoint of experience and in terms of sophisticated literary skills, White gives young readers the experience they need to transcend their own innocence as readers."[90] Norton D. Kinghorn argued that Charlotte, not Wilbur nor Fern, is the protagonist of the novel, and that "the web symbolizes the persuasive capability of language."[91] Janice M. Alberghene concluded that "*Charlotte's Web* does not merely tell about the writer's experience; it shows and creates that experience right before the reader's willing eyes."[92] Helene Solheim connected *Charlotte's Web* to White's other writing to argue that the book "is not at the periphery of White's work but at its center."[93]

In his acceptance speech for the Laura Ingalls Wilder Award in 1970, White explained "two or three strong beliefs [he had] about the business of writing for children." "I feel I must never kid them about anything; I feel I must be on solid ground myself. I also feel that a writer has an obligation to transmit, as best he can, his love of life, his appreciation for the world. I am not averse to departing from reality, but I am against departing from the truth."[94] The statement might have applied to his adult writings as well.

ASSESSMENTS AND APPRECIATIONS

The earliest published recognition of White's talent came in a long article on the success of the *New Yorker* in *Fortune*, August 1934, which set the pattern for subsequent studies of the magazine.[95] No history of the *New Yorker* can be complete without an examination of White's contribution to the tone and style of the magazine, a style Russell Maloney described in one such article as "modest, sly, elliptical, allusive, prim, slightly countrified, wistful, and (God help us) whimsical."[96] Interest in the process of composition by which he achieved that style has led several scholars to examine manuscript evidence.[97]

Toward the end of his life, reviewers of retrospective collections, the letters, and the biography by Scott Elledge recalled the range of White's achievements.[98] His death brought forth an additional outpouring of assessment and eulogy in the obituary notices of numerous publications.[99] White has been credited with having "restored [the essay] to a good name, something it had not enjoyed in journalistic circles since the Edwardians,"[100] and many critics would agree with the assertion that "[a]s an essayist, as a humorist, as a stylist he was one of America's masters."[101] Yet even White's admirers continued to worry about whether he was a major writer or a minor one.[102]

Since White's death, the personal or familiar essay has experienced some revival, and with it a self-conscious examination of the form by many of its most prominent practitioners. Like White's reviewers (and to a certain extent, like White himself, particularly in the often-cited introduction to *Essays of E. B. White*), these practitioners trace their roots to Montaigne, Addison and Steele, Lamb and Hazlitt, and Thoreau. For some, like Epstein or Lopate, the line of descent becomes uncomfortable when it reaches White; his mantle is not easily assumed, perhaps because his style is not really separable from his personality—to adopt the one, you have to adopt the other. The exploration of "voice" in White's essays has been the focus of three articles. Carl Klaus has closely examined the voices that White uses in some of his major essays, voices more distant from one another than might at first be imagined; Ken Smith proposes that White often uses "contesting discourses" in his essays, playing one voice against another; Richard Nordquist identifies the various personae White adopts in his essays as "forms of imposture."[103]

Clifton Fadiman attempted to get at the heart of the identification of White's voice with his style when he praised White's wartime editorials, claiming that "E. B. White is a major writer ... because his ideas and sentiments are large and basic and because, within the limitations of his chosen style and form, he writes about them perfectly."[104] Warren Beck found that

"White's writings, however personal, abound in that wide-ranging awareness and response essential to an achievement of literature's fullest dimensions."[105] William Howarth touched on the profound nature of White's essays when he noted that, for the clipbooks, "White chose his most durable works, culled from files of ephemera and arranged in chapters that describe his world: the city, the farm, the planet, the dying fall of youthful memory. Those are a poet's themes; White's gift and fate was to write them in plain, clear prose on glossy magazine pages."[106] Anita Silvey observed that he "was a man in love with beauty, with human freedom, and with nature. He possessed a boundless capacity for wonder about life, about everything we can see, feel, and touch."[107] As sentimental as that remark may seem, the evidence of White's life, in spite of his melancholy, points to its truth.

Support for the essential truth of that position comes from those celebrators of White's life who take his writing personally. Roy Barette, his eighty-eight-year-old neighbor and a practicing columnist, noted that White spoke fondly of writing ("It is wonderful to see words following one another across the paper the way my geese waddle up, head to tail, from the pond") and confirmed that White truly felt about life the way he claimed he did when he said, "Life's meaning has always eluded me and I guess always will. But I love it just the same."[108] Susan Allen Toth identified White as one of the two major influences on her writing. "Thinking of White as a man who knew fear, anxiety, and self-doubt, but who still reveled in life, I continue to want him as a guide. It is not easy to try to write prose, or live a life, with his humor, resilience, and staying power. But White's essays, stories, and letters reaffirm the 'invitation to life's dance' and tell the reader 'that the music is played for him, too, if he will but listen and move his feet.' "[109] The material in quotes was taken from White's essay on the influence of Thoreau, a relationship Caskie Stinnet recalled when writing of his own pilgrimage to Blue Hill, Maine, in imitation of White's pilgrimage to Walden Pond in *One Man's Meat*.[110]

John Updike also spoke personally in his remarks upon the occasion of White's receiving the 1971 National Medal for Literature. "White has figured in my life the way an author should figure, coming at me from different directions with a nudge, a reminder, a good example. . . . He writes as one among us, not above us, a man pulling his moral weight while keeping a level head and now and then letting loose with a song."[111]

REFERENCES AND BIOGRAPHIES

The only full-length study of E. B. White, Edward C. Sampson's volume in the Twaynes United States Authors Series, is still a valuable overview.[112] A. J. Anderson's *E. B. White: A Bibliography*, a standard source for tracking both White's writing and critical works on him, has been superseded by Katherine

Romans Hall's *E. B. White: A Bibliographic Catalogue of Printed Materials in the Department of Rare Books, Cornell University Library*, an indispensable work which nonetheless needs to be corrected and updated.[113] Scott Elledge's *E. B. White: A Biography* is a thorough, thoughtful, and sympathetic work; Linda Davis's *Onward and Upward: A Biography of Katharine S. White* makes an excellent companion to it, providing the best look at Katharine's life as an editor, and bringing a fresh perspective to the White's long marriage; Beverly Gherman has provided a biography for children in *E. B. White: Some Writer*.[114] In contrast to these well-documented biographies, Isabel Russell's *Katharine and E. B. White: An Affectionate Memoir* is, unfortunately, an opportunistic, narrow, and myopic portrayal of the Whites in Katharine's final years, giving an unbalanced and unfair portrait of Katharine, while most interesting when recording daily minutiae that confirm the personal foundation of White's essays, letters, and paragraphs.[115]

Several constraints have obliged me to leave out material that would have lengthened this book to three times its present size. I regret not covering all the clipbooks, particularly the early paragraphs, humor, and poems, and giving *Trumpet of the Swan* short shrift. It may be argued that White merits two separate collections, one for his children's books, and another for his literary nonfiction, and indeed there is sufficient critical material to fill them. I have attempted to compensate in part through the notes to this introduction.

Among those to whom I must express gratitude for their encouragement and cooperation, the foremost is Carl Klaus, who has written with insight and originality on White and Montaigne, and who has been supportive not only of this work but also of a full-length study of E. B. White's composing processes. Under his tutelage at the University of Iowa, I was introduced to literary nonfiction and prose style, and I remain in his debt. I am also grateful to Rebecca Lukens of Miami University who contributed her insights on White's children's books so eagerly, and to Ken Smith and Dick Nordquist, who readily assented to contribute original essays. My own labors on the book have been considerably lessened at Central Michigan University through the support and assistance of Francis Molson, Carol Swan, and Carole Pasche, in the Department of English, and in Park Library, William Miles and the Interlibrary Loan Department. For the preparation of typescript I appreciate in particular the work of Gail Calvert and Jennifer Whittaker. Above all I have prized the sympathy, understanding, and encouragement of my wife, Susan Root.

Notes

1. Joseph Epstein, "E. B. White, Dark & Lite," *Commentary* 81 (April 1986): 56.
2. Phillip Lopate, "What Happened to the Personal Essay?" *Against Joie de Vivre* (New York: Poseidon Press, 1989), 82.
3. Will Cuppy, "Bluebirds and What Not," *New York Herald Tribune Books*, 8 Decem-

ber 1929, 5; Lee Wilson Dodd, "A Monograph with a Punch," *Saturday Review of Literature* 6 (7 December 1929): 506.

4. E. F. M., "Case for the Quo," *Christian Science Monitor*, 17 March 1939, 20.

5. Otis Ferguson, "No Hands," *New Republic* 99 (28 June 1939): 227.

6. "Humorist," *Time* 33 (6 March 1939): 61.

7. Beatrice Sherman, "Drifting Whither with E. B. White," *New York Times Book Review*, 5 March 1939, 3.

8. Irwin Edman, "1000 Reasons, All Good," *Saturday Review of Literature* 19 (18 March 1939): 7.

9. James Thurber, "E. B. W.," *Saturday Review of Literature* 18 (15 October 1938): 8–9; reprinted in *Credos and Curios* (New York: Harper & Row, 1962), 134–41, and in this volume; Leonard Bacon, "Humors and Careers," *Saturday Review of Literature* 20 (29 April 1939): 3–4, 22.

10. E. B. White, "Preface," *A Subtreasury of American Humor*, ed. E. B. White and Katharine S. White (New York: Coward-McCann, 1941), xviii.

11. E. V. R. Wyatt, review of *A Subtreasury of American Humor, Commonweal* 35 (2 January 1942), 273–74. See also Leonard Bacon, "How to Break a Rib," *Saturday Review of Literature* 24 (22 November 1941), 7–8; and Otis Ferguson, "Laughter, Not Immoderate," *New Republic* 105 (15 December 1941), 832.

12. *Quo Vadimus? or, The Case for the Bicycle* (New York: Harper & Row, 1939): 69–73.

13. Eda Lou Walton, "Light Verse," *New York Herald Tribune Books*, 26 May 1929, XI:6.

14. Review of *The Lady is Cold, Nation* 129 (14 August 1929): 177.

15. William Rose Benet, review of *The Fox of Peapack, Saturday Review of Literature* 19 (29 October 1938): 20.

16. David McCord, "Lightest of the Arts," *Yale Review* 28 (Winter 1939): 393–94.

17. Edward Hoagland, "The Voice of the *New Yorker*," *New York Times Book Review*, 8 November 1981, 3, reprinted in this volume.

18. D. Aldan, Review of *Poems & Sketches of E. B. White, World Literature Today* 56 (Autumn 1982): 699.

19. James Finn Cotter, Review of *Poems and Sketches of E. B. White, America* 144 (13 March 1982): 10.

20. Terry Teachout, "A Man of Medium Height," *National Review* 34 (17 September 1982): 1162.

21. Timothy Foote, "A Darker White," *Time* 119 (25 January 1982): 81; Gary Michael Dault, "Missives From a Waltzing Mouse," *Maclean's* 95 (18 January 1982): 58.

22. Hoagland, 3.

23. Edward L. Martin, *H. L. Mencken and the Debunkers* (Athens: University of Georgia Press, 1984), 174; Norris W. Yates, "E. B. White, 'Farmer/Other'," *The American Humorist: Conscience of the Twentieth Century*, 2nd ed. (Ames: Iowa State University Press, 1964), 299–320, reprinted in this volume.

24. Stephen L. Tanner, "E. B. White and the Theory of Humor," *Humor* 2 (1989): 43–53, reprinted in this volume.

25. Thomas Grant, "The Sparrow on the Ledge: E. B. White in New York," *Studies in American Humor* 3 (Spring 1984): 24–33, reprinted in this volume.

26. Herschel Brickell, "Books on Our Table," *New York Post*, 6 October 1934, 7; William Rose Benet, "For Future Historians," *Saturday Review of Literature* 11 (27 October 1934): 40.

27. Review of *Every Day is Saturday, New York Herald Tribune Books*, 14 October 1934, VII: 23.

28. Morris Bishop, "Introduction," in E. B. White, *One Man's Meat*, Harper's Modern Classics (New York: Harper & Row, 1950), vii.

29. Rose Feld, "E. B. White Surveys His World," *New York Times Book Review*, 14 June 1942, 8.

30. Irwin Edman, "Earthy, Humorous, Accessible," *New York Herald Tribune Books*, 14 June 1942, IX:2.

31. Henry S. Canby, ". . . But No Man's Poison," *Saturday Review of Literature* 25 (13 June 1942): 7.

32. Diana Trilling, "Humanity and Humor," *Nation* 155 (8 August 1942): 118.

33. Edward Weeks, "First Person Singular," *Atlantic Monthly* 170 (July 1942): 100.

34. Bishop, x.

35. Scott Elledge, "*One Man's Meat* by E. B. White," *Carleton Miscellany* 4 (Fall 1963): 83–87, reprinted in this volume.

36. Leonard G. Heldreth, "'Pattern of Life Indelible': E. B. White's 'Once More to the Lake'," *CEA Critic* 45 (November 1985): 31; Roger S. Platizky, "Once More to the Lake: A Mythic Interpretation," *College Literature* 15 (Spring 1988): 171–79. Both are reprinted in this volume.

37. Richard Cox, "Nonfiction in the Classroom: E. B. White's 'Once More to the Lake'," *CCTE Studies* 52 (September 1987): 20–27.

38. *The Letters of E. B. White*, edited by Dorothy Lobrano Guth (New York: Harper & Row, 1979), 277.

39. "Brave New Scanties," *Time* 48 (11 November 1946): 109–110.

40. Isaac Rosenfeld, "Chopping a Teakettle," *Nation* 163 (28 December 1946): 762–63. For a later objection in this same vein, see Anonymous, "Go Climb a More Meaningful Tree," *Commonweal* 51 (10 March 1950): 573.

41. Robert Warshow, "E. B. White and the *New Yorker*," *The Immediate Experience: Movies, Comics, Theatre & Other Aspects of Popular Culture* (Garden City: Doubleday, 1962) 105–108.

42. Warren Beck, "Call for Immediate World Government," *Chicago Sun Book Week*, 15 December 1946, 3. See also Charles Poore, "Pointers for Stateman or Skeptic," *New York Times Book Review*, 17 November 1946, 3, 58; and Mark S. Watson, "Mr. White Surveys the World," *Saturday Review* 29 (9 November 1946), 14–15.

43. Irwin Edman, "E. B. White, That Fine Goldsmith in Words," *New York Herald Tribune Weekly Book Review*, 10 November 1946, VII:5.

44. Irwin Edman, "The Wonder and Wackiness of Man," *New York Times Book Review*, 17 January 1954, 1. See also Joseph Wood Krutch, "The Profession of a New Yorker," *Saturday Review* 36 (30 January 1954): 15–16, reprinted in this volume.

45. Harvey Curtis Webster, "Sense and Style," *New Republic* 130 (15 February 1954): 19; "*The New Yorker's Addison*," *Nation* 178 (29 May 1954): 469.

46. Robert E. Sherwood, "E. B. White: A Treasury of that Modest, Wise, and Witty Master," *New York Herald Tribune Book Review*, 17 January 1954, 1.

47. Herbert Gold, "Hearth and Hurricane," *Saturday Review* 45 (November 24, 1962): 30, reprinted in this volume.

48. Wilfrid Sheed, "*The New Yorker* Code," *Jubilee* 10 (March 1963): 48–54. See also Webster Schott, "E. B. White Forever," *New Republic* 147 (24 November 1962): 25–26.

49. Edmund Fuller, "Multitude of Topics Touched by a True Master of Style," *Chicago Tribune Magazine of Books*, 21 October 1962, 2.

50. M. J. Arlen, "World of E. B. White," *New York Times Book Review*, 26 October 1962, 24. See also Stanley Walker, "E. B. White's Civilized Way of Saying Things," *New York Herald Tribune*, 21 October 1962, 5.

51. W. J. Weatherby, "A Modern Man of Walden," *Manchester Guardian Weekly*, 14 February 1963, 14.

52. Richard Freedman, "The Quiet Wit of E. B. White," *Washington Post Book World*, 6 November 1977, E3, reprinted in this volume.

53. Eudora Welty, "Dateless Virtues," *New York Times Book Review*, 25 September 1977, 43.

54. Nigel Dennis, "Smilin' Through," *New York Review of Books* 24 (27 October 1977): 42, reprinted in this volume.

55. Spencer Brown, "The Odor of Durability," *Sewanee Review*, 86 (Winter 1978): 148.

56. *Writings from The New Yorker 1925–1976*, edited by Rebecca M. Dale (New York: HarperCollins, 1990).

57. Benjamin DeMott, "Books 1. Pick of the List," *Saturday Review*, 20 August 1977, 63.

58. Jean Stafford, "A Green Thumb in a Mass of Clenched Fists," *Saturday Review* 4 (11 December 1976): 61–63; John Updike, "Books: Of Beauty and Consternation," *New Yorker* 52 (27 December 1976), 64–68; Malcolm Muggeridge, "The Compleat New Yorker," *Harper's* (March 1977): 94, 98–99; Richard Lee Strout, "The Great White Way," *New Republic* 178 (29 April 1978): 2.

59. Edmund Fuller, "The Public Face of a Private Man," *Wall Street Journal*, 17 January 1977, 14; Stefan Kanfer, "Tongue and Groove," *Time* 108 (20 December 1976): 25; Anatole Broyard, "Seriously Unserious," *New York Times Book Review*, 7 December 1976, 39.

60. Roderick Nordell, "The Lofty with the Mundane," *Christian Science Monitor*, 5 January 1977, 23; John B. Breslin, review of *The Letters of E. B. White, America* 135 (25 December 1976): 21; Frank X. J. Homer, review of *The Letters of E. B. White, America* 136 (7 May 1977): 18; George Core, "A Mask and an Unveiling," *Sewanee Review* 85 (Spring 1977): lixx–lx.

61. Wilfrid Sheed, Review of *The Letters of E. B. White, New York Times Book Review*, 21 November 1976, 1.

62. Donald Hall, "E. B. White on the Exercycle," *National Review* 29 (10 June 1977): 671–72, reprinted in this volume.

63. Spencer Brown, "White of the Rueful Countenance," *American Scholar* 47 (Spring 1977): 240, reprinted in this volume.

64. Granville Hicks, "Literary Horizons: Clarity, Clarity, Clarity," *Saturday Review* 42 (1 August 1959), 13.

65. Israel Shenker, "E. B. White Rehones His Verbal Razor," *New York Times*, 3 May 1972, 49, 76; Roderick Nordell, "Rules for Good Writing," *Christian Science Monitor*, 28 May 1959, 11; review of *The Elements of Style, Christian Century* 76 (26 August 1959): 973; Shaun O'Connell, "E. B. White's Letters Provide a Constant Delight," *Boston Sunday Globe*, 9 January 1977, 100; Dorothy Parker, "Book Reviews," *Esquire* 52 (November 1959): 28.

66. Hyman Enzer, Review of *The Elements of Style, Journalism Quarterly* 36 (Fall 1959): 493–94.

67. Robert Cluett, *Prose Style and Critical Reading* (New York: Teachers College Press, 1976), 86; Louis T. Milic, "Rhetorical Choice and Stylistic Option: The Conscious and Unconscious Poles," in *Literary Style: A Symposium*, ed. Seymour Chatman (New York: Oxford University Press, 1970), 77–94; Louis T. Milic, *Stylists on Style: A Handbook with Selections for Analysis* (New York: Charles Scribner's Sons, 1969), 461–63; William H. Whyte, Jr., "You, Too, Can Write the Casual Style," *Harper's* (October 1953): 87–89; Richard Ohmann, "Use Definite, Specific, Concrete Language," *College English* 41 (December 1979): 390; Robertson Davies, "The Pleasures of an Ornate Style," *Mirabella* (March 1990): 64.

68. Monroe Beardsley, "Style and Good Style," in *Teaching High School Composition*, ed. Gary Tate and Edward P. J. Corbett (New York: Oxford University Press, 1970), 289–302.

69. Berel Lang, "Strunk and White and Grammar as Morality," *Soundings: An Interdisciplinary Journal* 55 (Spring 1982): 29–30.

70. *The Points of My Compass* (New York: Harper & Row, 1962), 122.

71. *Letters*, 464.

72. John Wesley Fuller, "Prose Styles in the Essays of E. B. White" (Ph.D. diss., University of Washington, Seattler, 1959); Dale Everett Haskell, "The Rhetoric of the Familiar

Essay: E. B. White and Personal Discourse," (Ph.D. diss., Texas Christian University, 1983); Michael Dennis Quigley, " 'The Germ of Common Cause': History, Rhetoric, and Ideology in the Essays of E. B. White," (Ph.D. diss., University of Oregon, Eugene, 1989).

73. *Letters*, 266–67, 368n; Ursula Nordstrom, "Stuart, Wilbur, Charlotte: A Tale of Tales," *New York Times Book Review*, 12 May 1974, 8, 10.

74. Malcolm Cowley, "Stuart Little: Or New York Through the Eyes of a Mouse," *New York Times Book Review*, 28 October 1945, 7, reprinted in this volume. See also May Lamberton Becker, "Books for Young People," *New York Herald Tribune Weekly Book Review*, 21 October 1945, 4.

75. Alice H. G. Phillips, "Of Mice and Men," *Times Literary Supplement*, 1 April 1988, 367. See also Rosemary Carr Benet, "Mrs. Little's Second Son," *Saturday Review of Literature* 28 (8 December 1945): 26.

76. Peter F. Neumeyer, "*Stuart Little*: The Manuscripts," *Horn Book Magazine* (September/October 1988): 598.

77. Anne Carroll Moore, "The Three Owls Notebook," *Horn Book Magazine* 28 (December 1952): 394.

78. Jennie D. Lindquist, review of *Charlotte's Web*, *Horn Book Magazine* 28 (December 1952): 407–408.

79. Margaret Ford Kieran, review of *Charlotte's Web*, *Atlantic Monthly* 140 (December 1952): 101; Polly Goodwin, review of *Charlotte's Web*, *Chicago Sunday Tribune*, 16 November 1952, sec. 4, p. 4; "The Little More, The Little Less," *Times Literary Supplement*, Children's Book Section, 28 November 1952, vii.

80. P. L. Travers, "Tangible Magic," *New York Herald Tribune Book Review*, 16 November 1952, 38. See also P. L. Travers, "Christmas Books I: My Childhood Bends Beside Me," *New Statesman and Nation* 54 (29 November 1952): 639.

81. Eudora Welty, "Life in the Barn Was Very Good," *New York Times Book Review*, 19 October 1952, 49.

82. Michele Murray, "Mr. White's *Trumpet of the Swan* Is an Elegaic if One-Key Pastorale," *National Observer*, 10 August 1970, 21.

83. Margaret Hentoff, "Little Private Lives," *New York Review of Books* 15 (17 December 1970): 11.

84. John Updike, review of *The Trumpet of the Swan*, *New York Times Book Review*, 28 June 1970, 4

85. Gerald Weales, "The Designs of E. B. White," *New York Times Book Review* (24 May 1970): 40, reprinted in this volume.

86. Rebecca J. Lukens, "The Child in Us All," (unpublished essay); Rebecca J. Lukens, *A Critical Handbook of Children's Literature* (Glenview, Ill: Scott, Foresman, 1976).

87. Roger Sale, *Fairy Tales and After: From Snow White to E. B. White* (Cambridge, Mass: Harvard University Press, 1978), 258.

88. Peter F. Neumeyer, "What Makes a Good Children's Book? The Texture of *Charlotte's Web*," *South Atlantic Bulletin* 44 (1979): 75, reprinted in this volume.

89. John Griffith, "*Charlotte's Web*: A Lonely Fantasy of Love," *Children's Literature* 8 (1979): 117.

90. Perry Nodelman, "Text as Teacher: The Beginning of *Charlotte's Web*, *Children's Literature*, vol. 13 (New Haven: Yale University Press, 1985), 126.

91. Norton D. Kinghorn, "The Real Miracle of *Charlotte's Web*," *Children's Literature Association Quarterly* 11 (Spring 1986): 8.

92. Janice M. Alberghene, "Writing in *Charlotte's Web*," *Children's Literature in Education* 16 (1985): 42, reprinted in this volume.

93. Helene Solheim, "Magic in the Web: Time, Pigs, and E. B. White," *South Atlantic Quarterly* 80 (Autumn 1981): 405, reprinted in this volume.

94. "Laura Ingalls Wilder Acceptance," *Horn Book* 46 (August 1970): 350–51.

95. Ralph Ingersoll, "The *New Yorker*," *Fortune* 10 (August 1934): 72–86, 90, 92, 97, 150, 152.

96. Russell Maloney, "Tilley the Toiler: A Profile of the *New Yorker Magazine*," *Saturday Review* 30 (30 August 1947): 10. See also Dale Kramer, *Ross and "The New Yorker"*, (New York: Doubleday, 1951); Jane Grant, *Ross, "The New Yorker" and Me*, (New York: Reynal, 1968); William Howarth, "E. B. White at the *New Yorker*," *Sewanee Review*, 93 (Fall 1985): 574–83; Gerald Weales, "Not for the Old Lady in Dubuque," *Denver Quarterly* 8 (Summer 1973): 65–83.

97. See especially Neumeyer, "Stuart Little: The Manuscripts"; Peter F. Neumeyer, "The Creation of *Charlotte's Web*: From Drafts to Book," part I, *Horn Book*, (October 1982): 489–97, and "The Creation of *Charlotte's Web*: From Drafts to Book," part II, *Horn Book*, (December 1982): 617–25; Peter F. Neumeyer, "The Creation of E. B. White's *The Trumpet of the Swan*: The Manuscripts," *Horn Book* 61 (January/February 1985): 117–28; Scott Elledge, "E. B. White at Work: The Creation of a Paragraph," *E. B. White: A Biography* (New York: W. W. Norton, 1984), 359–67; Nancy R. Comley et al., "Writing and Rewriting," *Fields of Writing: Readings Across the Disciplines*, 2nd ed. (New York: St. Martin's Press, 1987), 755–69; Douglas L. Hunt, "Introduction: About Essays and Essayists," *The Dolphin Reader* 2nd ed. (Boston: Houghton-Mifflin, 1990), 1–16.

98. George Bain, "In Praise of Writing Meant to be Read," *Maclean's* 97 (23 April 1984): 43; Thomas Ichniowski, review of *Essays of E. B. White, America* 138 (11 March 1978): 194–95; R. Thomas Ost, review of *Essays of E. B. White, Antioch Review* 35 (Fall 1977): 459.

99. See Paul Gray, "A Master of Luminous Prose—E. B. White: 1899–1985," *Time* (14 October 1985): 105; Jolene Roehlkepartain, "Simplicity: the Heart of E. B. White," *Christian Century* 102 (30 October 1985): 966; Merrill Sheils, "To Be Clear, Brief, Bold," *Newsweek* (12 October 1985): 79; "The Years With White," *Nation* 241 (12 October 1985): 329.

100. Russell Lynes, "The Divided Life of Stuart Little's Father," *New York Times Book Review* (26 February 1984), 9–10.

101. "The Talk of the Town: E. B. White," *New Yorker* 61 (14 October 1985): 31.

102. D. J. Enright, "Laurel—or Brussels Sprouts?" *Encounter* 50 (April 1978): 70–75.

103. Carl L. Klaus, "On the Voice(s) of E. B. White" (unpublished essay); Ken Smith, "Contesting Discourses in the Essays of E. B. White" and Richard L. Nordquist, "Forms of Imposture in the Essays of E. B. White," both original essays written for this volume.

104. Clifton Fadiman, "In Praise of E. B. White, Realist," *New York Times Book Review*, 10 June 1945, 1.

105. Warren Beck, "E. B. White," *College English* 35 (April 1946): 181.

106. Howarth, 575.

107. Anita Silvey, "In a Class by Himself," *Horn Book* 62 (January/February 1986): 17.

108. Roy Barrette, "A Neighbor's Farewell," *Yankee* 50 (February 1986): 127.

109. Susan Allen Toth, "E. B. White," in *How to Prepare for Your High-School Reunion and Other Midlife Musings* (Boston: Little, Brown, 1988), 164.

110. Caskie Stinnett, "A Letter to E. B. White," *Down East* (January 1989): 88, 107–109, 111.

111. John Updike, "Remarks on the Occasion of E. B. White's Receiving the 1971 National Medal for Literature on 1971 December 2" in *Picked-Up Pieces* (New York: Alfred A. Knopf, 1976), 437.

112. Edward C. Sampson, *E. B. White* (New York: Twayne Publishers, 1974).

113. A. J. Anderson, *E. B. White: A Bibliography* (Metuchen, NJ: Scarecrow Press, 1978);

Katherine Romans Hall, *E. B. White: A Bibliographic Catalogue of Printed Materials in the Department of Rare Books, Cornell University Library* (New York: Garland, 1979).

114. Scott Elledge, *E. B. White: A Biography.* (New York: W. W. Norton, 1985); Linda H. Davis, *Onward and Upward: A Biography of Katharine S. White* (New York: Harper & Row, 1987; Beverly Gherman, *E. B. White: Some Writer* (New York: Atheneum, 1992).

115. Isabel Russell, *Katharine and E. B. White: An Affectionate Memoir* (New York: W. W. Norton, 1988).

THE CLIPBOOKS

♦

One Man's Meat

◆

. . . But No Man's Poison

Henry S. Canby

A book like *One Man's Meat* is sure to give one what I call the itch of continuity, which is not at all the same thing as the continuous itch. Most books are like the pools or puddles or streamlets you come across in a day's hike. They have just rained down from the general atmosphere or run down from the landscape. But, after a while, perhaps in a wooded valley you see a deep-currented, purposeful stream, and say this must be the main line, this comes from somewhere significant, and is going somewhere for results. And yet it may be a small and modest stream.

I read, whenever I find them, Mr. White's narrative essays with their peculiar effect of casual conversation from a cracker barrel that leaves you scratching your head, and saying "that fellow has really *said* something." And then because they are so definitely American, so peculiarly our humor, and our half-sad, half-buoyant philosophy, the itch to place him in the American strain diverts me from my natural enjoyment of what I have read. Listening to the radio, it would seem that the world is in a precarious balance between the importance of the world's largest-selling beauty soap and the world's widest-spread predicament. The first radio words after the announcement of Pearl Harbor were "Give mother foot comfort for Christmas." Television is going to be the test of the modern world, for it will make sights seen over the air more real than we are able to be ourselves. The current struggle is between

Reprinted from *Saturday Review of Literature* 25 (13 June 1942): 7. Reprinted by permission.

nationalism and internationalism, but you have to have more of the first before you can do anything about the second. The least fraternal organization in the world is a fraternity, since it is based on exclusiveness. And yet—"It is all," as Mr. White says, "thoroughly cock-eyed." Yet even when we listen, at the radio, to the familiar voice which has marshmallows in place of tonsils, we know that there is something here for which a free nation is fighting—and hoping it can be done a little differently when we are through.

I am being less than just to Mr. White's sane and exploratory philosophy, which begins like a speaker at a banquet with seemingly irrelevant banter and ends in wisdom. But this is his method, and, fortunately, there have been one or two like him in every American generation. It is not the line of Washington Irving, who belongs to the school of urbane and genteel irony. It is not the line of Walt Whitman, who began in Irving's manner, but dropped it as soon as he learned how to write for himself. He gave the best answers to Mr. White's question, how can you have your own country and the world both. It is a simple answer—get the exclusiveness out of your fraternity. Mr. White knows it, of course, but he is more interested in leading questions than in dogmatic answers. He belongs (as I see) with Mark Twain and his tradition of serious fun-poking, and with Thoreau and his tradition of serious topsy-turvy. If Thoreau had not seen an overworked man plodding down a Concord road with a farm on his back, Mr. White certainly would, on Wall Street or in Maine, with stocks and bonds or summer boarders as the burden on living. It was Thoreau who suspected that the great Atlantic Cable would be used to bring news of some royal child's toothache or measles, and Mr. White who notes that we have harnessed the ether waves in order to advertise soap or gasoline.

I place him, therefore, unhesitatingly, with our cracker-box tree-stump philosophers. With the characteristic of American fellows who hold back their punches until they have done a little humorous shadow-boxing, which gives them a chance to get the audience friendly and laughing and confuse the opponent; then biff, smash comes the punch. It is the main stream of the homely American humorists, which begins in the eighteenth century, and regarded as literature; includes Franklin, Jackson, and Lincoln, as well as wisecrackers like Artemus Ward; and Thoreau and Mark Twain and Don Marquis and Robert Frost. It is a country sound at the core that can keep this kind of humor going, and yet not forget its Washingtons, its Jeffersons, its Emersons, its Woodrow Wilsons, its Hawthornes, and Hemingways. It is a nation that, fortunately, is nourished on more than one kind of meat.

One Man's Meat by E. B. White

Scott Elledge

Tuesday. Sat down first thing after breakfast to write something on E. B. White's *One Man's Meat*, but was diverted by a leaflet called "A Prose Appreciation Test for Senior High School." It came in the mail I brought last night from the village post office; but when I got home there were better things to do than look at anything so unrelated to the kind of life I'm trying to lead here in Maine, in August, by the sea. When I looked into it this morning, I was only trying to delay the start of a job I was afraid I couldn't bring off, but I may have told myself that after all I should look at the material (*material* is not a word you're likely to find in White—when he deals with "material," he makes you see why the thing and the word are ridiculous). I'm on a committee that plans to spend $50,000 on research in teaching literature in elementary and junior high schools, and I *should* take our responsibilities seriously. The theory is that if it's taste that good teaching produces, then we can evaluate good teaching by measuring the development of taste in pupils. This particular test was sent to our committee as an example of the kind of "instruments" now being used to test taste. It is straightforward enough. Each question consists of four 75-word passages on a common subject, "A Fire," "Spring," "Homecoming," "Tryst," and so on. All the test-taker has to do is rank the four passages according to their "Literary merit." But in question after question that proved to be more than I could do. Question X, "Literary Criticism," is a good sample of what troubled me:

1. That Miss West has a personality is evident to anyone familiar with her work. A personality, however, is not three-dimensionally revealed except in that form of work which comes closest to the heart and life of the worker. To write pungent and terrifyingly sane criticism is a notable thing, but to write novels of tender insight and intimate revelation is a far more convincing thing. *The Judge* is such a novel.

2. Robert Frost, whose verse is modern without being "queer" and local (he comes from New England) without being provincial, is one whom all poetry lovers will want to know at least. A two-dollar collection of his work published by Henry Holt is an especially

Reprinted from *Carleton Miscellany* 4:4 (Fall 1963): 83–87. Reprinted by permission of Carleton College.

delightful edition. And I can almost guarantee that if you have ever wandered through meadows and down lanes in Vermont, for instance, or Tennessee, you will instantly appreciate the lines which begin "Something there is which does not like a wall."

3. Catherine Merrill North is one of the best writers of the present day. She has written five books, the last of these being the recently published "Women Wear Hoods." Her plot, style, atmosphere, and characterization are always of the first order. Nobody ever read a North story without being a better man or woman for it. The reading public should be grateful to Mrs. North for the fine work she is doing. May "Women Wear Hoods" be quickly succeeded by another book by Mrs. North!

4. George Eliot might be classified as one of the greatest if not the greatest realist of the analytical or psychological order. But this would, to our mind, be a one-sided and incomplete estimate of the chief character in her writing and genius. Truthful rendering of life and character may have been one of the chief motives to composition, and a fundamental requisite to the art of her fiction, but it remained a means to a further end—the ultimate end—of her writing, as it no doubt was the fundamental stimulus to her imagination and design. And this end and motive make her an idealist and not a realist in fiction.

Any student conditioned to make the "right" response to *that* test would think that, whatever "merit" there might be in *One Man's Meat*, it was certainly not "literary." All White's work, from *Quo Vadimus* (now in paperback) through *The Points of My Compass*, is so free from signs of "literary merit" that your heart sinks when you think of trying to imitate him. You feel the way he says he felt whenever he thought of his ambition to write as well as Don Marquis. Who knows where he got his taste, or how to account for it? No doubt he learned from such "teachers" as Professor Strunk at Cornell, editor Harold Ross at the *New Yorker*, and editor Katharine White in Maine and Manhattan. In various essays he has admired Ring Lardner, FPA, and James Thurber. Not only in "Walden" but throughout *One Man's Meat* it is easy to hear what sound like echoes of Thoreau. But there is no telling where he found the passion to write well in a style free from the rhetoric associated with the phrase "literary merit."

It is easier, and safer, to speculate about his influence on us—that is, on people about my age who think and talk about style. In college in the thirties we were taught to admire Ruskin and Pater, Carlyle and Emerson, but we needed no help to admire the polished colloquial tone, the studied informality, the controlled freedom of "The Talk of the Town." We didn't know who wrote "The Talk of the Town"; but someone told us that E. B. White was the best of its contributors and we wished that we could write as well as he. When we began to teach English composition, we tried to persuade freshmen to believe that "Farewell, My Lovely" had a tone, a diction, a rhythm, an attitude—had a style more worth imitating than that of their home-town minister, their favorite newspaper columnist, or some other orator.

Many things contributed to our preference for prose that could get along very nicely without phrases like "contributed to our preference for." It was a time when Donne's vernacular sounded better than Milton's decorum, and we all praised such direct and colloquial openings as "I wonder, by my troth, what thou and I did till we loved"; and "For God's sake, hold your tongue and let me love!" (White has some fine openings, too: "Miss Nims, take a letter to Henry David Thoreau." "I would like to hand down a dissenting opinion in the case of the Camel ad which shows a Boston terrier relaxing." "One summer, along about 1904, my father rented a camp on a lake in Maine and took us all there for the month of August. We all got ringworm from some kitten and had to rub Pond's Extract on our arms and legs night and morning, and my father rolled over in a canoe with all his clothes on.") Yeats had said that when we argue with the world what we write is rhetoric, but when we argue with ourselves, we write poetry; and that interesting half-truth had its effect. But week in and week out for about twenty-five years our taste was influenced by the kind of mixture of Thoreau-like simplicity and anti-Dubuque urbanity that was the *New Yorker* of E. B. White.

One other thing the "Prose Appreciation Test" reminded me of is White's skill in taking off from such items. Lesser men can find such "texts" and intuit the sermons (or satires) latent in them, but lesser men despair of writing them. White wasn't afraid to try to do something with the text, to tease it, to squeeze it, to preach his hilarious homily, that was still intensely, passionately moral.

Thursday. No serious critical essay these days can omit at least a chapter on the persona, the mask, the voice, the character of the narrator. Among recent works of criticism is one called *The Voices of Coleridge* and another called *Milton's Epic Voice*. The author of the latter is so entranced by the idea of a speaking voice as a being independent of Milton that she says (but doesn't mean to) that Milton organized *Paradise Lost* along lines suggested to him by his "inspired narrator." And things are going to get worse before they get better. The *Carleton Miscellany's* own Wayne Booth is not responsible for the bullish state of voice criticism, but the "success" of *The Rhetoric of Fiction* is not going to help matters. Anyway. Don Marquis, Ring Lardner, Robert Benchley, and James Thurber all developed "voices," and their cadences we came to know so well we could have identified them by the sound of their voices coming from the next room. What they had in common was the voice of a humorist (different as their accents were); they were always performing as we wanted them to, always acting the part they had created. But the voice of White is the voice of a writer, as Howard Nemerov has said the voice of Wallace Stevens is the voice of a poet. All the way through *One Man's Meat* White reminds us that he thinks of himself as a writer, and he makes us feel that he is being as honest with us and with himself as he can be—as free of a pose, a mask, or a voice as we would like to be when we talk to someone we love. At any rate, *I* don't want to read anything about the difference between the "I" of the essays and the "real" E. B. White. The distinction here seems pointless: the honnête homme is a man who does not pretend to be an honnête homme.

Friday. Auden says, "Speaking for myself, the questions which interest me most when reading a poem are two. The first is technical: 'Here is a verbal contraption. How does it work?' The second is, in the broadest sense, moral: 'What kind of a guy inhabits this poem? What is his notion of the good life or the good place? His notion of the Evil One? What does he conceal from the reader? What does he conceal even from himself?'"

Reading *One Man's Meat*, written between 1938 and 1941, reminds me that my students are right in thinking of those years as a period in history. The essays are full of wonderfully concrete impressions of things and events and attitudes and feelings that belong to history—like back numbers of *Harper's Magazine.* But what makes the book a classic, what makes it possible to read the Foreword without a sense of the irony that colors most statements of self-evaluation read in aftertimes, is simply "the guy who inhabits the work." "Here then is a book [White wrote in the Foreword in 1942] in time of swords, a thought or two in time of deeds, a celebration of life in a period of violent death. Here is a record of an individual pursuing the sort of peaceable and indulgent existence which may not soon again be ours in the same measure. I offer "One Man's Meat" not with any idea that it is meaty but with the sure knowledge that it is one man—one individual unlimited, with the hope of liberty and justice for all."

Marquis, Lardner, Benchley, Thurber, all made us see the truth of the unheroic. We saw ourselves in the fears and awkwardnesses, in the ignobility, of the anti-hero. But the courage of the quietly desperate man who wrote *One Man's Meat* gave a wry dignity to all frightened little readers who despaired not only of the world but of themselves, of their power ever to write as well as White, or ever to be as painstakingly honest in life, or ever to give their art and their life the integrity that shines out from the works of E. B. White.

Humanity and Humor

Diana Trilling

Between July, 1938, and December, 1941, while the Second World War was getting under way, Mr. White was turning his place in Maine from a vacation retreat into a working farm with chickens, pigs, and sheep. He still had to earn his living by writing, and the essays in this volume—most of them for *Harper's*—were composed on the run, as it were, between the hen-house and the radio. They are divided between E. B. White the farmer and E. B. White the paragrapher of current affairs, whose talent has made such an impress on the front pages of the *New Yorker*, but the interplay of the two personalities is close and healthy; his devotion to his farm spares Mr. White no responsibility in the world, and his worldliness gives an added dimension to his farm. Unlike most literary people who return to the soil, Mr. White is a person of sensibility, not a sentimentalist, and when, for instance, he helps deliver a lamb, he has a decent self-consciousness but no need to glorify himself. An individual and a gentleman, he isn't out to sell you the idea that a farm is any man's meat. The record of his adventure shows not the slightest trace of being directed against you: peculiar among literary farmers, Mr. White didn't leave the city in order to leave you behind, nor is it any part of this effort to outsmart you on new territory. He will respect you and leave you alone as long as you respect him and leave him alone; this would be his definition of democracy, and he is ready to die for democracy. Vulgarity is something Mr. White takes into account by the way; he helps fumigate it out of existence with his fine aseptic prose.

The kinship with Thoreau is explicit throughout this book but there is also Mr. White's implicit kinship with Montaigne. Obviously, compared to the great humanist, Mr. White's powers are on a minor scale; in the matter of style, real as his gifts are, we question whether his felicity has not sometimes been achieved by going around rather than over intellectual hurdles. But as we read the diary he kept in the First World War, we recognize how compellingly the humanistic tradition had already claimed him, even as a young man. Perhaps this isn't remarkable—young men often reach a kind of climax of intellectual decency in their college years, after which their development is a

Reprinted from *Nation* 155 (8 August 1942): 118. Reprinted by permission of The Nation Company, Inc. © 1985.

steady retrogression justified in the name of "reality"—but what is remarkable is that Mr. White has held fast to this heritage into maturity and through a period in the world's history in which, on the liberal as well as the reactionary front, it has been so tempting to pervert mind to the uses of power.

I recall only one essay in the volume that deals specifically with the temptations that writers face in a troubled society. Nevertheless, every line Mr. White writes—whether he is dealing with egg-production or the Townsend plan, country schools or Anne Lindbergh (his analysis of "The Wave of the Future," incidentally, is a small masterpiece, one of the best things in the book)—supports in practice this single statement of his literary creed. It is January, 1939, and Mr. White has been informed that a certain writer, stricken by the cruel events of the world, has vowed never again to write anything that isn't significant and liberty-loving. "I have an idea that this, in its own way, is bad news," writes Mr. White. "Having resolved to be nothing but significant he is in a fair way to lose his effectiveness. . . . Even in evil times, a writer should cultivate only what naturally absorbs his fancy, whether it be freedom or cinch bugs. . . . A literature composed of nothing but liberty-loving thoughts is little better than the propaganda which it seeks to defeat. In a free country it is the duty of writers to pay no attention to duty. Only under a dictatorship is literature expected to exhibit an harmonious design or an inspirational tone." And he sums up: "A writer must believe in something, obviously, but he shouldn't join a club."

Well, Mr. White has joined no club except a society called Friends of the Land, but he believes in many good things. Being a humanist himself, he is a firm believer, for one thing, in man's humanity.

"Once More to the Lake": A Mythic Interpretation

Roger S. Platizky

In E. B. White's deceptively simple autobiographical essay "Once More to the Lake," the proverbial still waters run more deeply than one might at first suspect.[1] The narrative—which comes close to being fictive—appears to be just another variation on the "You can't go home again" theme. A man decides to revisit old haunts—a lake and campsite in Maine where he and his family used to vacation every summer in August. The man, now about his father's age, returns to the lake with his son. Before reaching the site, he wonders how time and the encroachments of civilization will have marred what he calls "this holy spot" (49). Upon arrival, however, he begins to sustain the illusion that nothing has changed and "there have been no years," a phrase he repeats resolutely and self-deceptively. But the narrator's illusion is shattered when the son steps into dripping bathing trunks after a noontime thunderstorm and, as he does, his father suddenly feels "the chill of death" in his groin (54). While White's theme appears rather conventional, the ritualistic setting of "Once More to the Lake" and the mythic conflict between father and son reveal a pattern that unifies the work in an unexpected way.

The complete title of White's essay, "Once More to the Lake (August 1941)," immediately conveys a tension between experiential time (the time of memory) and historical (or clocked) time that pervades the work. "Once More" implies a hopeful indeterminacy about a kind of time that can be repeatedly experienced or recaptured. At the same time, "Once More to the Lake" may mean one last time to the lake. The phrase "Once More" also has resonances of ritual. Milton's "Lycidas," for instance, an elegy infused with the theme of death and rebirth, begins with such a phrase.[2] In the same title, the date (August 1941), tucked away as it is in parentheses, is not merely a neutral autobiographical statistic, but also a reminder of World War II, revolution and change—a sign of the inexorability of historical time.[3] Thus two ways of perceiving time are immediately available in the title. Throughout the essay, the speaker will try to make signs of clocked time in his environment (e.g., the outboard motors) subordinate to aspects of the setting (memories of fishing)

Reprinted from *College Literature* (Spring 1988): 171–79. © 1988 by West Chester University.

which permit him to sustain his illusion that time has not marred his "holy spot."

The narrator wants to sustain the illusion first because he had idealized this campsite in Maine as a child—"none of us ever thought there was any place in the world like that lake in Maine. We returned summer after summer—always on August 1 for one month" (49). Returning to this cherished spot "summer after summer—always on August 1" created a ritual pattern for the summer retreat, a pattern that could well seem like a magical sign of constancy in a world of flux. When he returns to the lake, the speaker still secretly longs for that security. Unconsciously, he imagines that if he returns to the same spot at the same time of year with his son (whom he takes to mirror himself in youth), and re-enacts all the summer rituals of his childhood—waking up at the same time in the morning, walking on the same trails, fishing with the same bait, eating the same kind of pie—he will, as if by homeopathic magic, become a participant in nature's seasonal return. This ceremony of return for renewal is enacted to convert his retreat into a rebirth—from the adult back to the child, with the ubiquitous August sun and the amniotic lake seemingly promising their magic of constancy. According to Philip Rahv, "the essential function of myth" is that it releases man "from the flux of temporality, arresting change in the timeless, the permanent, the ever recurrent conceived as a 'sacred repetition.' "[4] By calling the lake a "holy spot" and referring to its stillness as that of a cathedral (49–50), the narrator consecrates his past and all the memories the lake and campsite contain.

The speaker also consecrates the lake setting because the illusion of permanancy that the setting conveys belies the threat of mortality for the speaker, who is no longer young. Early in the essay, the speaker betrays his fear of mortality with imagery as he compares the lake-site of his childhood with the setting of his adulthood. "I have since become a salt-water man, but sometimes in the summer there are days when the restlessness of the tides and the fearful cold of the sea water and the incessant wind which blows across the afternoon and into the evening make me wish for the placidity of a lake in the woods" (49). In contrast to the regressive placidity of the lake whose fresh water, motionless and life-bearing, holds the memories of childhood, "the restlessness of the tides" (governed by the mutability of the moon in its archetypal cycle of death and rebirth), "the fearful cold of the sea," and "the incessant wind" that blows "across the afternoon and into the evening" imagistically project the aging speaker's anxieties about mortality and change. The ebb and flow of years incessantly proceed, like history, into the "afternoon" and "evening" of one's life and culture. The speaker, who has to be in or approaching middle age (if his first visit to the lake was in 1904 and this one with his son is in 1941), is metaphorically in the "afternoon" of his life, dreading the tide of evening and yearning to return to the placid morning of his existence.

It is for this reason that all the events at the lake that are perceived by the speaker as pleasurable occur in the morning, and most that are sensed as unpleasurable take place in the afternoon. It is in the morning when the speaker and his son go fishing and when memories are most clear and fertile. "I remembered clearest of all the early mornings, when the lake was cool and motionless, remembered how the bedroom smelled of the lumber it was made of and of the wet woods . . . (49). It is in the afternoon, on the other hand, that the thunderstorm brings with it a revelation of "the chill of death." It is also in the noontime heat of summer that the speaker describes how the tennis court net sags "in the dry noon, and the whole place steamed with midday heat and hunger and emptiness" (51).

Ironically, the speaker in his need to return does not permit himself to see that the fearful tides, the cold of the sea, and the placid lake—all being forms of water—are part of one system, just as the morning and afternoon sunshine are modifications of the same light, and just as the seasons of childhood and adulthood are merely stages of the same ineluctable process. Jung has said that the "afternoon of human life must have a significance of its own and cannot be a pitiful appendage to life's morning."[5] White's speaker, however, to use Jung's phrase, tries to carry "over into the afternoon the law of the morning," and this phenomenological error leads to his rude awakening.

Furthermore, the speaker tries to black out all traces of what the setting insistently reveals—the "elementary idea" that life lives on life.[6] The very act of fishing attests to this: the speaker uses dead bait to catch live fish, then eats the fish to sustain himself (and his memories of fishing as a child). The idea that time, like man, like the water, and all forms of life is a preserver and destroyer both is implicit (but unrecognized by the speaker) in the imagery White uses to paint one of the idyllic early morning fishing scenes:

> It was the arrival of this fly [a dragonfly] that convinced me beyond any doubt that everything was as it always had been, that the years were a mirage and there had been no years. The small waves were the same, chucking the row boat under the chin as we fished at anchor, and the boat was the same boat, the same color green and the ribs broken in the same places, and under the floorboards the same fresh-water leavings and debris—the dead helgramite, the wisps of moss, the rusty discarded fishook, the dried blood from yesterday's catch. (50)

Paradoxically and ironically, the "constants" that assure the speaker that there have been no years are simultaneously images that represent mutability, erosion, and death. The "wisps of moss," the "fresh-water leavings and debris," "the rusty discarded fishook" and the oxydized green-colored boat, the "dead helgramite" used to catch fish, the "dried blood from yesterday's catch," and the personified broken ribs of the boat all imply the deteriorative and inexorable qualities of time and process. The "trustworthy" lake, therefore, becomes the medium of flux for all these things, man-made and natural. By translating all of these images into positive signs that nothing has changed, the nostalgic speaker closes off his vision to the corrosive and paradoxical qualities of the lake and of time.

Averse to change, the speaker allows himself to embark on a mythic path of chronological primitivism in his quest for sameness, constancy, immortality. The believer in chronological primitivism maintains that the earliest stage of human history is the best and that childhood, both cultural and personal, is better than maturity.[7] Similarly, in White's essay, the speaker not only tries to stop the flow of time for himself, but he also rhapsodically tries to maintain an ideal image of his country in the beloved summertime. "Summertime, oh summertime, pattern of life indelible, the fade-proof lake, the woods unshatterable, the pasture with the sweetfern and the juniper forever and ever, summer without end; . . . the cottages with their innocent and tranquil design, their tiny docks with the flagpole and the American flag floating against the white clouds in the blue sky" (52). With the American flag floating mystically "against the white clouds in the blue sky," the speaker's nostalgia is not only for his own past, but also for the past of his country. The pastoral images of "life indelible," "sounds unshatterable," "the sweetfern and the juniper forever and ever" belong mythically to the images of the golden age or prelapsarian state when nature's abundance was inexhaustible, when man and nature were a brotherhood, and when man had no reason to fear time and death. By having America partake of "summertime, pattern of life indelible" in his paean to nature, the speaker may be mythically trying to revive the Edenic potential of America, a time when all was tranquil, agrarian, innocent, fertile, and golden. In this case, the speaker would be like other questers in myth: by making a ritual return to his cherished lake, he is also attempting to revitalize the agrarian ideality of his culture.

E. B. White, however, uses irony several times in this section to undercut the mythical efficacy of his celebrant's idealism. First, White includes in the "Summertime" paean a reference to American postcards "that showed things looking a little better than they looked" (52). Then, he also demythifies the purer spirit and innocence of "the American family at play" by having his speaker wonder for a moment "whether it was true that the people who drove up for Sunday dinner at the farmhouse were turned away because there wasn't enough chicken" (52). Here the references to untrustworthy postcards and discriminatory (rather than democratic) Sunday farmhouse dinners serve a similar function to what the "rusty discarded fishook" and "dead helgramite" did in the earlier passage on fishing: the latter shatters the illusion of time and nature's benevolence while the former challenges the speaker's overly idealistic view of America and its family ethics.

White also uses irony in his depiction of the father/son relationship in the narrative. Ideally, the child, like the morning of an age, should represent to the chronological primitivitic sensibility the fullest potentiality for growth. But the "creepy sensation" the speaker feels as he begins to confuse his identity with his son's in the following passage suggests otherwise: "I began to sustain the illusion that he [the son] was I, and therefore, by simple transposition, that I was my father. This sensation persisted, kept cropping up all the time we were there. . . . I seemed to be living a dual existence. I would be in the middle of a simple act, I would be picking up a bait box or laying down a table fork, or I would be saying something, and suddenly it would be not I but my father who was saying the words or making the gesture. It gave me a creepy sensation" (50).

The speaker's identity confusions between his own father, himself, and his son indicate not only a longing for the return of the father (White's father died in August 1936), but also an unconscious wish for immortality.[8] That is, if the father could be his own father (past), himself (present), and his own son (future) at the same time, there would be no years, because he would be, like the lake, eternally regenerative. Historical time and change, then, could not pose the threat that they do in this narrative. The "creepy sensation" occurs, in part, because it is physically and psychologically dizzying and decentering to conceive of oneself as existing in three different times and identities simultaneously without being immobilized. Heraclitus once stated that a person "cannot step twice into the same river"[9] even though the river gives one the illusion that this could be done. But the speaker in White's essay tries to step in and out of different desired times and personalities as though he felt he could be truly whole only by doing this. Ironically, such attempts decenter the self and lead to psychic fragmentation. Paradoxically, the speaker can only stay whole by remaining part; to become one with the setting or the son or the father would cause him to lose his own identity.

The speaker's ultimate inability to fuse identities with his son is also inevitable since a generation gap exists between the nostalgic father and his more progressive son. This can be seen in his son's love for the same outboard motors that threaten the father's illusion that there have been no years. "The only thing that was wrong now, really, was the sound of the place, an unfamiliar nervous sound of the outboard motors. This was the note that jarred, the one thing that set the years moving. . . . My boy loved our rented outboard . . ." (52). In contrast to his progressive son, the speaker prefers the old inboard motors with the "sedative" noises they made (52). Not surprisingly, the speaker also liked the way you could go into reverse with the older motors, "if you learned the trick" (52). The son, however, has new tricks of his own both to practice and learn in the present. Ironically, the father, who wants to see the son as a mirror image of his own youth, has brought historical time to the lake in bringing his son.

In addition, the relationship between father and son, as described by the father during their fishing ritual, seems to founder on unconscious sexual jealousy. This is suggested by the traditional double entendre on "fly" and "rod" in the following passage: "We stared silently at the tips of our rods. I lowered the tip of mine into the water. . . . I looked at the boy who was silently watching his fly, and it was my hands that held his rod, my eyes watching. I felt dizzy and didn't know which rod I was at the end of" (51). Mythically, this fishing scene, reminiscent of the Fisher King and the quest for regeneration through immersion in water, could imply that the older fisherman (also representative of a former culture now in transition) wishes he could retain his potency by changing sexual identities with his son, whose potential for fertility is at its dawn. In ironic modernization of the myth, the older fisherman instead of willingly relinquishing his power to the youth looks on with unconscious envy. This interpretation helps to clarify the last scene in which the speaker suddenly feels "the chill of death" in his groin as his son pulls his "dripping trunks" up "around his vitals" (54). Thus, the son becomes both the preserver and destroyer of the speaker's illusion of constancy. At the same time that the son may perpetuate the father's image genetically by someday giving birth and his name to another son, the son will also usurp his father's place both in the water and historically. As in Donald Hall's modern poem "My Son, My Executioner," the son paradoxically becomes both "the instrument of immortality" and "the document of bodily decay."[10] Therefore, like the lake, the periodicity of nature, and time itself, the son becomes a representation of the elementary idea that life lives on life.

The scenes that finally prove revelatory for the speaker in "Once More to the Lake" are the climactic thunderstorm and its aftermath. As the sky begins to darken, the speaker describes the storm as being "like the revival of an old melodrama that I had seen long ago with childish awe" (54). In this statement, there is a fusion and separation between past and present modes of perception. The adult who can now critically disclaim as a "revival of an old melodrama" something he has seen "long ago with childish awe" is beginning to deflate his idealistic belief that "there had been no years." That there will be an ominous, revelatory quality to this storm is forecast by the image of "the gods grinning and licking their chops on the hills" (54). The whole atmosphere of the storm is one that shows nature to be not only regenerative, but also appetitive. Even the archetypal calm that follows this storm is described ambiguously. "Afterward the calm, the rain steadily rustling in the calm lake, the return of light and hope and spirits, and the campers running out in joy and relief to go on swimming in the rain, their bright cries perpetuating the deathless joke about how they were getting simply drenched, and the children screaming with delight at the new sensation of bathing in the rain, and the joke about getting drenched linking the generations in a strong indestructible chain. And the comedian who waded in carrying an umbrella" (54).

Taken out of context, this passage would seem wholly optimistic about the human condition in a world of change. Yet, when the passage is taken within context, one notices the "nervous" words "deathless," "drenched" and "screamed" as well as the equally nervous overuse of "and" as a connective in search for security in external proofs of "the return of light and hope and spirits." But as we have seen throughout the narrative, this speaker is too needy of such proofs to be an objective recorder or interpreter of them. In contrasting the children's delightful new sensation of bathing (the speaker does not go into the water) with the speaker's new sensation—"the chill of death"—one sees how ironic this euphoric calm is with regard to human destiny. The mythical gods are "grinning and licking their chops on the hills" at the cosmic joke of man's being positioned in a universe of deathless time and death-in-time. But the speaker, holding on to the vestiges of mythic belief in a kinship with nature that is "indestructible," is like the "comedian who waded in carrying an umbrella." Perhaps only a comedian can embody the paradoxes of birth and death, regeneration and decay, and still see the humor in them. Perhaps this is man's hope. But "Once More to the Lake" ends with the word "death," and one is left wondering how long this comedian will be able to wade in that lake of memories before a new and even stronger storm turns his time-weary umbrella inside out.

Notes

1. E. B. White, "Once More to the Lake," *The Norton Reader*, ed. Arthur M. Eastman, et al. (New York: Norton, 1977), 49–54. Hereafter, all references will be to this text, and all page numbers will be recorded parenthetically within the essay. This is one of many college anthologies in which White's popular essay has been reprinted. Two other commonly used college anthologies in which the essay appears are *Life Studies: A Thematic Reader*, ed. David Cavitch (N.Y.: St. Martins Press, 1983), 117–224; and *The Dolphin Reader* (shorter), ed. Douglas Hunt (Boston: Houghton Mifflin, 1987), 578–93.

2. Richard P. Adams, "The Archetypal Pattern of Death and Rebirth in Milton's 'Lycidas,'" *Myth and Literature: Contemporary Theory and Practice*, ed. John B. Vickery (Lincoln: U of Nebraska P, 1966), 187–91.

3. A former student, Gary Harencak, brought to my attention the allusions to World War II in "Once More to the Lake."

4. Phillip Rahv, "The Myth and the Powerhouse," *Myth and Literature: Contemporary Theory and Practice*, ed. John B. Vickery (Lincoln: U of Nebraska P, 1966), 111, 114.

5. Jung is quoted by Joseph Campbell in *The Masks of God: Primitive Mythology* (N.Y.: Penguin Books, 1979), 123.

6. Joseph Campbell discussed the archetypal idea of life living on life in a televised interview with Bill Moyers, Friday, April 17, 1981.

7. Chronological Primitivism is defined and illustrated in *The Dictionary of the History of Ideas*, III: 577–78.

8. Douglas Hunt and Melody Richardson Daily, *Instructor's Guide to the Dolphin Reader* (Boston: Houghton Mifflin, 1987), 207.

9. Michael C. Stokes, "Heraclitus of Ephesus," *The Encyclopedia of Philosophy*, III: 477–81.

10. Donald Hall, "My Son, My Executioner," *An Introduction to Literature*, 6th ed., ed. Barnet et al. (Boston: Little, Brown, 1982), 431.

"Pattern of Life Indelible":
E. B. White's "Once More to the Lake"

Leonard G. Heldreth

Describing his craft, E. B. White wrote in 1964 to Scott Elledge: "I was interested in your remarks about the writer as poser, because, of course, all writing is both a mask and an unveiling, particularly in the case of the essayist, who must take his trousers off without showing his genitals. (I got my training in the upper berths of Pullman cars long ago.)"[1] White's own essay, "Once More to the Lake," written twenty-three years before, embodies his philosophy, for it is both a mask and an unveiling. The smooth narrative of the father's nostalgic journey with his son, as placid until the end as the surface of the lake itself, has charmed millions of readers and has been reprinted extensively. Yet, the seemingly casual narrative is carefully constructed upon the basic pattern of human generation, the physical transmission of life—a pattern which is hardly noticeable until White's ending when son replaces father as procreator. The architecture and major themes of the essay can be most clearly and specifically understood through an examination of two patterns of exposition: cyclical images of three generations of men and images of masculine sexuality.

Cyclical repetition begins in the first paragraph of the essay: "We returned summer after summer—always on August 1st for one month."[2] This remembered pattern is then contrasted with the narrator's present position in life: "I have since become a salt-water man, but sometimes in summer there are days when the restlessness of the tides and the fearsome cold of the seawater and the incessant wind which blows across the afternoon and into the evening make me wish for the placidity of a lake in the woods." The references to saltwater (with connotations of sweat, tears, and maturity), to relentless wind and restless tides (associated with passing time and inevitable death) characterize the middle age of the narrator, who now finds himself vulnerable and yearns sometimes for the fresher water and more sheltered life of his youth. The age of the narrator is paralleled by the time of year (August, archetypal end of summer) and the wind blowing "across the afternoon and into the evening."

This contrast between the narrator's present life and his remembered

Reprinted from *CEA Critic* 45 (November 1985): 31–34. Reprinted with permission.

youth leads to a feeling of *deja vu* as he sees his son repeating the actions of his own boyhood. Behind the duality of father and son is a larger, three-fold relationship involving the narrator's father. "I began to sustain the illusion that he [the son] was I, and therefore, by simple transition, that I was my father. This sensation . . . was not an entirely new feeling, but in this setting it grew much stronger. I seemed to be living a dual existence. I would be in the middle of some simple act . . . and suddenly it would be not I but my father who was saying the words or making the gesture." The illusion established by returning to boyhood haunts and patterns of existence cannot, however, be maintained; for the narrator knows his father is dead, and that "the road under our sneakers was only a two-track road. The middle track was missing, the one with the marks of the hooves and the splotches of dried, flaky manure. There had always been three tracks to choose from in choosing which track to walk in; now the choice was narrowed down to two. For a moment I missed terribly the middle alternative." The track associated with horse-drawn vehicles and the time of his father is gone. The three potential roles once open to the narrator—son, father, grandfather—are now narrowed to two, for with the death of his father, his role as son ends. Only two paths remain: father and grandfather. This realization, early in the essay, of the now limited options and the narrator's missing "terribly the middle alternative" anticipates the symbolic chill in the groin of the last paragraph where the choices are again reduced.

Generation, in the sense of procreation, has traditionally offered one method of transcending time, of achieving immortality. Through perpetuating their names and estates through male offspring, men have symbolically recreated themselves, escaping time. This relation of father and son, of a boy echoing his father's masculine experience, is at the very core of White's account; and the sexuality, which each generation inherits and which physically yokes "the generations in a strong indestructible link," ties the father and son together in parallel images throughout the essay. For example, as the two walk into town, the father has "trouble making out which was I, the one walking at my side, the one walking in my pants."

At the beginning of the essay, the boy seems hardly aware of his sexuality. Since his actions during the visit to the lake repeat the father's activities at a similar age, we assume the boy to experience the same emotions as his father felt canoeing along the shore. Sexual stirrings, generally a contradictory mass of primitive drives and romantic ideals, are reflected in the descriptions of the lake, which has "places in it which, to a child at least seemed infinitely remote and primeval" but which has also "this unique, this holy spot" with "the stillness of a cathedral." The father tries to recall his own feelings as a boy, remembering the "country girls," the courting couples on the small steam boat, and "what it had felt like to think about girls then."

The father knows, despite the boy's present innocence, that he is maturing; as he remembers his adolescent feelings and transfers them to his son, so also he seems to recall that sexual activities in early adolescence are usually solitary ones. His description of the boy's relationship with the boat contains what seems to be a description of masturbation. "My boy loved" the boat and "his great desire was to achieve singlehanded mastery over it, and authority, and he soon learned the trick of choking it a little (but not too much), and the adjustment of the needlevalue." The rest of the paragraph, describing the boy's handling of the "old one-cylinder engine with the heavy flywheel" until he "felt he had complete mastery over his motor" and could keep it from leaping "ahead, charging bull-fashion at the dock," continues the metaphor. While White and his son Joe were vacationing at Belgrade Lakes that summer, he wrote to his wife about the boat: "We now have a perfectly enormous outboard motor on our rowboat, which I am unable to start, except semi-occasionally. This is deeply disappointing to Joe. When the motor chooses to start, it leaps into a frightful speed, usually knocking us both down in the boat" (*Letters*, p. 215). The language of the letter is quite different from and much less developed than that of the essay.

In the fishing scene, the parallels of masculine sexuality between father and son become more explicit. Reliving his boyhood experiences, the narrator finds "the same damp moss covering the worms in the bait can." The fishing rods seem quite phallic: "I looked at the boy, who was silently watching his fly, and it was my hands that held his rod, my eyes watching. I felt dizzy and I didn't know which rod I was at the end of." It is only a step from the confusion of rods to the parallel of groins at the end.

As the essay moves toward its conclusion, the emphasis on generation and sexuality becomes more emphatic. The thunderstorm, almost a cliche of sexual symbolism, prepares the reader for the inevitable last lines. The appearance of the storm reminds the father of his earlier attitudes toward such storms and of their importance to him: "It was like a revival of an old melodrama that I had seen long ago with childish awe." And despite his present casual attitude, he acknowledges the implicit power in it: "The second-act climax of an electrical disturbance over a lake in America had not changed in any important respect. This was the big scene, still the big scene." The continued description of the storm completes the image: the familiar onset of desire, "the whole thing was so familiar, the first feeling of oppression and heat"; the growing crescendo of the act, "the premonitory rumble. Then the kettle drum, then the snare, the bass drum and cymbals"; finally, "crackling light against the dark," with the image of the old lascivious gods "grinning and licking their chops in the hill." The aftermath is "the calm, the rain rustling in the calm lake, the return of light and hope and spirits." Then there is "the joke about getting drenched linking the generations in a strong, indestructible chain."

But such chains must break, and fathers and sons must inevitably separate. When the boy sees other people swimming after the storm, he announces, symbolically leaving his father for society, that he is "going in too." The boy has apparently been naked throughout the storm, at ease in the company of his father, but now he covers himself as he goes to join the social rites and the comedian with an umbrella. "He pulled his dripping trunks from the line where they had hung all through the shower and wrung them out."

The trunks are the central image in a progression from *pants* (two paragraphs earlier) to *groin* two sentences later, and the choice of garment here enables White, through a pun, to tie the boy into the cycle of generations (or generators). Earlier in the essay, describing visits to the lake with his father, the narrator remembered "the great importance of the trunks and your father's enormous authority in such matters . . . the trunks to be unpacked, to give up their rich burden." The narrator, as a boy, was fascinated with his father's sexual authority, just as his son with the boat is also trying to attain "mastery over it and authority." Now, as an adult, the father accepts his sexual position as casually as he accepts the storm. The wonder is gone: "you sneaked up in your car and parked it under a tree near the camp and took out the bags and in five minutes it was all over, no fuss, no loud wonderful fuss about trunks." Through the word play on *trunks*, White links grandfather, father, and son.

In the last lines the father watches the boy "languidly, and with no thought of going in." His impotence contrasts with his description of the boy's "hard little body, skinny and bare." As the boy draws the trunks up over his "vitals" (a much more effective word here than "genitals," "privates," or other similar synonyms, for it indicates the life-giving properties), the father sees the naked boy wince at the touch of the "soggy, icy" trunks. Writing to a young girl, Marilyn Boyer, in 1961, White said about this passage: "So when the little boy in the essay puts on a cold, wet bathing suit, the man feels the chill, as though *he* were experiencing it. Only for him it is truly a chilling experience, because it suddenly seems to foreshadow death" (*Letters*, p. 350). The narrator cannot ignore the evidence that he sees: his son is becoming a young man and will inevitably replace him as a progenitor as he replaced his father. And with that realization, he finds that "suddenly my groin felt the chill of death."

Thus the major themes come together in the last paragraph of the essay. The separation of parent and child is brought to its metaphoric inevitability. The overlap between past and present, between illusion and reality, is removed: the narrator is neither his father nor his son; and while he will achieve a limited immortality through successive generations, he, as a physical being, is faced squarely with approaching death, a death which has already removed his father. The passage of time, whatever illusion he may conjure, cannot be denied. But for a few days he has relived through his son the experience of being a boy on the edge of manhood; and in the experiences of his son and all the sons to follow, only through the repeated archetypes of human life, will be found that "summertime, oh summertime, pattern of life indelible, the fadeproof lake, the woods unshatterable, the pasture with the sweetfern and the juniper forever and ever, summer without end."

Notes

1. *Letters of E. B. White*, ed. Dorothy Lobrano Guth (New York: Harper and Row, 1976), p. 516.

2. *Essays of E. B. White* (New York: Harper and Row, 1977), p. 197; all references to the essay are to this edition. White was forty-two on July 11, 1941; in late July he visited the Belgrade Lakes with his young son Joe, and in October he wrote the essay for his column in *Harper's Magazine*.

The Second Tree From the Corner

◆

The Profession of a New Yorker

JOSEPH WOOD KRUTCH

The most remarkable thing about E. B. White is not that he is a good writer—though good writers are scarce enough—but that he should be the particular kind of good writer he is: highly personal, persistently oblique, and generally concerned less with the Queen than with the little mouse under her chair.

Any writer's conference could have told him that this would never do. Nowadays successful writers are often dull, fanatical, pompous, long-winded, incoherent, and sometimes illiterate, but they are "objective," their pages bristle with facts, and they "deal with an important subject." Mr. White breaks all the rules. He doesn't even know that the familiar essay is dead. And yet, for all this self-indulgence, he has managed somehow to achieve what Max Beerbohm called in his own case "a very pleasant little reputation." How come?

Take as an example his new book, "The Second Tree from the Corner," which seems to be precisely what every publisher knows won't sell. It is a mere collection, and a very miscellaneous one at that. There are two or three essays, a good many paragraphs from *The New Yorker*'s "Talk of the Town," two reprinted introductions to other books, and even quite a bit of verse mixed in with the prose. A mere scrapbook if there ever was one and composed of nothing except "fugitive" pieces. As any publisher would say to almost any

Reprinted from *Saturday Review of Literature* 36 (30 January 1954): 15–16. Reprinted by permission.

other writer, the thing has no unity either external or internal—except perhaps the unity of a personality which is not a thing anybody now cares about. "What's your theme, Mr. White? What's your message? People have no time for this sort of thing in a dangerous world. The only kind of non-fiction that sells is the 'What You Ought to Know About . . .' kind. In fact, even that is hardly good enough. 'What You Don't Dare Not Know About . . .' is better. Good God, Mr. White, you are even genteel." And yet the chances are that "The Second Tree from the Corner" will not do too badly.

Perhaps the explanation is merely that Mr. White is good enough in his own special way to prove an exception to all rules, but if that is too simple then we shall have to fall back upon the more inclusive mystery of *The New Yorker* itself and say that Mr. White published principally in a magazine whose devoted readers are convinced that it can do no wrong even when it goes in for the sort of thing not to be tolerated anywhere else.

One sometimes gets as tired of admitting *The New Yorker's* virtues as the Athenians did of hearing Aristides called "The Just." At such moments one can argue that it has much to answer for and that no single influence on the taste of the public ought to be so strong. It helped kill the familiar essay at the same time that it popularized certain substitutes for it. By inventing the all-too-readable "profile" with its stress upon eccentricity, it made soberer attempts to assess personalities or achievements seem dull. Avoiding cliches it established cliches of its own, and *New Yorker*-type fiction is as readily recognizable as *The Saturday Evening Post* type. It put the fear of not being "smart" into the hearts of people who had no business caring whether they were smart or not. It made all sorts of writers, artists, and editors turn themselves into unsuccessful imitators when they might better have gone their own ways. It even reached across the ocean to corrupt *Punch*. It redefined the chic, but no matter how the chic may be defined it tends to become the enemy of everything else. One of Oscar Wilde's characters made, apropos another character, the famous remark, "He always behaves like a gentleman—a thing no gentleman ever does," and a sort of extension of that remark suggests what *The New Yorker* has always striven to avoid. Intellectually as well as in every other respect it has always been aware of the difference between the false chic and the true—which changes from moment to moment. And on the whole it has been astonishingly successful in never being caught with last year's hat. In fact, it has finally got to the point where any hat it chose to wear became, *ipso facto*, the right one.

Worst of all, it has come to dominate a large group of devoted readers who take their every cue from its pages. The lady from Dubuque and the gentleman from Kansas City recognize one another as "my kind" by exchanging recollections of this cartoon or that paragraph. In fact, the members of certain groups have come to communicate almost exclusively in references to the sacred writings as successive instalments appear week after week.

If it had not managed to remain fresher than anyone would have supposed possibly it would be intolerable. Why hasn't it gone stale? Most of the old-time staffers seem modestly inclined to insist that the late Harold Ross is the answer and of him they have made a legend which they seem to believe in even more firmly than anyone else does. But what was his secret—if it really was his?

In part, no doubt, it was the realization that one can change just a little without seeming to change at all. Thus, though *The New Yorker* was born in the reckless Twenties, though as late as 1935 Wolcott Gibbs was protesting in the introduction to one of the first "Annuals" that the magazine had formulated no political philosophy and had "no intention of beginning now," it soon found in Mr. White a man who could introduce paragraphs about World Government and thus supply at least the minimum of "social conscious-ness" which had become indispensable without making it seem out of place on the next page but one to a Peter Arno cartoon.

At least equally important was the related policy which permitted its contributors to differ widely so long as they could, nevertheless, be made to confine their divergencies within a certain framework. One would be tempted, off-hand, to say that Mr. White is a "typical *New Yorker* writer." And in certain respects he is. His manner is debonaire, so that even when discussing World Government or country life he manages to suggest that he is, nevertheless, a man who knows his way about town. When he lapses from "smartness" the lapse is deliberate and of course he writes with that almost finicky awareness of "good usage" which it is said Mr. Ross, otherwise a rough diamond, paradoxically insisted upon. But once all this has proved that he "belongs" he can be permitted to indulge in what would otherwise seem the wildest eccentricity.

For instance, one of the best pieces in the present volume is concerned with his well-known enthusiasm for Thoreau and tells how remembered sentences from "Walden" keep rising to his lips. "I go into a restaurant, we'll say, at the lunch hour, and the headwaiter approaches me, accusingly. 'All alone?' he asks. 'I feel it wholesome to be alone the greater part of the time,' I reply. Or I am walking along a street and meet an acquaintance—someone I haven't seen in a long time and don't care if I never see again. 'Where y'been all this time?' he demands. 'If a man does not keep pace with his companions,' I retort, 'perhaps it is because he hears a different drummer'."

What business have such fancies as these in *The New Yorker*? Would Thoreau himself have been a welcome contributor? What would he have thought of a magazine which was "smart" first of all and is predisposed to favor stories and sketches whose scene is a bar—especially a bar which is either very elegant or very low? Yet Mr. White manages to get in not only quotations from Thoreau but also sentiments of his own which are decidedly Thoreauish. By what miracle can a passage like the following be made to seem chic? "Man's separation from his mother, Nature . . . becomes more complete with every passing year, and may finally reach the point of artifice where, to maintain life at all, we will have to resort to a recording—some recollection of the natural world, some grunting noise that takes us back to reality and stirs us to accept the half-forgotten sources of our original supply." That such things *can* be got in is, of course, a credit to Mr. White and to *The New Yorker* as well.

Perhaps, then, we shall just have to fall back upon our original explanation of Mr. White's improbable success: he is a good writer. After all, it will hardly do to explain him in terms of *The New Yorker* when you have to explain a good deal of *The New Yorker* in terms of him.

The Wonder and Wackiness of Man

Irwin Edman

It is high time to declare roundly what a good many people have long suspected, that E. B. White is the finest essayist in the United States. He says wise things gracefully; he is the master of an idiom at once exact and suggestive, distinguished yet familiar. His style is crisp and tender, and incomparably his own. A city-dwelling Thoreau holed up very frequently on the first page of the *New Yorker*, but from that Tower of Irony remembering Maine, where he lived part of the time, and Walden Pond, where Thoreau lived briefly.

Mr. White some years ago published a collection, at once hilarious and at moments profound, called "Quo Vadimus," the title piece of which was really about where are we all going anyway? Mr. White's book of collected essays, "One Man's Meat," is required reading, or selections from it, in many high schools in the United States. Even people who know these facts do not perhaps always realize that this is the same E. B. White who has written two children's books, the excellent "Stuart Little," and the near perfect Charlotte's Web."

He has been for over twenty-five years an editor of the *New Yorker* and has written virtually for all departments of the magazine, except racing and feminine fashions. He has even done a cover. He is known only by his work, which is perhaps as it should be.

His subject, that of any first-class essayist, is mankind, its follies, its humor, its passions, its predicaments. His themes are, more often than not, contemporary man as he lives—particularly in the city of New York. When he writes of the country, it is mostly of his other favorite animals: there is a tribute to the hen, and a heartfelt piece on the death of a pig. Even modern city man with his urban plights Mr. White sees, as any reflective writer must, in the context of the weather, the seasons, the sky and the eternal.

In the midst of brooding over the thunderous implications of the head-lines, he paused to observe a leaf falling in a tiny garden in a New York backyard. Like the chief character of the title piece, he is aware amid the gadgets, the alarms, the fakes and cheapnesses, as well as the splendor of the city, of the glistening ecstasy of "the second tree from the corner" caught in

Reprinted from *New York Times Book Review*, 17 January 1954, 1. Copyright © 1954/5462/1970/77 by the New York Times Company. Reprinted with permission.

a certain light, and of the eternal and recurrently human facts, a child happy on a swing while pundits in the Pentagon calculate the exactitudes of atomic firepower.

He weighs the meaning of the United Nations when one begins to think in terms of the wide and simple fact of our common humanity. He considers humor and begins by saying it cannot be analyzed, yet he manages to say trenchant things about it. "Beneath the sparkling surface of these dilemmas flows the strong tide of human woe." "Humor plays close to the big, hot fire, which is truth and the reader often feels the heat."

One feels the heat, or the banked fires, of Mr. White's humor, too, the warmth of his quiet dedications and of his moral integrities. It is in "The Retort Transcendental" in which phrases of Thoreau leap to the lips of the essayist in reply to current banalities or foolishness. The writing is often ablaze with deep feeling about important matters, about freedom which, it is clear, is in Mr. White's scale of values the most important of all. One feels the heat, too, of his passion for life, however troubled, for mankind, however foolish, and for New York, however maddening.

One feels it perhaps most in that sheer masterpiece of a parable, or a short story (is it?), a mystic's radiant avowal mildly entitled "The Second Tree From The Corner." The writing bears in every sentence Mr. White's signature, from the beginning "Have you had any bizarre thoughts lately?" asked the doctor, to the passage in which the troubled non-hero responds to the psychiatrist's question, "What is it you want?" "As he walked Trexler meditated on what he wanted. Trexler knew what he wanted and what, in general, all men wanted, and he was glad in a way that it was inexpressible and unattainable. He was satisfied to remember that it was deep, formless, enduring and impossible of fulfillment."

As one reads these prose pieces, ranging from longish essays and short, short stories (most but not all of which have appeared in the *New Yorker* or elsewhere), to paragraphs that one recalls from the *New Yorker* (and about which at the time one had felt Mr. White's touch), one is haunted by the desire to analyze the secret of these telling and economical effects. They add up to (or perhaps "fuse into" would be better) this writer's style, which is one with his substance. The wit is marked at once by penetration and by compassion, the nobility is without affectation, and the homespunness is unaffected, too.

There is a constant communicated sense of the wonder and the wackiness of man, the care for the exact phrase and the delight in the breezy candor of the vernacular. "Body and soul always ravaged by the internal slugging match." This writing is clearly the product of sedulous art, but it has the flame of spontaneity and the grit of independence both as to mode and spirit.

The story of Mr. Volente returning to his beloved New York on a languid summer dawn has the freshness of a countryman still wide-eyed at the marvel of New York; it has also the affection nourished on knowledge in a knowing city mind. The true poetry of feeling breaks through even a casual paragraph on the Business Show, and there is authentic poetry, too, in some of the excellent light verse here included, warmth in the wit and wisdom in the epigram.

One sometimes wonders what Thoreau might have written about, what he might have written like, if he had lived for the most part in New York City a century later than he lived in Concord, Mass. I suspect he would have written about some of the things E. B. White writes about and in something of the way he writes. He could scarcely have done it much better. Here is the Thoreau of our day, the play of mind, the uncorrupted seriousness, the dry unquenchable humor, all in danger now of coming to be regarded as and eventually perhaps coming to be un-American activities. This book is American prose and, one is tempted to say, Americanism at its best.

The Points of My Compass

◆

Hearth and Hurricane

HERBERT GOLD

The most important point of reference for understanding E. B. White's special gifts as a man of letters—and his special difficulties with these gifts—is the great American writer Henry David Thoreau, who pared down his life to the smallest practical elements. From within his stoical seclusion he screeched most eloquently at the rest of the world.

E. B. White has tried to live in society. He has had, and still has, a wife; one can almost say that he has also had a magazine, *The New Yorker*, much of whose best prose is either his or reflects his own wryly committed spirit. But the burden of grafting a Thoreauvian blend of stoical abstention and poetic concern onto *The New Yorker's* peculiarly discreet diction has weighed heavily on White. *The New Yorker* dislikes strong emotion strongly expressed, sustained argument argumentatively put forward. It is as if emotion and argument might keep the commuters reading past their stops on the train. White has been one of the architects of *The New Yorker's* style, and also one of its victims. Nevertheless, his real quality as a man and a writer has managed to survive. He has felt strongly about various matters, from the atomic bomb to urban noise. Wit and understatement and a contained rage result in a considerable achievement in this new collection, "The Points of My Compass," which is brilliant sentence by sentence, convincing paragraph by paragraph, but occasionally fades out into whimsy over the long stretch of an essay.

Reprinted from *Saturday Review* 45 (24 November 1962): 30. Reprinted with permission.

Dogs, hurricanes, village characters, Democrats, Republicans, Florida seasides, a girl circus rider, a coon, pigeons, and old railroads receive his nostalgic approval. The essay on Thoreau embodies a passionately sustained admiration, and this makes an exciting occasion. Modern times—its machinery, television, factory farming, city bustle, bad grammar—receives a dose of coolness through a series of cautious dry, humorous personal accounts. White has developed a trick that might be called the semisequitur. He often concludes one of these essays with a note of not-quite-relevant pedantry, as if to say, "Well, there I go, raising my voice again. But listen, what really concerns me is: The back kitchen got renovated."

He need not be so shy. He can compose a beautiful, helpless evocation of the weakness that overtakes a man moving out of an apartment, disposing of the accumulated years. Or he can pay a lively, funny, youthfully exuberant tribute to an old car—much superior to the Detroit product of 1958, he decided. (Moderate in most matters, he admits that he did buy a later model.)

At his best, raising his privileged voice, White vigorously protests the abuses of power and argues that the nation must function as "the true friend and guardian of sovereign man." He is passionate about Thoreau, about disarmament, about the need for rational states and international cooperation. He does not mince words in his prescription: world government. He notes that he was misquoted in the *Congressional Record* as urging "Supernatural cooperation," when what he actually urged was "supranational" means. It is an appropriate irony that a writer who joins a finicky concern with language to large humanitarian hopes was spooked by a typo. It leads him to wonder if maybe that's the way salvation will have to come—supernaturally.

In the meantime, despite the printers' revision of his ideas, E. B. White's complaints and celebrations will continue to provide some sense under the glare of the rockets. This supernatural, supranational man, wearing his bright orange cap in order not to be shot by the hunters, bears his good wits back and forth between Maine and New York, Cape Canaveral and the United Nations, the fading past and the dim future.

The Essays of E. B. White

◆

Smilin' Through

Nigel Dennis

One of the many interesting pieces in *Essays of E. B. White* is called "Some Remarks on Humor" and was originally the preface to an anthology of humor assembled by White and his wife and published in 1941. In it, White does his duty to the publishers like a man and talks about the essence of humor—why funny is so funny, what temperature the oven should be, and so on—but his heart is not in this unhappy duty; no man knows better that a dissertation on humor is bound to be worthless as information and painful as reading matter. So, he moves on smartly to the infinitely fascinating question, which nobody has managed to answer, of why Americans believe "that if a thing is funny it can be presumed to be something less than great, because if it were truly great it would be wholly serious."

"Wholly solemn" or "wholly grave" is what is meant here, because the whole point of White's argument is that a humorous response to life can be just as serious as a humorless one. How it has come about that a nation which produces humor in such abundance, and lives by it to such an extent that it would be unrecognizable without it, has concluded that humor is inferior nonetheless both in form and depth—this is either a most bewildering paradox or can be explained simply by itself: that of which there is no end, and which comes so easily to so many, cannot matter as much as a gravity which lies

Reprinted from *New York Review of Books* 24 (27 October 1977): 42–43. Reprinted with permission from *The New York Review of Books*. Copyright © 1977 by Nyrev, Inc.

outside the reach of the vulgar and makes the author seem more like a rare bird than a bird-brained one.

Thus, when White says of Finley Peter Dunne's Mr. Dooley that "the Irish dialect is difficult but worth the effort, and it smooths out after the first hundred miles," the correctness of the criticism is invalidated by the smile, and the statement needs rewriting in stolid form before its rightness can matter. Similarly, few people would rate W. C. Fields's disgraceful comedy as a serious social criticism of American hypocrisies; Fields was without the capacity to lapse into the shameless sentimentality that made Chaplin's comedy seem infinitely serious and inspired volumes of writing that are still painfully serious to read.

It would be wrong to argue that all great comedians have something to offer. The late-lamented Groucho gave only joy to millions of people—a gift that is not regarded as serious and is not to be ranked with a good hospital or a seeing-eye dog. Most American humorists fall into Groucho's category of clown and tumbler, and they pull down many funny foreigners in their fall. Few serious American students of French literature have noticed how funny Stendhal can be. We are never told that Dostoevsky wrote a story about a bureaucrat who was swallowed alive by a crocodile, leaving his wife "a sort of grass-widow." Even Tolstoy's unbelievably venomous humor respecting his two great hates, Wagner and Shakespeare, must be rendered glumly before it can be set before the serious student.

White shows that American humorists have accepted their secondary place in the scale of seriousness for many years. The greatest of them, Mark Twain, asserted that "humor is only a fragrance, a decoration"; he himself was essentially a preacher, he said (how strange for a man to think that essence and fragrance are separable!). Franklin P. Adams didn't think it was even profitable: "For the writers who amass the greatest gold have, it seems to me, no sense of humor. . . ." And the essayist Frank Moore Colby remarks, in an excellent passage on humor, that the pride taken by every American in his sense of humor is not a tendency that should be commended. "There are people whom nature meant to be solemn from their cradle to their grave . . . Solemnity is relatively a blessing, and the man who was born with it should never be encouraged to wrench himself away." Poets who wrench themselves away long enough to write light verse are careful, White says, to do so under an assumed name. Apparently their seriousness as poets would be dangerously reduced if they were heard to laugh. *The New Oxford Book of American Verse*, published last year, shows that this is as true today as it was in 1941. Gravity is the hallmark of that excellent volume. After James Russell Lowell, only Gwendolyn Brooks and E. E. Cummings risk the calamity of a smile. T. S. Eliot is pure sackcloth and ashes; all the work he put into cats gets a rejection slip.

White believes that things are different in England. "The *Punch* editors not only write the jokes but they help make the laws of England." It could be said that the laws have been an improvement on the jokes; but White's point is sound. Britain's problem is the opposite of America's. Too much gravity incurs suspicion. It indicates that the author has a mission, or a message, either of which is bound to create discomfort and unhappiness. Most of the century's most notable missionaries—Shaw, Chesterton, Belloc, Waugh—did their best to be serious as humorously as possible. Their native audiences took little interest in the United States except as a bottomless well of excellent humor. Thurber's and White's *Is Sex Necessary?* would have seemed to many of them a far more serious contribution to life in 1941 than the collected works of Theodore Dreiser.

But White has a second misfortune to be distressed about: he is not only a humorous writer but an essayist as well. He says of this fate: "I am not fooled about the place of the essay in twentieth-century American letters— it stands a short distance down the line. The essayist, unlike the novelist, the poet, and the playwright, must be content in his self-imposed role of second-class citizen. A writer who has his sights trained on the Nobel Prize or other earthly triumphs had best write a novel, a poem, or a play. . . ." His publishers think better of him. They say: "The *Essays of E. B. White* are incomparable; as one critic put it, he is 'our finest essayist, perhaps our only one.'" In fact, he is one of a great many; but since few of them need to struggle with the curse of humor, they not only escape the humiliation of second-class citizenship but are often not recognized as essayists at all. Some are even indistinguishable, in a bad light, from men whose sights are trained on the Nobel Prize.

On this matter there is an interesting comment by Harold Ross, quoted by White in his collected *Letters* of last year. Ross turned a cold eye on any piece of work that was what he called "writer-conscious"—work, that is to say, in which the author's sights were trained more on his own impressiveness than on his subject. Though the phrase was coined by a man who only edited a humorous magazine, it would be wise to take it seriously. "Writer-consciousness" is one of the toughest dragons in the field of authorship and carries off sociological and critical essayists as frequently as if they were virgins. One of White's achievements—which goes hand in hand with his deprecatory remarks about himself—is the extent to which he manages to avoid being "writer-conscious": his search is for the plain word and his concern is for the subject. If he doesn't always get the better of the dragon it is because the humorist is always fond of his humor and gets personally involved in his pursuit of it.

Still the question remains: What seriousness can be expected of a man who can only write essays and is inclined to smile? White has smoothed out this question somewhat by the selection he has made for this book: there are a number of pieces, mostly about civil liberties, which would meet the serious test with perfect solemnity, even though they have no serious theories behind them and no serious cliches to push them forward. There are also some dubious ones, such as the study of *Walden*, a book which White thinks was not written for the "plodding economist" (is this the way to talk?), and the lively piece on White's old professor at Cornell, William Strunk Jr., whose textbook, *The Elements of Style*, was largely a compendium of short rules—"Omit needless words"; "Make definite assertions"; "Avoid a succession of loose sentences." These rules, if followed today, would reduce most great works to slim volumes.

But the heart of the collection is the picture it presents of country life. A humorous undertow is running all the time, and the combination of this and the rural material is bound to startle the foreigner who depends not only on the press for his picture of America but on American writers who are first-class citizens with a vengeance. The French like to say: "There is a peasant inside every Frenchman"; but the idea of a sort of peasant living in an American can only seem absurd. Take this statement, for example: "I like the cold. I like the snow. I like the descent to the dark, cold kitchen at six in the morning, to put a fire in the wood stove. . . . I steal down in my wrapper carrying a pair of corduroy pants . . . and fill the kettle with fresh spring water . . . with a poker I clear the grate in the big black Home Crawford 8-20, roll up two sheets of yesterday's Bangor *Daily News*, and lay them in the firebox along with a few sticks of cedar kindling and two sticks of stovewood on top of that."

There must be something serious about this statement because of the shock it must give to innocent Frenchmen and many others. It is difficult for a foreigner to turn his back on an America that is not only entirely urban and electrical but forever verging on the criminal. He has lived with it for many years; it was as long ago as the Thirties that Alistair Cooke began his great pioneering struggle to present America as a place where people lived. White not only enters into this struggle with a cheerfulness that many serious natives would find objectionable; he even shows that the distress felt by Europeans over the loss of old ways and old institutions is felt with the same bitterness in his homeland.

There are a few other things to be said in favor of White. In his old-fashioned way, he omits needless words and avoids a succession of loose sentences. He continues the old tradition which has made humor America's best ambassador. Though only an essayist, he makes definite assertions and says shortly what others say at length. He will never win the Nobel Prize and will certainly never approach a Great Work; but he will always make sense, which is an achievement too. To conclude that he should be ranked among serious writers would only give offense to those who are; the most one can say is that he was thought to be serious by Harold Ross.

The Quiet Wit of E. B. White

RICHARD FREEDMAN

The essayist, says E. B. White in the foreword to this sterling collection, is "sustained by the childish belief that everything he thinks about, everything that happens to him, is of general interest."

This is the first assertion in the book, and the only disingenous one. For surely the interest inheres in what the essayist brings to his material rather than in the material itself. If the essayist is any good, what interests him necessarily interests us. Montaigne's kidney stones are more memorable than your Aunt Tillie's because they happened to Montaigne.

To mention White in the same paragraph as the inventor and supreme master of the essay form is not quite the wild inflation of literary values it might at first seem: the woods are not so full of wise men expressing themselves in this form that we can afford to get sniffy about our finest living practitioner of it, and if White lacks the Frenchman's ultimate profundity, he has a crusty charm all his own that radiates from every page he writes.

Whether he is holding forth on Fred the dachshund—surely the least sentimentalized but most memorable canine in recent literature—or on the vanished New York of the 1940's; on the Model T Ford, Thoreau, media meteorologists or the death of a pig, it is the quality of his mind that rivets the reader's attention to his subject matter. As Montaigne himself said, "I take the first subject that chance offers me. All are equally good."

The test of White's excellence as an essayist, then, is that he can entrance even when dealing with a subject which of itself may leave the reader gelid with indifference. In my case, at least, nature in general and farm life in particular have this numbing effect, yet filtered through White's mind and sensibility, even an account of his barnyard chores becomes as exciting as his account of the New York we agree on loving.

How does he accomplish this? His truly is the art which conceals art. The essays amble rather than sparkle, yet occasionally a cliche will be wrenched a half-turn into an epigram so poetically expressed that it coruscates with quiet wit: "An attractive half truth in bed with a man can disturb him as deeply as a cracker crumb." Or the humidity of Florida is such that "postage stamps mate with another as shamelessly as grasshoppers."

Reprinted from *Washington Post Book World*, 6 November 1977: E3. Copyright © 1977 by *The Washington Post*. Reprinted with permission.

More characteristically the epigram will be less flamboyantly witty, but will make a profound point about, say, the inner nature of democracy, the seeming artlessness of expression only enhancing the passionate conviction underlying it: "The concern of a democracy is that no honest man shall feel uncomfortable, I don't care who he is, or how nutty he is"; or as long ago as 1941, "Fraudulence has become a national virtue and is well thought of in many circles."

This latter observation springs from White's horror at the Floridian practice of painting oranges to look more orange than nature saw fit to make them. And here, perhaps, is the greatest gift of the essayistic mind: to extract a momentous truth from the most seemingly trivial event or artifact. Perhaps the finest of the 31 pieces in the collection does just that. It is the brief account, written 30 years ago, of the death by disease of a pig, told with such austere emotion that, without any fancy tricks, it becomes a metaphor of our universal helplessness in the face of death—for the mortality of all of us. If John Donne had been a Yankee farmer, he would have written this way.

The Yankee Farmer White most closely resembles, of course, is Thoreau. He paraphrases him ("my program is to simplify"), writes perceptively about him (the moving centenary tribute to *Walden* is included in this collection), and occasionally even improves on him: "The Canada jay looks as though he had slept in his clothes." Only in his admiration for cities and motor cars does White diverge from his master, and even then it's the New York of 1947, the Ford Model T, that he admires. Since then, the city seems "to have suffered a personality change, as though it had a brain tumor as yet undetected," and the self-starter has taken the fun out of driving, "I can still feel my old Ford nuzzling me at the curb, as though looking for an apple in my pocket."

White is a nostalgic man, whether he is bemoaning the deaths of railroad passenger service or the St. Nicholas Magazine, but he never wallows in nostalgia for its own sake, nor does he let it blind him to current realities. Even in 1947 he saw that New York could easily "explode in a radioactive cloud of hate and rancor and bigotry," and the fact that so far it hadn't done so was no guarantee that it never would.

In the self-abnegating seamlessness of his prose it is easy to forget that, as an artist, too, he is so far from being buried in the past that he was almost the sole creator of one of the most underrated, but I think most likely to endure, modern prose styles—that of the *New Yorker*, a style easier to deride than to imitate successfully.

The Poems and Sketches of E. B. White

◆

The Voice of The New Yorker

EDWARD HOAGLAND

E. B. White is 82, and it's a pleasure to report that, as far as this reader can tell, all the principal decisions of his life were for the best. He married happily when he was 30, the same year in which his first two books were published. Four years later he bought a summer house on the coast of Maine, to which he retired in 1957 with great contentment, after many years of close, witty and even occasionally definitive observation of New York City. He had set his sights on becoming a superb essayist, rather than a novelist or poet, and chose a fledgling magazine called the *New Yorker* as his vehicle. The rest is history, one might almost say. He made his name synonymous with the word *essay* on this side of the ocean for a couple of decades, and in effect became the voice of the *New Yorker*—for which we are indebted both to him and to the magazine.

There are times, reading an E. B. White book of essays, when you think he must be the most likable man of letters alive. This is as it should be in a collection of personal pieces; and if you are some kind of writer yourself, you probably want to try to imitate him. He developed a professional commentator's ability to "rise to any occasion"—a trade fair on Eighth Avenue, an adman's grammatical gaffe in the newspaper, an atomic test in the Pacific, a threatening notice from the Humane Society about his busy dachshund, which

Reprinted from *New York Times Book Review*, 8 November 1981: 3, 36–37, 39. Reprinted by permission of the author.

is wearing a Maine license tag. He holds a new baby to his ear like a conch shell, walks his young son to a fussily progressive nursery school, discusses the love life of bees and snails from readings in the library, goes house hunting in a sketch entitled "Growing Up in New Canaan."

Because Mr. White did not leap outward to an independent career the way such other *New Yorker* stalwarts as Edmund Wilson, John O'Hara and John Updike did—who published a distinguished body of material that would have been unpublishable there—one sometimes wondered whether he had sacrificed part of his potential for being a voice for himself by being the voice of the magazine. Though the question cannot be answered with assurance by a stranger, again the evidence is that he did exactly what he ought to have. This collection of poems and sketches—many of them slightly experimental, many not published in the magazine—reveals no unpopular ideas, no unfashionable or contentious crotchets that he might have picked up and worked on at one time and then laid aside in the squeeze of meeting a professional deadline. There is no anger in him that threatens to get out of hand, no bent for a rigorous or painful self-examination. He was not a poet—fewer than 10 of the 63 poems included strike me as much good—and not a fiction writer either. The sketches which resemble short stories are nowhere near the caliber of those which amount to short essays. As a result, the book should not be a reader's introduction to Mr. White. A better choice for that purpose would be the selection of his essays published in 1977, or his chronicles of country and city living, "One Man's Meat" and "The Second Tree From the Corner," or a masterly children's book like "Stuart Little," or his "Letters" (1976).

Nonetheless, some lovely snippets are collected here. In "Twins" he visits the zoo to see a moose calf and discovers two newborn deer. "Heavier than Air" is about the fear of flying; and "Fin de Saison—Palm Beach" speaks for itself.

And "Commuter":

> Commuter　　one who spends his life
> In riding to and from his wife;
> A man who shaves and takes a train
> And then rides back to shave again

And from "Pigeon, Sing Cuccu!":

> Beside the Fifty-ninth Street lake
> Old men, alive and toothless.
> Applaud the plundering of the drake
> And grin when love is ruthless.

An essayist, unlike a novelist or dramatist, need not be overly concerned with "plot," and so there have been many essayists besides Mr. White who have turned their attention to animals. Like most poets, an essayist is likely to be temperamentally quite self-absorbed, and thus may find it easier, less obtrusive, to muse about himself partly by way of speculating on the nature of beasts. Also it is a means of avoiding being controversial while edging into controversy, as of course George Orwell did in "Animal Farm." And, like poets, essayists are simply "alone" more than a novelist—whose head is clamorous with "characters"—and so they may be more observant of the dog, the cat, the fox, the cedar waxwing in the backyard.

Mr. White has written wonderfully about pigs, geese, coons, crows, hackmatacks after a hurricane, about small-town gossip, continuity and tragedy. He is practically always authoritative on Maine, but there do tend to be two E. B. Whites in a span of essays—the Maine democrat and the Manhattan sophisticate, if not to say aristocrat, who sometimes rises to occasions you wish he hadn't risen to. Coyly, for the Bryn Mawr Alumnae Bulletin, he describes being a Bryn Mawr husband; and, earlier, has inflicted on us a lengthy, supercilious account of the servant problem on East 48th Street: "Now the relatives of domestics are an even more mysterious band of people than domestics themselves. I knew from experience that sometimes they didn't even have names. I also knew that they never had telephones, although they sometimes lived in the same building with a telephone. . . . She arrived about nine that morning, with fourteen-month-old child in rather bad repair." (One wishes for an E. B. White to ridicule this piece as in White's famous poem taking off on Louis Broomfield's "Malabar Farm.")

His better city essays over the years have been datelined "Turtle Bay," and my only objection to the genre is that—in contrast to himself as country man—he can be disingenuously selective when he's being a New Yorker. City wealth and city poverty aren't savage in Mr. White's New York; and it is not only from hindsight that one can argue with him. He has imbued Manhattan's Turtle Bay with a false innocence, as if the neighborhood hadn't stopped being a real turtle bay 300 years ago.

Yet he can also be refreshingly blunt. In the preface to his 1977 collection of essays, he wrote, "The last time I visited New York, it seemed to have suffered a personality change, as though it had a brain tumor as yet undetected." One should not fault the man for having been a moderate who didn't make more waves, didn't speak louder than came naturally to him. He has worked with the best will in the world through a whole lifetime to say things well, and he has sometimes said hard things, like a writer for the ages, as well as saying them well.

In "The Age of Dust," we see Mr. White hanging a swing in an apple tree for a little girl. Then he goes into the house to continue reading an article in the Bulletin of Atomic Scientists about radioactivity. It is a remarkably humane weapon, the author of the article suggests, because "it gives each member of the target population a choice of whether he will live or die." After an attack, the little girl, in other words, should hold "a folded, dampened handkerchief" over her mouth and walk out of the city in which she lives.

"I went outdoors again to push the swing some more for the little girl, who is always forgetting her handkerchief. At lunch I watched her try to fold her napkin. It seemed to take forever," says Mr. White, envisioning her, with many other small girls, entering the Broadway subway and emerging at 242nd Street and walking north, clutching a folded handkerchief askew across her mouth.

THE CHILDREN'S BOOKS

♦

Stuart Little

♦

Mrs. Little's Second Son

ROSEMARY CARR BENET

Although "Stuart Little" may be listed as a children's book, and children will undoubtedly be the excuse for getting it into the house, it is for all ages, all shapes and sizes of readers who like the light fantastic tone. The exact number of years of the reader won't matter here any more than it does with "Alice," "The Wind in the Willows," some of Milne, or indeed the work of Walt Disney, who created that other popular mouse.

What is "Stuart Little" about? A mouse. Well, what was "The Wind in the Willows" about? A toad. But not the usual mouse or toad; neither one belongs to the general run of the animals-in-waistcoats school of writing. The first three sentences here will give the reader a definite idea as to whether this is or is not his meat. "When Mrs. Frederick C. Little's second son was born, everybody noticed that he was not much bigger than a mouse. The truth of the matter was the baby looked very much like a mouse in every way. He was only about two inches high; and he had a mouse's sharp nose, a mouse's tail, a mouse's whiskers, and the pleasant shy manner of a mouse."

The humorous, wise quality found in E. B. White's other work is reflected here in miniature. Stuart's conversation, towards the end of the book, with an earthy, much traveled telephone repair man who likes the North, has something of the philosophy of "One Man's Meat." There is a matter-of-factness about all Stuart's adventures that keeps them from being too whimsical and

Reprinted from *Saturday Review of Literature* 28 (8 December 1945):26. Reprinted by permission.

that gives them substance and charm. "Before he was many days old, he was not only looking like a mouse but acting like one too,—wearing a grey hat and carrying a small cane."

There is bound to be a charm about the miniature. Thumbelina is apt to be more popular always than Gargantua. Again, of course, one must qualify that statement by adding, for some people. Others *may* prefer elephants and the scale of Grand Central Station. At any rate there are many fine, small details about Stuart's fine, small life; the bed made from four clothes-pins and a cigarette box, the skates fashioned from paper clips, the dime rolled along like a hoop. Since the other Little son, George, is normal size, these all present family problems. Stuart's life in New York, his mistrust of Snowbell, the sinister family cat, his tour on the open road, all give us life in a new dimension, a mouse's eye view of things.

It is easy to see, by the way, from Garth William's illustrations why Stuart mistrusts Snowbell.

This is Mr. White's first venture into the present field. He began "Stuart Little" for a niece who was six years old at the time but had "grown up and was reading Hemingway" before he finished. "Oh, fish feathers," as Stuart Little once said, "size has nothing to do with it. It's temperament and ability that count!" That applies to "Stuart Little" the book, too.

Stuart Little: Or New York Through the Eyes of a Mouse

Malcolm Cowley

Although Mr. and Mrs. Frederick C. Little were normal persons in every way, their second son looked very much like a mouse. Stuart, as they named him, had a mouse's sharp nose, a mouse's whiskers and a mouse's tail. At birth he was so small that a three-cent stamp would have carried him anywhere in the United States. At the age of 7, when he was fully grown, he weighed three and one-half ounces and was a little more than two inches tall, not counting the tail. He wore a gray hat and twirled a little cane.

In his pleasant, mouselike manner, shy but inquisitive, he was always getting into scrapes. Once he tried to do gymnastics on the cord that hung from the window blind, to impress the household cat. The blind rolled up and Stuart was imprisoned there all morning. Once he tried to go skating in Central Park; but a dog chased him, and he had to hide in a celery grove on top of a garbage can. The can was emptied into a truck, the truck was emptied into a scow, and Stuart was carried out to sea. He would have drowned that time, except for a friend of his, a little wrenlike bird named Margalo, who let him cling to her feet and carried him back to his own window sill.

When Margalo flew away to the north the following spring, Stuart went searching for her in a toy automobile with a real engine. He would drive into a filling station and say, "Five, please."

"Five what?" the attendant would ask, looking down at the car not half so big as a scooter.

"Five drops," Stuart would answer in a firm if squeaky voice. "Better look at the oil, too," he would say before riding off to look for a brownish bird, in much the same spirit as Galahad seeking the Grail.

Little Stuart is a very engaging hero, and "Stuart Little" is an entertaining book, whether for children or their parents. If I also found it a little disappointing, perhaps that is because I had been expecting that E. B. White would write nothing less than a children's classic. He has all the required talents, including a gift for making himself understood. He never condescends to his readers: if they happen to be younger than the audience he reaches through the New Yorker, he merely takes more pains to explain his story. Style is even more important in children's books than in those for adults, because one often reads aloud to children, and a bad style wearies the reader, not to mention what it does to the listeners. Within his own range of effects, Mr. White has the best style of any American author: clear, unhackneyed and never tying the tongue into knots.

He has, moreover, a talent for making big things small and homely, as if he saw the world distinctly through the wrong end of a telescope; or as if—to change the figure—he took his readers down the rabbit hole and showed them the bottle that Alice found there, the little bottle with "Drink Me" printed on the label. The liquid in the bottle had a sort of mixed flavor of cherry tart, custard, pineapple, roast turkey, toffy and hot buttered toast; and when Alice drank it, she began shrinking until she was only ten inches high, so that she could look through a tiny door into the loveliest garden you ever saw. But the garden that Mr. White describes in his essays is the world as a whole, and the effect of smallness is deceptive—just as the effect of bigness is deceptive in the authors who imitate Walt Whitman; they describe a world that is really bare and simple, whereas Mr. White's world merely gives, through art, the effect of simplicity.

With this combination of talents in the author, one has high hopes for the book, and Mr. White doesn't always let us down. His dialogue is good from beginning to end. Each of the separate episodes is entertaining, and one at least is uproarious—I mean the boat race in Central Park with Stuart braving the storm at the wheel of a toy yacht. The day he spends as a school teacher is an effective fable about the San Francisco Conference: "Nix on swiping anything" and "Absolutely no being mean" are the two fundamental laws he proposes for a world organization, and I doubt that our statesmen could improve on them.

But the parts of "Stuart Little" are greater than the whole, and the book doesn't hold to the same mood or move in a straight line. There are loose ends in the story, of the sort that make children ask, "What happened then?"—and this time there isn't any answer. For example, a gray Angora cat plans to climb through the window and eat the little bird who is the heroine of the story. Margalo is warned and flies away; but we never learn what happened to the cat when she prowled through the house at night. We never learn what happened to Stuart as he pursued his search for Margalo: did he ever find her? Did he return to his family? Mr. White has a tendency to write amusing scenes instead of telling a story. To say that "Stuart Little" is one of the best children's books published this year is very modest praise for a writer of his talent.

Charlotte's Web

◆

What Makes a Good Children's Book? The Texture of *Charlotte's Web*

Peter Neumeyer

What makes a good children's book? The very question elicits expressions of despair. Might as well ask, "What makes a good book?" But the question is not impossible to answer. Denseness of texture would be a simple and defensible reply. And what is "denseness of texture?" It is close warp; close woof. Many threads per inch. Denseness is allied to richness. There's simply a lot there, a lot put into the book, by an author with many resources, and consequently a lot to consider by a reader with developed capacities.

Take E. B. White's *Charlotte's Web*, and contemplate it, from the discreet word all the way to the mythopoeic dimension.[1]

I. THE WORD

The most discreet attribute in a book is the individual word. The words of *Charlotte's Web* are distinctive and describable. The book opens: "'Where's Papa going with that ax?' said Fern to her mother as they were setting the table for breakfast." The words are simple and basic. "Simple" and "basic" are

Reprinted from *South Atlantic Bulletin* 44:2 (May 1979), 66–75. Reprinted by permission.

not terms to cover numinous impressions. They mean that the words are not Latinate, but are short, commonplace, and that they bespeak their homely Anglo-Saxon origins.

Book endings are almost as instructive as their openings. *Charlotte's Web* ends: "It is not often that someone comes along who is a true friend and a good writer. Charlotte was both" (p. 184). "Charlotte was both" is the last sentence of the book. Charlotte, the feminine of Karl, is, unlike Cher or Sherry, both spawned antiseptically of electronic parents, a true, almost, a chivalric name. "Was" and "both" bespeak their ancient lineage on their very face. And the antithesis, the longer period followed by the almost shockingly short sentence, is classic.

Point one, then, *Charlotte's Web* is a book in which much of the language is distinctive for its pure and primordial pedigree.

II. CHARACTERS AND LANGUAGES

The main characters in *Charlotte's Web* have, in good novelistic tradition, names suggestive of the characteristics of their owners, and—in manner to be explored later—crucial to the most basic nature of the book.

The farm family owning the famous pig is named Arable. The plowable farm—arable. The Plowables own the land to be plowed. One Arable child has an intimate relationship with all natural creatures. Fern Arable, of course. The Fern is a plant so ancient that its earliest evidences are fossilized, are paleographic.

Mrs. Arable is simply Fern's mother, or Mrs. Arable. She dreams of deep freezers, as any generic missus would. And Mr. Arable is Mr. Arable simply, *The Farmer*, not further distinguished, and thus a cousin of Lenski's pasteboard "Farmer Small."

The pig is Wilbur, with all respects to a possible Wilbur reader of this piece, an amiable if perhaps somewhat lumpish name. About Charlotte's name, or Templeton, the rat's, I have no more to say, for the reader can, if he knows the personages involved, make inferences as plausible as mine.

White, then, uses simple English language, and gives his characters names that are appropriate and suggestive. In addition he gives to those characters, human and animal, language such as is befitting to their person, or describes them in language appropriate to character. Thus Templeton, the rat, incarnation of physical and moral putridness, is introduced first as he "crept stealthily along the wall and disappeared into a private tunnel that he had dug between the door and the trough . . ." (p. 30).

"Dug," "door," and "trough," are surreptitious and plough-nosed words. Not open, clean, easy words with healthy pure vowels and crisp consonants, but "ough" words, of off sound, and deceptive in their very spelling. "Dung," "Dugs," "Dinginess"—we can make a catalogue of such words.

Later, still about Templeton, White says, "A rat can creep out late at night . . . [eating from] . . . discarded lunch boxes containing the foul remains of peanut butter sandwiches" (pp. 122–23). The word "creep" is one of White's deceptively simple felicities, reminding us of Swift's use of the same word in describing the Lilliputians' groveling sycophancy—"leaping and creeping," cowering and fawning.

How pure, how simple, by contrast, the straight-forward address of simple Wilbur (like Squire Allworthy in *Tom Jones*). "'Attention please!' he said in a loud, firm voice. 'Will the party who addressed me at bedtime last night kindly make himself or herself known by giving an appropriate sign or signal!'" The bull-horn sensibility of the opening, and the ingenuous covering of all bases—"himself or herself [affirmative action!] . . . sign or signal"— betoken a cerebral circuitry in pig that has all the convolutions of a railroad track in arable Kansas. Truly, "by their words ye shall know them." And *this* is the manner in which the true dramatist, the real negative capability, delineates character.

One may pursue the subtlety of White's play with individual words one degree further. In fact, one must do so to understand all that is happening in this seemingly simple book.

Templeton, who, as he told Wilbur, prefers to spend his time "eating, gnawing, spying, and hiding," (p. 29) eats Wilbur's food from the trough during the rainstorm, sending Wilbur into a fit of depression which makes Lurvy, the hired man, force medicine down the ailing pig's throat. A sad, a bitter day indeed!

The sentence, "Darkness settled over everything" has the tone of Haydn's *Creation*, and tells us we shall have to do with an epic, even if a mini-epic like a rape of the lock, for example. Or, a close call for a pig. The phrase foreshadows, and we shall return to the matter of epic later.

To continue with the subject of wordplay by the author: when Wilbur learns how the seemingly cruel spider, Charlotte, puts her net-caught prey out of its misery: "Wilbur admired the way Charlotte managed. He was particularly glad that she always put her victim to sleep before eating it. 'It's real thoughtful of you to do that, Charlotte,' he said" (p. 48). Note, a book that begins "Where's Papa going with the ax?", a book preferring always to see the real world there, and eschewing all obfuscation—such a book using the doily and antimacassar euphemism, the genteelism, "put to sleep" for the simple word "kill" or "dead", and juxtaposing the phrase outrageously with the eating of the "deceased." ("Would you like to view the remains?" Charlotte might now ask.)

There is still more fun to be had with words when the Zuckermans get pig Wilbur clean for the fair. Enjoy simply the slop glob word choice as Mrs.

Zuckerman says of Wilbur, " 'Every time Lurvy slops him, the food runs down around the ears. Then it dries and forms a crust. He also has a smudge on one side where he lays in the manure.' ' "He lays in clean straw,' corrected Mr. Zuckerman" (p. 120). Half the funning is the vivid word choice. The other, subtler half is grammatical, of course, for Zuckerman "corrects" his wife—the word "corrects" most significantly and purposefully White's—about Wilbur's bed, which is straw, not manure. But the word "correct," favorite of school marms, is juxtaposed with the incorrect use of the word "lay," that other obsession of the guardians of the language. " 'He lays in the manure.' 'He lays in clean straw,' corrected. . . ." And the notion of correctness pertaining to straw and manure is hip to thigh with a mistake in "correctness" pertaining to one of the language's silliest grammatical fetishes.

When White is serious, his words are serious and to the point. There are no circumlocutions, no euphemisms, no fancy talk when there's writerly work to be done, as when, at the beginning of Chapter XIII, White has to set the stage naturalistically, explaining economically and precisely the web of a spider, with its orb and radial lines. No verbal high jinx here, and if you don't know what orb and radial lines are, and can't tell by the picture, you'd better ask someone.

And finally, fittingly, on the matter of words, the plot itself is to turn on a simple word, and the tension and the suspense regarding the identity of a single word.

Wilbur, at the fair, turns out not to win the blue ribbon, not to be the largest, biggest, fattest pig. Again there rises the spectre of his being slaughtered for bacon. Clearly, as we know must be the case in stories such as this, rescue must come from somewhere. But from where? Templeton, the rat, creeps once again, and typically, into the garbage and the foul remnants scattered about the fairground. There, among deviled ham sandwich and wormy apple, he finds a bit of old newspaper from which he tears a—the—word. What word? It will be the talisman, the instrument of Wilbur's salvation as sweet Charlotte in her dying last act weaves neatly into the center of her final web the great word, HUMBLE. Similarly to the manner in which comparable situations are handled in *Winnie the Pooh* ("trespassers," or "North Pole") nobody is completely certain of the word's proper use. They have the dictionary definition all right—more or less—"Not proud," and "near the ground." How fitting for Wilbur, says Charlotte. He is indeed not a proud pig, and he is, physically speaking, "near the ground."

White renders with enormous skill the very slight misconstrual of words, as such misconstrual takes place among children and students, and occasionally foreigners, when they look up a word in the dictionary and use it, but have not the custom of the word, and therefore slightly, only slightly, mistake, using, more or less, the dictionary equivalents, but in a manner in which one who is really in possession of the word would not.

And the joke continues with the human beings in the next chapter. Next morning everyone climbs out of the truck at the Fair Grounds. " 'Look!' cried Fern. 'Look at Charlotte's web! Look what it says!'

The grownups and the children joined hands and stood there, studying the new sign.

' "Humble," ' said Mr. Zuckerman. 'Now ain't that just the word for Wilbur!' " (p. 149). And later an admiring woman, looking at the livestock, points out that Wilbur 'Isn't as big as the pig next door, . . . but he's cleaner. That's what I like.'

'So do I,' said another man.

'He's humble, too,' said a woman reading the sign on the web (p. 151).

The glorious non-sequitur is authorial genius of a sort almost to defy analysis. Wilbur is not *not* humble; nor is Humble the word anyone would think to describe him. The word is simply askew for the occasion, a good and literally "found" joke. The magic word is itself common and unpretentious, simple, yet misunderstood, and it turns out, in all its—not wrongness, but simply irrelevance—to be the "open sesame" that clinches Wilbur's salvation and sinecure.

III. The Sentence

White is artist of the word. He is also artist of the sentence. The marvelous dictional simplicity of the opening has been commented on. That the first sentence, "Where's Papa going with that ax?" is almost as simple an interrogative as is possible in our language is noteworthy. And between that exemplary opening and the closing, White continues play with syntax, only one instance of which I will here point out, a verbal cousin to what in music is called a crab canon. Fern's brother, Avery, is swinging from a rope in Zuckerman's barn. The illustration, matching text, graphically shows the pendular rope—the rope swing—and the act of swinging which White renders. "Avery straddled the rope and jumped. He sailed out through the door, frog and all, into the sky, frog and all (p. 70)." The syntactic mimesis of the act by the syntax—up, down, up—is noteworthy, as are numerous other and kindred word games in the text.

But more stunning even than White's first sentence is the conclusion to *Charlotte's Web.* ". . . . It is not often that someone comes along who is a true friend and a good writer. Charlotte was both" (p. 184). This penultimate sentence has the neoclassical poise, balance, distance, and decorum, the proverb-like conclusiveness, of a line from, say, Johnson's "The Vanity of Human Wishes." It stands classically, drawing its credibility from the clarity of its expression. Exegesis would be but a diminution of the impact of its brevity: *Charlotte was both*.

IV. The Plot and The Rhetoric

Beyond matters of diction and syntax, further expertise is demonstrated by White in his control of basic authorial techniques, such as plotting. *Charlotte's Web* is a skillfully plotted tale, a well-told tale using foreshadowing, and standing up to the old Sheherezade test—will you leave the story teller's head on one more night to hear the outcome? "Will loveable pig Wilbur be left alive or butchered? Can Charlotte save him?"

"Hello!" says a dumb bumbling sheep to Wilbur at the outset. "Seems to me you're putting on weight. . . . Well, I don't like to spread bad news . . ." (p. 49). Like the first rejections of Lear by Goneril, such a note bodes ill. From then on in *Charlotte's Web*, the incidents follow inevitably, fate seems inexorable, and, in fact, we have no cheap romance, but tragicomedy in which salvation comes hand in hand with the cathartic ending in which Charlotte is sacrificed for the continuity of her species.

There are suspenseful barbings of the hook enroute, as when Mr. Arable says to Zuckerman, the hired hand, ". . . wonderful pig. . . . It's hard to believe he was the runt of the litter. You'll get some extra good ham and bacon, Homer, when it comes time to kill *that* pig" (p. 125). (And the name, Homer, for the farmhand—the unlikely combination, Homer Zuckerman—will come into its own too.)

As for White's authorial stance, it is omniscient, as when he says of the newly introduced spider, Charlotte, "[u]nderneath her rather bold and cruel exterior, she had a kind heart, and she was to prove loyal and true to the very end" (p. 41). No doubt, then, that White has in mind the total shape and the outcome of the story. Occasionally, too, White permits himself an aside to the audience, either to children reading the tale, or to their parents, as when Charlotte, explaining webs to Wilbur, says "Did you ever hear of the Queensborough Bridge?" "What do people catch in the Queensborough Bridge—bugs?" (p. 60) asks Wilbur, and you must note the felicitous little touch of "in," not "on" the Queensborough Bridge, since Wilbur is thinking still syntactically about webs (*in* webs), not bridges (about which one, of course, says "on"). The grace of White's ironical asides may be fully appreciated when compared with similar attempts by no less than Thackeray in *The Rose and the Ring* (1855), archly addressing the parents over the heads of children so that the effect is really none other than the author breaking faith with his audience.

The matter of authorial stance is complicated, too, when White successfully violates that first injunction for children's authors: "Don't have talking animals." For the first two chapters, indeed, only the human beings talk. Then, later, when the animals do seem to talk, the stunt is pulled off so neatly that, even with the text in front of one, one is hard put to decide whether Fern can actually understand the animals. We never do hear a conversational exchange between Fern and the beasts.

V. The Tradition

Having noted White's artistry, ranging from diction to sentence structure, to rhetorical and authorial stance, there remains only the analysis of the largest dimension of the tale, the demonstration that this seemingly slight children's story flows in the mainstream of Western literary tradition, drawing for its names, themes, even its plot, from rich classical backgrounds, and, insofar as these themselves mirror deepest archetypical truths, drawing on primordial human manifestations.

First, the epical connotations of "Darkness settled over everything" (p. 29), and of Mr. Zuckerman's first name, Homer, have been suggested. *Charlotte's Web*, both according to the author's oft-stated intent, and from ample internal evidence, is in the mainstream of the Western literary tradition, a tradition traceable at least three millenia, beginning in the ninth century B.C. with Hesiod's *Works and Days*, and carried on through Virgil's *Eclogues*, and then on through such 18th century achievements as Thompson's "The Seasons." And indeed, as in Thompson, and in Haydn, the book is interspersed with lyrical intermezzos in a minor key, celebrating the beauties of the rural year. Thus, mid-plot and action, in Chapter VI, we find: "Early summer days are a jubilee time for birds. In the fields around the house, in the barn, in the woods, in the swamp—everywhere love and songs and nests and eggs. . . . On an apple bough, the Phoebe teeters and wags its tail and says 'Phoebe, phoebe!': The song sparrow, who knows how brief and lovely life is, says 'Sweet, sweet, sweet interlude . . .'" (p. 43).

Note in this excerpt not only the exaltation of the seasons, but the melancholy theme of *et in arcadia ego*—in the midst of life, there comes death. Moodful contemplations of the time—of year or of day—pervade the book, as when Fern is at the barn and, though knowing it is suppertime, cannot bear to leave. "Swallows passed on silent wings, in and out of the doorways, bringing food to their young ones. From across the road a bird sang "Whipoorwill, whipoorwill!". . . . he [Lurvy] loved life, and loved to be a part of the world on a summer evening" (p. 62).

Such a passage is kindred to Collin's odes, to Young's "Night Thoughts," and by way of them, to the Roman, and through them, to the Greek pastoral.

The same chapter ends:

"Good night, Charlotte" said Wilbur.

"Good night, Wilbur!"

There was a pause.

"Good night, Charlotte!"

"Good night, Wilbur!"

"Good night!"

"Good night" (p. 65).

The evening approaches. The night cometh. . . .

White himself (the letter to me notwithstanding) was fully aware of what he was about, as we may see in his recently published *Letters*, in which repeatedly there occur such statements as White's telling Gene Deitch, who intended to film the book, ". . . the film should be a paean to life, a hymn to the barn, an acceptance of dung."[3] Ten years earlier, writing to Louis de Rochemont, White had already called *Charlotte's Web* a "hymn to the barn. . . . pastoral, seasonal . . ."[4] And if further supporting evidence of the arcadian sources of the book is needed, note merely the name of the one understanding choral interpreter of the relationship of nature's beasts to the natural child, and to the lapsarian adults—Dr. Dorian.

Secondly, as significant as the generic placement of the book, is its clear place in the archetypical tradition: Life out of Death; Birth and Renewal out of the Ashes. Out of the winter earth springs new life, and out of the death of Charlotte comes her progeny and her immortality. "We're leaving here on the warm updraft," the ballooning spiders call to Wilbur. "This is our moment of setting forth." (p. 179) And we readers may ponder back to the long history of setting forth in literature—Adam and Eve at the end of *Paradise Lost*, Gawain, the Grail questers, Huck on his river, and Stuart Little, White's mouse creation of five years earlier. In Stuart's book, *Stuart Little*, the last sentence reads ". . . . he peered ahead into the great land that stretched before him . . . the sky was bright, and somehow he felt he was headed in the right direction."[5]

The dying first, and the setting forth, were crucial to White as he worked and contemplated his book. We have again the evidence in the *Letters* of White's repeated exasperation with those who would trivialize the story, making it meaningless by altering the conclusion, eliminating Charlotte's death, and giving the book a happy ending.[6] As White well knew, the great theme of the book was its core. As he wrote in 1973, " 'Charlotte' was a story of friendship, life, death, salvation."[7]

To set forth such a historically and anthropologically basic and primal theme, using authorial resources but a few of which I have adumbrated, is to write with denseness of texture on a subject of sufficient magnitude. And to do that is to write greatly. Written perhaps with children in mind, *Charlotte's Web* is a great book.

Notes

1. I venture my thesis notwithstanding the fact of E. B. White's twitting me, saying how lucky he was when writing the book "that I didn't know what in hell was going on. To have known might easily have been catastrophic." (Unpublished letter to the author, April 20, 1977.)

2. E. B. White, *Charlotte's Web* (New York: Harper & Row, 1952), p. 1.

3. Ed. Dorothy Lobrano Guth, *Letters of E. B. White* (New York: Harper & Row), p. 614.

4. *Letters*, p. 481.

5. E. B. White, *Stuart Little* (New York: Harper & Row, 1945), p. 131.

6. *Letters*, pp. 531, 532, 550, 585.

7. *Letters*, p. 645.

Writing in *Charlotte's Web*

JANICE M. ALBERGHENE

My acquaintance with *Charlotte's Web* was long delayed. I first read it at 25, an age at which many of my contemporaries were anticipating the pleasures of rereading it with the infants they at present cradled in their arms. I approached the book, however, in much the same way I would have as a child. I scrutinized its cover and wondered about the title: who was Charlotte, and if she was so important, why was the book called *Charlotte's Web* instead of *Charlotte and Her Web*? The first page or two of the story hardly answered these questions. Feeling sneaky but determined, I turned then to the book's last page and read, "It is not often that someone comes along who is a true friend and a good writer. Charlotte was both" (p. 184). The child reader in me nodded familiarly at the words "true friend"—most children's books got around to this topic one way or another—but when I saw "good writer," I resumed my role of adult critic. Even the co-author of *The Elements of Style* would, I thought, be hard pressed to explain to children what the term "good writer" signified. Surely White had used that last phrase lightly; he could not have meant to explore what it means to be a "good writer" in a children's book. But he could, and he did.

At first glance then, it seems odd that few critics have commented on Charlotte's writing.[1] More importantly, if skilled readers pay little conscious attention to Charlotte as a writer, what attention do children pay? Dr. Dorian, a character who appears midway through *Charlotte's Web*, offers a broad hint during a conversation with Mrs. Arable. She is worried about eight-year-old Fern's claim that "animals talk to each other." Asked his opinion, he says that he has never heard an animal talk, "But that proves nothing. It is quite possible that an animal has spoken civilly to me and that I didn't catch the remark because I wasn't paying attention. Children pay better attention than grownups" (p. 110).[2]

The attention Fern pays to the animals' talk is a deep absorption. She is reflective, but she is not self-conscious—she is thinking, but she isn't thinking that she's thinking. Readers of *Charlotte's Web* are sometimes startled to discover Fern at the end of Chapter 13 ("Good Progress"). The chapter falls into two halves, with the break signaled by a space of several blank lines as well as by

Reprinted from *Children's Literature in Education*, 1985: 32–44. Reprinted with permission.

a brief change in scene to the dump where Templeton scavenges advertising slogans for Charlotte's campaign to save Wilbur. The remainder of the chapter concerns Charlotte's review of the slogans, Wilbur's audition for the word "radiant," and Charlotte's soothing Wilbur with two stories followed by a lullaby. Only then does White mention Fern: "When the song ended, Fern got up and went home" (p. 104). Although White does not state the exact time of Fern's arrival, the reader knows that she has heard the song, and White's use of the word "when" indicates that Fern has been present for some time—for the mulling over of words, for checking the chosen word's match with the living being it is meant to describe, and for the storytelling before the lullaby. And in fact, the next chapter begins with Fern's telling her mother, "Charlotte is the best storyteller I ever heard" (p. 105). Fern follows up her praise of Charlotte by telling her own versions of the stories.

I would like to suggest that the child reader's experience with words and storytelling is similar to Fern's, not only in this chapter, but throughout the book. Starting with the moment the reader first meets Charlotte as a "small voice" invisible in the darkness (p. 31), she prompts the reader to consider and experience language in increasingly sophisticated ways, from the literal meanings of words to casting words into stories and speeches. Please note, in this connection, that the child reader's experience of languages is *similar* to Fern's, but it is not identical. For some readers, Wilbur provides an even closer parallel. Wilbur is Charlotte's first pupil—he is the character addressed out of the darkness by the "small voice." As he matures under Charlotte's guidance, so does his use of language, until he too can make a speech worthy of a "good writer." By saying this I am not claiming that children become good writers by the time they finish *Charlotte's Web*. Children do, however, have numerous opportunities to experience language from the inside out—from the perspective of storyteller or writer.[3] Charlotte's role in that process is the subject of the rest of this article.

Charlotte's Web is as distinctly American as the county fair its characters attend. Yet Charlotte does not conform to many of American society's widely held presuppositions about writers. Despite their being condoned or even admired as the price of creativity, the traits the presuppositions refer to characterize the writer as eccentric at best. At his worst, he is a self-centered egotist who is "fierce, brutal, scheming, bloodthirsty" in the service of his art. These adjectives are, of course, the ones Wilbur uses to describe Charlotte at the beginning of their friendship. The narrator, however, immediately tells the reader that Wilbur is "mistaken about Charlotte. Underneath her rather bold and cruel exterior, she had a kind heart, and she was to prove loyal and true to the very end" (p. 41).[4] Charlotte's altruism is commendable, but encouraging the child reader to identify closely with her is problematic, because, among other things, Charlotte dies at the end of the book. Rather than being the reader's second self, Charlotte is the reader's inspiration. One of the reasons this occurs is because Charlotte is Wilbur's inspiration. Right at the beginning of the book, the child reader is encouraged to sympathize with Wilbur's point of view; he is just a little pig and he does not want to die.

The reader's sympathies for Wilbur are first enlisted by Fern, who is "only eight" (p. 1). She stands in for the reader who is old enough to nurture something more helpless than herself, but young enough to know what it is like to be subject regularly to someone else's control, no matter how benevolent that control may be. On hearing that her father plans to kill Wilbur because he is little and a weakling, Fern cries: "The pig couldn't help being born small, could it? If I had been very small at birth, would you have killed me?" (p. 3). Fern's championing the weak and powerless Wilbur is an action children fervently support. Some of the readers of *Charlotte's Web* have questioned why at the end of the book Fern forgets Charlotte and Wilbur and runs off with Henry Fussy at the County Fair. One reason is that the reader simply does not need Fern anymore. The reader's involvement with Wilbur and Charlotte is so complete that seeing Fern's reactions to the more private events of the fair (Fern does witness Wilbur's public triumph) would be superfluous to the point of distraction. The reader's own sensitivity to words, a sensitivity coached by Charlotte, is what counts.

Language is more irritating and befuddling than it is enlightening and pleasurable until Charlotte appears. Wilbur, at the beginning or the book, is newly separated from Fern, on his own for the first time, and unsuccessful in his attempts to communicate. He cannot understand what others are saying; neither can he make himself understood to his listeners. When a lamb tells him, "Pigs mean less than nothing to me" (p. 28), the literal minded Wilbur entangles himself in a scholastic debate over how anything can be less than nothing. To a rat who tells Wilbur, "I hardly know the meaning of the word (play)," Wilbur futilely responds by giving him a list of synonyms: "to have fun, to frolic, to run and skip and make merry" (p. 29). Literal replies are the naive respondent's only mode of discourse. Wilbur's responses are funny to the reader who is old enough to have learned that "less than nothing" and "hardly know the meaning of the word" are figurative expressions; but at the same time, the reader sympathizes with Wilbur's attempts to make himself understood.

Charlotte's first contact with Wilbur is his introduction to the most easily appreciated extraliteral quality of words: how they sound. Charlotte is heard, not seen: ". . . out of the darkness, came a small voice. . . . It sounded rather thin, but pleasant" (p. 31). In the morning Charlotte adds meaning to sound with her greeting of "Salutations!" Wilbur's response is slightly hysterical: "Salu-*what*?" he cried.

"Salutations!" repeated the voice.

"What are *they*, and where are *you*?" screamed Wilbur.

"Please, *please*, tell me where you are. And what are salutations?"

"Salutations are greetings," said the voice. When I say 'salutations,' it's just my fancy way of saying hello or good morning. Actually, it's a silly expression, and I am surprised that I used it at all" (pp. 35–36). In this one short exchange, Charlotte both explains the meaning of a word and says something about it as language—"it's a silly expression." Although she says that she is surprised that she used the word, the reader is not. Silly expressions are fun to use, especially when one knows how to pronounce them. In this connection, note that Wilbur's "Salu-*what?*" breaks the word in half and makes the reader pause to sound it out.

"Salutations" is just the first of a series of words that Charlotte defines for Wilbur. "Untenable," "sedentary," "gullible," "versatile," "magnum opus" and "languishing" also become a part of his, *and the reader's*, vocabulary. This results each time from Charlotte's using the word and Wilbur's asking what it means. Wilbur's reactions to the successive words show his emotional maturing and his increasing sophistication regarding language. For example, Charlotte uses "gullible" to describe humans. The pig's response to hearing what it means is the opposite of his hysterical reaction to "Salutations." "That's a mercy," Wilbur says, and then lies down and goes to sleep (p. 67). "*Magnum opus*" is a term Charlotte uses to correct Wilbur's impression that her egg sac is a "plaything." Wilbur immediately accepts the explanation of the Latin term and curiously asks exactly what the sac contains (pp. 144–45). "Languishing" is a word Wilbur hesitates to ask Charlotte to define. He hesitates because he has noticed that the spider's voice sounds sad, and he does not want to "bother" her (p. 146). In this sequence of terms, Wilbur's early babyish excitability gives way respectively to relaxation, curiosity, and consideration for someone else's well being.

Having a large vocabulary and using it in her conversation is by no means Charlotte's only claim to being a writer. She demonstrates her skill with words in two other, and very important, ways. One involves the selection and actual writing of words in her web. This is Charlotte's public authorship. Her private storytelling also shows that she is a writer. Public and private authorship alternates throughout the book in ways that artfully encourage the reader to imitate each kind of composing.

As the distinction suggests, Charlotte's public authorship is the more striking of the two kinds of composing. Ironically, however, only the reader, the animals, Fern, and one very singular adult character know or believe that Charlotte is special because she is the author of the words which appear in her web. These words refer to Wilbur and a trick that Charlotte plays on the gullible humans in order to save Wilbur's life. Charlotte figures, quite rightly, that the humans will see the words as a sign that Wilbur is very special and should not meet the ordinary pig's fate of becoming bacon and sausage links. Only three humans raise the possibility that it is the spider who is remarkable. The first is Mr. Zuckerman, who shakes his head and does not even finish his sentence (p. 79). The second is Mrs. Zuckerman, who makes the suggestion as a tart response to her husband's nearly scaring her out of her wits by telling her that she had better sit down before he tells her something. Mrs. Zuckerman shifts her attention to the pig after she sees that Charlotte is an unremarkable looking grey spider (pp. 80–81). The third adult who suggests that the spider is marvelous is Dr. Dorian, who, as noted earlier in this essay, states that it is possible that animals do talk. He also says, ". . . I don't understand how a spider learned to spin a web in the first place. . . . The web itself is a miracle" (p. 109). The exclusions of adults (with the exception of the pro-child Dr. Dorian) from the group of believers in Charlotte serves to strengthen the child reader's involvement with the words in the web—the child knows that *she* knows the *real* story.

The reader in fact has participated in the choosing of the words for the web. Charlotte chose the first slogan, "Some Pig," by herself. For the second slogan, Charlotte calls together the barn animals and asks for suggestions. As the suggestions are put forward, it is hard for any reader not to start thinking of suggestions of her own. "Pig Supreme" is rejected by Charlotte because "it sounds like a rich dessert" (p. 88). The word "terrific," however, meets with Charlotte's approbation even though Wilbur objects that he is not terrific: "That doesn't make a particle of difference. . . . People believe almost anything they see in print" (p. 89). Charlotte later softens this cynical bit of advice by telling Wilbur, "You're terrific as far as *I'm* concerned, . . . and that's what counts" (p. 91). The reader learns several important things here. She learns that the connotations of words are important, but she also learns that most people are not conscious or critical enough of what they see in print. Sensitivity to language is important in both the sending and receiving of words.

Wilbur demonstrates his sensitivity to the words in the web by discovering that he feels sensations or emotions appropriate to the various words. Although Wilbur at first objected that he was not actually "terrific," by the time Charlotte has finished writing the word in her web and people have come to marvel over seeing it, ". . . Wilbur, who really *felt* terrific, stood quietly swelling out his chest and swinging his snout from side to side" (p. 96). Charlotte tests the aptness of the next word, "radiant," by asking to see Wilbur "in action." The pig obliges by racing, jumping, and doing a back flip. Charlotte decides to use the word even though she has reservations, whereupon Wilbur announces, "Actually . . . I *feel* radiant" (p. 101). Although his outward appearance belies the adjective, the word does describe Wilbur's inner self. The italics in the above quotations are White's. They emphasize that Wilbur subjectively feels the words' applications. The pig's reaction shows that a good writer affects her audience. Charlotte is careful to mull over the meanings of the next (which is also the final) word she writes. Satisfied that "humble" is "Wilbur all over" (p. 140), she incorporates the adjective into the center of her web. Wilbur reacts by looking "very humble and very grateful" (p. 149). The team of Wilbur and Charlotte provides a model of responsive reader and responsible author.

Charlotte concretely delineates artistic responsibility in the scene in "Good Progress," where the reader sees her weave "terrific" into her web.

Charlotte has no audience as she writes, but for the witnessing reader. Her isolation emphasizes her close connection to the word she is actually drawing out of her own body.[5] Charlotte only uses words that are literally a part of her, and her craftsmanship is clearly evident as she labors in the dark—an apt metaphor for the artist at work.[6] Earlier in the story, Mrs. Zuckerman's "It seems to me we have no ordinary *spider*" (p. 80) implied what readers already knew: the author of "Some Pig" was "Some Spider." The adjective she chose referred to herself as well as to her subject. The same applies to the word she writes now and to the words she will write in the future. Charlotte *is* "terrific." She fits Webster's definition: "exciting, or adapted to excite, great fear or dread." Wilbur, for example, is horrified when he sees Charlotte wrap a fly and then listens to her discussing her love of blood (p. 38). Yet Charlotte is also "terrific" in the colloquial sense of being wonderful. "Radiant" certainly describes both Charlotte and her weaving: eight legs radiate out from her body, and radial lines emanate from the center of her web.

Finally, the last word Charlotte writes is the most telling of all. She writes with no desire for personal fame; she wants to focus attention on Wilbur, not herself. "Humble" aptly characterizes this goal. It is, moreover, a wonderfully understated reference to what Wilbur once called Charlotte's "miserable inheritance" through generations of spiders of trapping and weaving as a way to make a living (pp. 39–40). In a discussion of *Stuart Little*, Peter Neumeyer states that "White always uses established classic themes," and he points out "the classical note of *et in arcadia ego*" and "the name of Dr. Dorian (the Dorians—the early inhabitants of fabled Arcadia) and farmer Zuckerman's first name, Homer" in *Charlotte's Web*.[7] Considering this information, it is therefore not unreasonable to suggest that White may have recalled the story of Arachne when he decided on "humble" as the last word for Charlotte's web. Arachne was a young Lydian weaver who boasted that her work rivalled that of Athena, goddess of crafts. Although warned by Athena about her presumption, Arachne shrugged off the advice. Athena then wove a tapestry depicting mortals punished for their arrogance by the gods. Arachne retaliated by portraying some of the gods' scandals. Enraged, Athena struck the girl with a shuttle and turned her into spider (hence the zoological classification Arachnida to which spiders belong). Ever since that time, spiders have crept into corners to spin their webs.

I remember being told this story as a child. It was presented as an explanation for the perennial war that exists between housewives intent on spotlessness and spiders intent on creating cobwebs. Charlotte's "humble," however, is much more than a plea not to be swept out with the dirt from under the rug—or in this case, from under the tie-ups. "Humble" is Charlotte's reversal of Arachne's hubris. She does play a trick on *her* gullible Olympians, the Zuckermans et al., but she plays the trick out of love, not pride. Her writing fools adults into seeing the truth about Wilbur, a truth that child readers did not need to be fooled into seeing. Neither do they *need* to know the story of Arachne to understand that Charlotte's position as a writer is a humble one. "Some Spider" was overlooked in the excitement about "Some Pig." I specifically mention Arachne, then, not as an example of a connection a child reader is likely to make, but rather as an example of the kind of connection that *Charlotte's Web* prepares him to make. The "Some Pig" incident clearly raises for even very young children the issue of writing as self-expression. This is just an issue that becomes more and more complicated as one becomes literate, as can one's interpretation of "humble."[8]

The trick is to keep a sense of perspective, as well as a sense of humor. White's sense of perspective and his sense of humor are in full swing in the passage where Charlotte works on her second slogan. The physical act of writing, routine that it is to adults, is enormously complicated to young children. For them, forming letters is analogous to Charlotte's spinning. Charlotte must think carefully about every move she makes. She begins by deciding what kind of thread (dry or sticky) to use. This is very like choosing among pen, pencil, or crayons. Charlotte next decides to write double-lined figures so they will stand out. This is a favorite device of children shortly after they have mastered the basic shapes of letters. In the following passage, Charlotte has just completed the "E" in "TERRIFIC" and is starting on the first "R": " 'Now for the R! Up we go! Attach! Descend! Pay out line! Whoa! Attach! Good! Up you go! Repeat! Attach! Descend! Pay out line. Whoa, girl! Steady now! Attach! Climb! Attach! Over to the right! Pay out line! Attach! Now right and down and swing that loop around and around! Now in to the left! Attach! Climb! Repeat! O.K.! Easy, keep those lines together! Now, then, out and down for the leg of the R! Pay out line! Whoa! Attach! Ascend! Repeat! Good girl!' " (p. 94). The concentration that distinguishes Charlotte's work also characterizes the effort of any novice printer who with fat pencil in hand leans over a sheet of wide-ruled manila practice paper. Note too that following the above description of the "R's" creation further implicates the reader in Charlotte's writing. Really following White's description means visualizing to the point of tracing with a finger or a pencil the movements the spider made.

Interesting or intriguing as this imitation may be, it is only one of two kinds of imitating that *Charlotte's Web* inspires. The second kind of imitating is much richer, for here the reader is invited to do no less than tell stories herself. Fern, and then much later, Wilbur, provide the reader with examples of following Charlotte's lead. The first instance of Fern's imitating Charlotte is the occasion of Charlotte's making a speech to welcome the new goslings to the barn. Charlotte says: " 'I am sure, . . . that every one of us here will be gratified to learn that after four weeks of unremitting effort and patience on the part of our friend the goose, she now has something to show for it. The goslings have arrived. May I offer my sincere congratulations!' " (p. 44). Fern later tells her parents: " 'Well, when the first gosling stuck its little head out from under the goose, I was sitting on my stool in the corner and Charlotte was on her web. She made a speech. She said: "I am sure that every one of us here in the barn cellar will be gratified to learn that after four weeks of unremitting effort and patience on the part of the goose, she now has something to show for it." Don't you think that was a pleasant thing for her to say?'" (pp. 53–54). Fern's reporting is close, but not exact. She inserts "in the barn cellar," and omits "our friend," and the last two lines of the speech. The point here is the pleasure of making a speech, not the importance of imitation for its own sake.

The second occasion of Fern's repeating what Charlotte has said even more clearly shows Fern's excitement in storytelling. After his try-out for the word "radiant," Wilbur asks Charlotte to tell him a story. She begins "Once upon a time" (p. 102), but what follows is a fish tale delivered in the frenetic style of a ringside announcer. A cousin of hers found a small fish in the web she had built over a little stream: "There was the fish, caught only by one fin, and its tail wildly thrashing and shining in the sun. There was the web, sagging dangerously under the weight of the fish."

"How much did the fish weigh?" asked Wilbur eagerly.

"I don't know," said Charlotte. "There was my cousin, slipping in, dodging out, beaten mercilessly over the head by the wildly thrashing fish, dancing in, dancing out, throwing her threads and fighting hard" (pp. 102–103). Like many a child, Wilbur then begs for another story. Charlotte complies, but this story is much shorter—only two sentences, compared with the previous narrative, which runs about three paragraphs in its entirety. Once again Charlotte talks about a cousin, this time one "who was an aeronaut . . . 'A balloonist . . . My cousin used to stand on her head and let out enough thread to form a balloon. Then she'd let go and be lifted into the air and carried upward on the warm wind'" (pp. 103–04). These are the stories Fern had in mind when, in a passage mentioned earlier, she praises Charlotte's storytelling. Charlotte *is* a fine storyteller, one who can spin a fish tale as well as she can spin a web.

The effect the story has on Fern is still more evident in the version she gives her mother:

> "Charlotte never fibs. This cousin of hers built a web across a stream. One day she was hanging around on the web and a tiny fish leaped into the air and got tangled in the web. The fish was caught by one fin, Mother; its tail was wildly thrashing and shining in the sun. *Can't you just see* the web, sagging dangerously under the weight of the fish? Charlotte's cousin kept slipping in, dodging out, and she was beaten mercilessly over the head by the wildly thrashing fish, dancing in, dancing out, throwing . . ."
>
> "Fern!" snapped her mother. "Stop it! Stop inventing these wild tales!"
>
> "I'm not inventing," said Fern. "I'm just telling you the facts."
>
> "What finally happened?" asked her mother, whose curiosity began to get the better of her. (p. 106)[9]

The italics in the above passage are mine. They are there to draw attention to Fern's excited visualizing of the scene that Charlotte recounted. Fern was so affected by the story, and is so effective in retelling it that her mother, a woman who believes that "Spiders can't talk," wants to hear the end of the story. Mrs. Arable even agrees, after hearing the aeronaut story, that being a balloonist would be quite pleasant (pp. 105, 106).

As is only fitting, Wilbur provides the reader with a final example of Charlotte's inspiring language that heightens one's awareness of the life around and within oneself. Charlotte is now dead, and all but three of her children have ballooned off to find new homes. At their suggestion, Wilbur has collaborated in giving each of the three a name. Naming is sacral; it demonstrates that the speaker identifies and knows the spirit and essence of the person or object named. The collaborative aspect of Wilbur's naming emphasizes the power of language to create community and shared understanding. This is a power which can transcend death and make the past come alive in the present. The following speech "on this very important occasion" shows how much of this power Wilbur owes to Charlotte: "'Joy! Aranea! Nellie!' he began. 'Welcome to the barn cellar. You have chosen a hallowed doorway from which to string your webs. I think it is only fair to tell you that I was devoted to your mother. I owe my very life to her. She was brilliant, beautiful, and loyal to the end. I shall always treasure her memory. To you, her daughters, I pledge my friendship, forever and ever'" (p. 182). Wilbur's speech closely echoes the cadences of Charlotte's greeting to the goslings, but the substance of the text is Wilbur's response to the present. Whereas Fern repeated Charlotte's speech with minor variations, Wilbur shows that he has learned how to make new speeches for new occasions. Wilbur owes not only life, but also language, to the grey spider. The reader owes White not only her glimpse of the humble experience of one writer, but also her (the reader's) own initiation into a community of writers. *Charlotte's Web* does not merely tell about the writer's experience; it shows and creates that experience right before the willing reader's eyes.

Notes

1. Among those who have, see John Griffith, "*Charlotte's Web*: A Lonely Fantasy of Love," *Children's Literature*, 8 (1980), 117: "It is sad that Charlotte is gone, but it's funny to think of her as a good writer, since her entire published canon was only five words." Griffith goes on to say, however, that "In an important way, this is the right epitaph: a true friend and a good writer. . . . One of the clearest marks of *Charlotte's Web* as the fantasy of a lonely, yearning imagination is the importance it places on language as the means through which 'spirit is laid against spirit.' The highest and best love, in this story, is that which expresses itself through words." Peter F. Neumeyer defends Charlotte's "entire published canon" in his entry for the *DLB*, 22, *American Writers for Children, 1900–1960*, 343: "And if Charlotte's . . . is deemed a rather minimum prose sample, one must recall rule 13 of Strunk and White's *Elements of Style*:

'Omit needless words,' and White's own statement in an interview, 'The main thing I try to do is to write as clearly as I can.' Charlotte was clear."

2.   Also in this connection, see White's comment, "In *Charlotte's Web*, I gave them [children] a literate spider, and they took that." E. B. White, "On Writing for Children."

3.   In "Text as Teacher: The Beginning of *Charlotte's Web*," Perry Nodelman presented a related argument. He focused on the ways in which the first two chapters of *Charlotte's Web* teach the reader how to read the remaining twenty.

4.   For a different view, see Roger Sale, "Two Pigs," in *Fairy Tales and After: From Snow White to E. B. White*, p. 261: "White then drops a stitch, as it were, and ends this chapter with a needless reassuring note about Charlotte's true kind heart. . . ."

5.   In this connection, see White's comment in the *Letters of E. B. White*, p. 346: "And remember that writing is translation, and the opus to be translated is yourself."

6.   For information on White himself at work, see Peter F. Neumeyer, "The Creation of *Charlotte's Web*: From Drafts to Book, Part I" and "Part II". See also Scott Elledge, "E. B. White at Work: The Creation of a Paragraph," in *E. B. White: A Biography*, pp. 359–67.

7.   Peter F. Neumeyer, "E. B. White," *DLB*, 22, *American Writers for Children, 1900–1960*, 338, 344.

8.   See White's comment in the foreword to *The Second Tree from the Corner*, p. xi: "Whoever sets pen to paper writes of himself, whether knowingly or not, and this is a book of revelations: essays, poems, stories, opinions, reports, drawn from the past, the present, the future, the city, and the country."

9.   See also E. B. White, "Mr. Forbush's Friends," in *Essays of E. B. White*, p. 176: ". . . once I liberated a hummingbird from a spider's web."

THE LETTERS

◆

The Letters of E. B. White

♦

White of the Rueful Countenance

SPENCER BROWN

If men will impartially, and not asquint, look toward the offices and function of a poet, they will easily conclude to themselves the impossibility of any man's being the poet, with out first being a good man.

—Ben Jonson

I sound as though I were contemptuous of poets; the fact is I am jealous of them. I would rather be one than anything.

—E. B. White

It is a defensible paradox to describe E. B. White as a poet. He writes nimble verse, he is a good man, and he is often poetical in his prose. Now he invites us to look over his whole accomplishment; White would never call it his oeuvre: "I seldom use a word or phrase borrowed from any language except English (because I don't know any other language)." The occasion is the publication of his letters, at a time when he and his wife are fortunately still around to help the editor, although White apologizes for being still alive: "Ideally, a book of letters should be published posthumously." Readers who have admired and loved his pictures of farm life, his incomparable books for children, and his phrases mingling the unexpected and the inevitable, will be equally delighted by the letters. "They would not find me changed from him

Reprinted from *The American Scholar*, 46:2 (Spring 1977), 237–8, 240, 254. Copyright © 1977 by the Phi Beta Kappa Society.

they knew—Only more sure of all I thought was true." And here we are back in poetry.

White is a sort of prose Frost. Like Frost, he would choose to be a plain New England farmer—"With an income in cash of, say, a thousand / (From, say, a publisher in New York City)." He would differ in being much richer. From the twenties on, he was permanently, if loosely, attached to *The New Yorker*. He augmented a good salary by writing extra pieces for it and other magazines, and by collaborating with Thurber on *Is Sex Necessary?* (a book that made his father "ashamed"). *The New Yorker*, financially sickly in the lush twenties, began to flourish during the depression. White and his wife, Katharine, who was a tower of strength and a pillar of sanity in the magazine's sedulously cultivated chaos, were always comfortably off.

He differs from Frost, too, in being a willing rather than a reluctant farmer. He obviously loves pigs, sheep, the birthing of lambs, the brooding of hens and geese, the preparation of incubators, the digging out of rocks. He loves boats, calling himself more brave than skillful as a sailor. He endures cheerfully the attention of several generations of dogs—dogs of investigative and panhandling ways and low morality. Over and over in his letters he announces his immediate retirement from *The New Yorker*; he is going back to Maine and will do nothing but farm. Three months afterward, he is in active correspondence with Harold Ross and lesser editors. Six months later, the letters erupt from a city address or from *The New Yorker* office. But even then, he sees himself as a small-town boy who now lives on a farm and really farms it.

It is a genuine pose, whose roots are in solid reality and among whose advantages are the ability to view an urban or national or international problem with new eyes and a sometimes embarrassing honesty. Yet in E. B. White it is the style that matters, not the ideas. There is practically nothing in White's collected work to disturb his audience or shock a Norman Cousins. He protests the firing of the holy Hollywood Ten (that decalog-rolling required for good standing in the liberal lodge), but he is under no illusions about the possible reform or future beneficence of Communist countries. He is distressed by contamination (he seems not to use the word *pollution*) but believes Eisenhower's decision to resume bomb testing was wise. He stands for total freedom of the press, as a sort of religious tenet, but he hates pornography. He refuses to join any organization and has no use for pacifists, but he would solve the problems of war and peace by instituting world government. The windmills he tilts against are huge, unreachable, and thus harmless. He is the White of the Rueful Countenance.

In all this he is the poet. Poets rarely offer us anything like an original philosophical or scientific or political discovery. They only reflect such discoveries. The true discoverers, the thinkers, are usually so excited by attaining, or blundering on, big truths that they rush their findings into equations or undistinguished prose.

White's discoveries are personal, paradoxes that assist in molding his style; in large part they are his style. He has hay fever and loves haying. He is allergic to the horses that help in the haying, and he loves horses. He is specifically and unashamedly and totally American. Without vainglory he just accepts American things, the data he lives happily with. He also enjoys poking holes in American technology and pompous American verbosity. Three letters to Ross fulminate against the stapler. When Ross gives him a de-stapling machine, he continues the war, even after he must admit that the machine is better than he had a right to expect. He grants the new slick cars their mechanical perfection but hates them because he can't get into them easily and they have too little ground clearance for leaving the tar (Maine speech for "hard road"). He loves the old high cars, especially Model Ts.

In 1922 he crossed the continent in a Model T. In Louisville he became probably the only poet in history to recoup his losses at the racetrack by writing a sonnet and getting it published for twenty-five dollars in a local paper. He got a newspaper job in Seattle. When it dried up, he went to Alaska, first-class part of the way, working the rest. Although he was only twenty-three, his letters home display minute observation and descriptive humor; his style was forming.

His mature style is so much part of us that we find it hard to characterize. Some years back, a favorite English department quip was to parody the cumbrous title of a Hopkins poem with "The Blessed Thomas Stearns Eliot Compared to the Air We Breathe." Most of us could make a case for "The Blessed Elwyn Brooks White Compared to the Air We Breathe."

White always disclaimed responsibility for *The New Yorker*. He always ostensibly deferred to Ross or Katharine White. But a careful reading of the *Letters* will reinforce the suspicion that he was *The New Yorker*: its vocabulary, its way of looking at things, its tone. He set the tone even by his manner of denying his influence, and through *The New Yorker* he was enormously influential. His gradual withdrawal from the magazine may have accelerated its current evolution toward the plantigrade-political.

Of course it is brash to discuss White's style; bat boys do not publicly analyze Ted Williams's stance and swing. But as far as we may permissibly see, the man is the style—quirky, interested in everything, a snapper-up of unconsidered trifles, the perfect journalist whose declared ambition is to be a journalist. He eschews connectives, but everything connects, in rhythm. It is speech rhythm with the cagey devices of classical rhetoric: repetition, understatement, hyperbole, anticlimax, climax, the withholding of information until the right word comes along to make the sentence and the information end like the fall of a hammer. Above all it is perception of the absurd, the ironic, the pathetic, the rueful. It is half unswerving honesty and half play-acting, sturdy preciosity and innocent sophistication. For all its apparent ease, its parturition must be painful; White salutes the craft of writing for "the beartraps, the power, and the glory."

In praising the style of his friend Morris Bishop, White describes himself: "I like to think of those sentences turned out just right, in their little hats set jauntily on one side and their starchy shirtfronts immaculate." White is the perfection of the lapidary-colloquial. Keep the reader off-balance; never give him the word he expects. Much humor is the puncturing of pomposity, but in order to puncture it you must create it. White is a master at creating off-pomposity, like an off-rhyme.

Relentlessly contemporary and with no evident literary roots, White makes his base only in New York and on the Maine coast. He claims he never reads. But his diabolically adept parodies suggests he is a secret student of many styles. Forster, Thoreau certainly, Menchken possibly, and Stevenson possibly (although he denies having read *Aes Triplex*) may have gone into his development. Moreover, many letters sound right out of Mark Twain's *Autobiography* or, with the necessary changes in spelling and punctuation, *Huckleberry Finn*. When Huck puzzles over questions of right and wrong, he concludes, "I reckoned I wouldn't bother no more about it, but after this do whichever come handiest at the time." White says, "I don't pretend to know what is good, what is bad. I go by instinct."

Pose or not, the style dazzles. Like other poets, of whom he need not be jealous, White makes us enjoy life more. He is the poet because he is a good man.

E. B. White on the Exercycle

Donald Hall

All winter, frozen into a New Hampshire farm, I have taken exercise by riding a stationary bicycle. It's been five miles a day every day, going nowhere, on this strange vehicle near the living room's castiron Glenwood. To defeat the boredom of such pedaling, I have been reading E. B. White's *Letters*. Five miles a day comes out to about 12 pages. I figure that the whole book consumed 285 living room miles, give or take a furlong. It's been a pleasant journey, although for a long time I felt sure that the *Letters*, like the bicycle, were not going anywhere.

I learned a few things, reading White's *Letters*. The first thing I learned was where *The New Yorker's* style came from. I don't mean the magazine's dear eccentricities of content—Ivy League football columns, racetrack chit-chat, thickets of factual data on anything; those large quantities came from Harold Ross. I mean instead *The New Yorker* tone of voice—at once self-mocking and self-assured, witty through comic juxtaposition, ironic and modest and uppity all together—which characterizes "Talk of the Town," and which the whole staff caught like a communicable disease from E. B. White. When Thurber caught it he could begin to be Thurber. Wolcott Gibbs caught it, anonymous drones who churned out Talk pieces caught it—and John Updike in one of his incarnations, and Brendan Gill.

One sees the start of The Style in White's *Letters*, in letters written before Ross called *The New Yorker* into existence. By this time, the familiar *New Yorker* style has dispersed itself among hundreds of writers not clever enough to write for the master's magazine. The Style turns up in the *Turnipgrower's Gazette*, looking slightly shifty-eyed. If he wades around in the monthly journalism of our day, White must feel at times like an imperfect Typhoid Mary, seeing so many weak imitations of the disease he carried.

But we must not blame him if his genius was semi-communicable. Most of his influence has been benign, for the elements of his style are elegant and forceful, brief, idiomatic, rhythmic, particular, and pointed. White's principles of prose resemble Ezra Pound's or George Orwell's—three rather different writers—but beyond the principles there is a cadence of feeling in White's

Reprinted from *National Review*, 10 June 1977, 671–72. Copyright © 1977 by *National Review*, Inc., 150 East 35th Street, New York, NY 10016. Reprinted by permission.

work that pervades and identifies him specifically. The Style is the man, and the man comes to seem The Style.

As I pedaled my way through the first three hundred pages, the consistency of The Style began to disturb me. It was like talking with someone who wore the same facial expression—a strange smile, a frown—whether he spoke of baseball or death, *New Yorker* business or the United Nations. Or it was like talking with someone who kept one note of irony, although you could not tell where in his mouth or his inflection the irony resided; even when he says I love you or I hate your guts, there is something self-mocking, something which while it gives is also taking away. The Style thus is strangely disconnected from the world it talks about, a Cheshire Cat's smile fading on the air. I suspect that Groucho Marx was remarking this quality when he referred to White as "a wraithlike figure who lives in a spirit world."

That sense of self-mockery means that even when White is most serious, you cannot quite fault him for what he says. He is modest about his notions— modesty like a pill-box three feet thick. I find myself wanting to be unfair to E. B. White and The Style. So I will try: over much of this book, I find him complacent, without a sympathy that extends into the world around him. The letters reveal a man class-bound. When he is political, his empathy is *principled*, rather than emotional, and I am suspicious of the principles. He advocates a federacy of nations, or he attacks the Salisbury/*Esquire*/Xerox menage; but— as when he censured Alexander Woollcott for providing testimonial advertising, years back—one senses that his defense of literature and the First Amendment resides as much in *good taste* as in moral principle.

This Style, we come to see, is a grid imposed on the world, a way to organize perceptions into sentences. Organizing perceptions, it delimits a world. I think The Style exists in order to limit the extent of empathy possible—and therefore the extent of vulnerability or hurt. It is language as carapace. Therefore when he observes—on a Mother's Day in New York City—that "the entire janitorial family [across the street] has blossomed into pink carnations," the characteristic adjective separates these working-class people from our feelings, our concerns, as effectively as if we were looking at them through aquarium glass—or through Eustace Tilley's monocle.

I said I wanted to be unfair. I have been unfair enough. This book is wonderful. As I pedal my way from page to page, turning healthier by the signature, I like the man E. B. White more and more. If The Style is the man, the man's daily improvised exercises in The Style of himself finally add up to E. B. White's best book. He is a writer at his best—one would have thought— in little things: essays, children's books, paragraphs, newsbreaks, satirical poems—yet willy-nilly, not knowing that he was doing it, he has written a large book, which is the book of his life, in this collection of letters.

It is the shape of this life that finally gives the book the dimensions that elsewhere his writing has lacked, and that moves him beyond style. White has never been afraid to touch on death—in his wonderful essay "Once More to the Lake," in *Charlotte's Web*—but he has only *touched* on death, precisely: *touched* on it and then drawn back. In general he has avoided confrontation with human suffering, protected as ever by the ironic and elegant shell of The Style.

But when he went to Maine, he began—it turns up in letter after letter— to look outside the coziness of this monoclass world, into the world of rural people among whom class is insignificant. More important, White and his beloved wife, Katharine, began to suffer—as we shall all suffer, if we do not kill ourselves earlier—the gradual debilitations of body, day to day, over the long road through aging toward death. As he and his wife suffer infirmity, pain, and the loss of their bright talents, acknowledged suffering enters White's prose. The Style enlarges, self-mockery is no longer possible, and he joins a dance of dying which unites him with the rest of humanity. Compassion and empathy become him; he is a noble and fine old man; and his firm and scrupulous language leaves him not at all, but serves him as by its example it serves us all. The stationary bicycle—life lived day by day, problems encountered, suffering endured—went somewhere after all.

ASSESSMENTS

◆

E. B. W.

JAMES THURBER

Once, a few years ago (how the time flies!) a gentleman came to the offices of *The New Yorker* and asked for E. B. White. He was shown into the reception room and Mr. White was told that someone was waiting for him there. White's customary practice in those days, if he couldn't place a caller's name, was to slip moodily out of the building by way of the fire escape and hide in the coolness of Schrafft's until the visitor went away. He is not afraid of process servers, blackmailers, borrowers, or cranks; he is afraid of the smiling stranger who tramples the inviolable flowers of your privacy bearing a letter of introduction from an old Phi Gam brother now in the real estate game in Duluth. White knows that the Man in the Reception Room may not be so easy to get rid of as a process server—or even a blackmailer: he may grab great handfuls of your fairest hours, he may even appropriate a sizable chunk of your life, for no better reason than that he was anchor man on your brother's high school relay team, or married the sister of your old girl, or met an aunt of yours on a West Indies cruise. Most of us, out of a politeness made up of faint curiosity and profound resignation, go out to meet the smiling stranger with a gesture of surrender and a fixed grin, but White has always taken to the fire escape. He has avoided the Man in the Reception room as he has avoided the interviewer, the photographer, the microphone, the rostrum, the literary tea, and the Stork Club. His life is his own. He is the only writer of prominence I know of who could walk through the Algonquin lobby or between the tables at Jack and Charlie's and be recognized only by his friends.

But to get back to the particular caller of six years ago whom we left waiting in the reception room. On that occasion, out of some obscure compulsion, White decided to go out and confront the man and see what he wanted. "I'm White," he told the stranger he found sitting alone in the room. The man rose, stared for a long moment at the audacious fellow in front of him, and then said, with grim certainty, "You are not E. B. White." White admits that his hair leaped up but it is my fond contention that his heart did, too. I like to think that he was a little disappointed when he realized, as he was bound to, that the man was wrong. I like to insist that he resumed his burden of identity with a small sigh. (Where the remarkable interview got to from the tense point to which I have brought it here I shall leave it to my memoirs to tell.)

In the early days of *The New Yorker* the object of this searching examination signed his first few stories and poems with his full name: Elwyn (as God is my judge) Brooks White. I cannot imagine what spark of abandon, what youthful spirit of devil-may-care prompted a poet who loves to live half-hidden from the eye to come out thus boldly into the open. He didn't keep it up long; he couldn't stand the fierce glare of polysyllabic self-acknowledgement. For some years now he has signed his casuals and his verses merely with his initials, E. B. W. To his friends he is Andy. It was a lucky break that saved him from Elly or Wynnie or whatever else one might make out of Elwyn in the diminutive. He went to Cornell and it seems that every White who goes there is nicknamed Andy for the simple if rather faraway reason that the first president of the University was named Andrew White.

It used to be a wonder and a worry to White's boss, Mr. Harold Ross, the mystic and wonderful editor of *The New Yorker*, that his favorite and most invaluable assistant avoided people, lived along the untrodden ways, hid by mossy stones, and behaved generally in what Ross was pleased to call an anti-social manner. For a restlessly gregarious man who consorted with ten thousand people from Groucho Marx to Lord Dalhousie it was difficult to comprehend the spirit of Walden Pond. As long ago as the late nineteen twenties there were hundreds of people who implored Ross to introduce them to the man who wrote, on the already famous first page of *The New Yorker*, those silver and crystal sentences which have a ring like the ring of nobody else's sentences in the world. White declined to be taken to literary parties, or to any other kind of parties, but one day Ross lured him to the house of a certain literary lady who, White was persuaded to believe, would be found alone. When the door of her house was opened to them, Ross pushed White into the hallway loud with the chatter of voices proceeding from a crowded living room, the unmistakably assertive voices of writers and artists. Ross made the serious mistake of entering the living room first. When he looked around for White, that shy young man had quietly disappeared. He had proceeded deviously through the house, to the disciplined dismay of the servants, out the back door, and over trees and fences, or whatever else may have been in his way, to the freedom he so greatly cherishes, leaving the curtsy, the compliment, and the booksy chat to writers who go in for that sort of thing.

"Isn't there," Ross demanded of him one time, "*any*body you would like to meet?" White gave this difficult question his grave consideration and said, at long last, "Yes. Willie Stevens and Helen Hayes." It is a proof of the reckless zeal and the devoted energy of Harold Ross that he instantly set about trying to get hold of Willie Stevens for the purpose of inviting him to a dinner in New York at which White and Miss Hayes were to be the only other guests. I am desolated to report that this little coming together could not be accomplished: Willie apparently knew too many people the way it was and declined the invitation with that gentle old world courtesy of which he was so consummate a master. Ross did manage finally to bring White face to face with Helen Hayes. Our hero, I am informed, was discontented and tongue-tied during their brief, jumpy conversation and was glad when it was all over. I suppose Miss Hayes was, too.

E. B. White was born in Mount Vernon, N. Y. He had an ordinary, normal childhood, monkeying with an old Oliver typewriter, shooting with an air gun at the weather-vane on his father's barn. At Cornell he charmed and astonished his English professors with a prose style so far above Cayuga's ordinary run of literary talent as to be considered something of a miracle. The *Cornell Sun* under White's editorship must have been the best written college newspaper in the country. After Cornell he drove a model T Ford across the country with a friend named Howard Cushman. When they ran out of money, they played for their supper—and their gasoline—on a fascinating musical instrument that White had made out of some pieces of wire and an old shoe or something. In Seattle the young explorer got a job as reporter on the *Times*, the kind of newspaper that did not allow you to use the verb "to mangle." Accurately reporting, one day, the anguished cry of a poor husband who had found the body of his wife in the municipal morgue, White wrote "My God, it's her!" and when the city editor changed this to "My God, it is she!" our wanderer moved sadly on to where they had a better understanding of people and a proper feeling for the finer usages of the English tongue. He became mess boy on a ship bound for Alaska, commanded by an old whaling captain, and manned by a crew who knew that a man says it's her when he finds her dead.

Shortly after *The New Yorker* was founded, its editors began to get occasionally manuscripts from an unknown young man named E. B. White who was a production assistant in an advertising agency. Harold Ross and Katharine Angell, his literary editor, were not slow to perceive that here were the perfect eye and ear, the authentic voice and accent for their struggling magazine. It took months, however, to trap the elusive writer into a conference and weeks to persuade him to come to work in the office; he finally agreed to give them his Thursdays. It is not too much to say that Andy White was the most valuable person on the magazine. His delicate tinkering with the works of *The New Yorker* caused it to move with a new ease and grace. His tag lines for those little newsbreaks which the magazine uses at the bottom of columns were soon being read joyfully aloud around town. His contributions to the Talk of the Town, particularly his Notes and Comment on the first page, struck the shining note that Ross had dreamed of striking. He has written a great many of the most memorable picture captions, including the famous one that has passed (usually misquoted) into song and legend, editorial and, I daresay, sermon: "I say it's spinach and I say the hell with it." He had a hand in everything: he even painted a cover and wrote a few advertisements. One day nine years ago he decided that some pencil drawings I had absently made and thrown on the floor should be published in *The New Yorker*, so he picked them up, inked in the lines, and, to the surprise of us all, including Ross, got them published in *The New Yorker*.

Andy White understands begonias and children, canaries and goldfish, dachshunds and Scottish terriers, men and motives. His ear not only notes the louder cosmic rhythms but catches the faintest ticking sounds. He plays a fair ping pong, a good piano, and a terrible poker (once, holding four natural jacks, he dropped out of the betting under the delusion that there were eight jacks in the deck and all he had was half of them). He has steadfastly refused to learn to play bridge or to take out life insurance. Once he offered an airplane pilot a thousand dollars to take him through a stormy dawn from Roosevelt Field to Chicago because a mysterious phone call had made him believe a friend was in great distress. The pilot had to make a forced landing in Pittsburgh, so that all White had to pay to see for himself that all was quiet along Lake Michigan was eight hundred dollars and his railroad fare from Pittsburgh. When a band of desperadoes stole his Buick sedan out of a quiet Turtle Bay garage and used it in the robbery of an upstate bank, White was suspected by the New York police of being the "brain guy" who devised the operations of a large and dangerous mob. For days detectives shrewdly infested his office, peering under tables, asking questions, staring in suspicious bewilderment at the preposterous array of scrawls, dentist's dates, symbols, phone numbers, photographs, and maps that littered his walls. Eventually they went shrewdly away but every time I hear the sirens scream, I think they are coming for White. The former suspect is a good man with ax, rifle, and canoe (for several years he was part owner of a boys' camp in darkest Canada), and he sails a thirtyfoot boat expertly. Two of his favorite books are "Van Zanten's Happy Days" and Alain-Fournier's "The Wanderer." In the country he is afflicted with hay fever and in the city with a dizziness that resembles ordinary dizziness only as the mist resembles the rain. He expects every day of his life that something will kill him: a bit of mould, a small bug, a piece of huckleberry pie.

Some years ago White bought a farm in Maine and he now lives there the year around with his wife, who was Katharine Angell. He spends most of his time delousing turkeys, gathering bantam eggs, building mice-proof closets, and ripping out old fireplaces and putting in new ones. There is in him not a little of the spirit of Thoreau who believed "that the world crowds round the individual, leaving him no vista, and shuts out the beauty of the earth; and that the wholesome wants of man are few." Now and then, between sunup and milking time, Andy White manages to write a casual or a poem for *The New Yorker*, or write a book. Many of the things he writes seem to me as lovely as a tree—say a maple after the first frost, or the cherry hung with snow. What he will go on to do in his forties and fifties I have no idea. If he simply continues to do what he has always done, it will be all right with me.

October 15, 1938

In Praise of E. B. White, Realist

Clifton Fadiman

It has been remarked—ever since Van Wyck Brooks pointed it out some decades ago—that the superior American writer often becomes famous, wealthy, influential, even more skillful, but only rarely becomes mature. Maturity still makes us uneasy. It is not irrelevant that the middle-aged heroes of the whisky advertisements have obviously been selected by virtue of their betrayal of no sign of any thought process whatsoever behind their photogenic distinction. Many of our writers find growing up not merely difficult but socially and emotionally unrewarding. Those who do insist on developing whether their readers like it or not are freaks.

E. B. White is such a freak.

He is also one of the most useful political thinkers in this country.

He is also one of the finest living writers of prose in this country.

This triad of statements will embarrass Mr. White, who not only writes as if he were a modest man—that's merely a trick—but actually is one. It may possibly arouse skepticism or even irritation in many others, including those who admire Mr. White for certain qualities that are as delightful as they are relatively unimportant. Agreed, he has the charm of a dozen Irishmen. He is a master of light verse. His sketches of country living are humorous and poetical. He is fey. He is whimsical. He is funny. He is beautifully absurd. Because he is all these things there is some danger that he will be considered a minor writer. I use the word danger advisedly. Thoreau was put down, is still being put down, as a "nature writer" and an eccentric. The truth is that we have not yet caught up with Thoreau, and unless we do so our democracy, which is identical with the globe's democracy, is by so much the more in peril.

In using the solemn word major I run some risk of alienating people, including the subject of this essay. Nevertheless, I will use the word major. E. B. White is a major writer. He is a major writer because his ideas and sentiments are large and basic and because, within the limitations of his chosen style and form, he writes about them perfectly.

In these remarks (intended not as a critical essay but merely as a longish advertisement constructed to induce you to buy a few of Mr. White's ideas) I propose to write about him as if he were major.

In the early years of the New Yorker magazine, edited then, now, and let us hope forever by the nonpareil Harold Ross, E. B. White contributed excellent light verse and various prose oddments. For about ten years prior to 1938 he wrote or rewrote the first page (Notes and Comment) each week. For several years thereafter he wrote small essays for Harper's magazine under the heading One Man's Meat, and is now back on Notes and Comment again. He has published a couple of books of light verse; "Quo Vadimus" (amusing sketches); "Is Sex Necessary?" (with James Thurber), still funny, and still reasonably wise; "Every Day Is Saturday," a collection of the New Yorker pieces; and "One Man's Meat," mainly from the pages of Harper's. During the approximately twenty years covered by the publication of these frail-appearing volumes he has grown from a paragrapher to a writer, from a light-fingered original humorist to a light-giving original thinker. That the New Yorker, which is primarily a magazine of entertainment, should have been his seminary and his graduate school is a tribute to the flexibility and vision of its editor. What hath Ross wrought?

A sentence or so back I spoke of Mr. White as an original thinker. I do not mean that you will find much that is "new" in him. I mean only that his mind naturally works from origins. His most casual remarks, and most of them are quite casual, come out of a sense not only of where man is but of what he started from. They are almost always based, though rarely explicitly, on an original, that is, fundamental, proposition which mankind when it is rational accepts as true. I have been casting about for a good short example of this kind of thinking and believe I will start with this one:

> Clubs, fraternities, nations—these are the beloved barriers in the way of a workable world; these will have to surrender some of their rights and some of their ribs. A "fraternity" is the antithesis of *fraternity*. The first (that is, the order or organization) is predicated on the idea of exclusion; the second (that is, the abstract thing) is based on a feeling of total equality. Anyone who remembers back to his fraternity days at college recalls the enthusiasts in his group, the rabid members, both old and young, who were obsessed with the mystical charm of membership in their particular order. They were usually men who were incapable of genuine brotherhood or at least unaware of its implications. Fraternity begins when the exclusion formula is found to be distasteful. The effect of any organization of a social and brotherly nature is to strengthen rather than to diminish the lines which divide people into classes; the effect of states and nations is the same, and eventually these lines will have to be softened; these powers will have to be generalized. It is written on the wall that this is so. I'm not inventing it, I'm just copying it off the wall.

It is my contention that this is original reflection. It goes back to an original abstract idea accepted by mankind when mankind is thinking rationally—the idea of fraternity. It demonstrates that college fraternities represent the opposite of this idea. The "practical" proof, if you must have one, of the soundness of the reasoning is that this paragraph is quoted as one of the basic arguments in the recent program of educational reorganization drawn up by a committee of Amherst College teachers. As a result it is probable that fraternities will be abolished at Amherst. The plain fact of the matter is that, if all college men could think, the mere attentive reading by them of Mr. White's half-dozen sentences would result in the immediate abolition of all fraternities, which in turn would constitute a radical step away from infantilism.

Mr. White is a very useful writer because he is an abstract thinker who does not write abstractly. His base is always a generalization, which is what makes him more than a journalist; but the development is always concrete. Here is an example: In October, 1940, he wrote a semi-joshing, semi-indignant piece on the design of the American motor-car. In the course of it he said, "The ultimate goal of automobile designers is to produce a car into whose driving seat the operator will sink without a trace." After enlarging on that nice (and true) point he went on to state: "The public's passive acceptance of this strange vehicle is disheartening, as is the acceptance by other peoples of the strange modern governments which are destroying them in a dulcet fashion. I think there will some day be an awakening of a rude sort, just as there will some day inevitably be a union of democracies, after many millions have died for the treacherous design of nationalism."

Now the parallel between the design of the motor-car and the "treacherous design of nationalism" (read Fascism) is more than a piece of wit. In the first place it is based on a true relationship: in both cases "the operator will sink without a trace." But underlying Mr. White's concrete statements are certain unmentioned abstract ideas: first, that liberty is a good; second, that passive acceptance, as against rational reflection, is an evil. For me this is philosophy quite in the Greek sense.

Philosophy is a calm vision of the whole, journalism an excited perception of the part. Mr. White once wrote that he liked the radio comments of the late Hendrik Willem Van Loon on the day's events "because he has made them seem like a part of a whole, not like an isolated moment in time." This is profoundly true, and it is just as true that if radio commentators in general dared to talk about the events of the day as part of a whole the network officials would in unison shriek, "controversial." The result is that rational reflection is for the most part barred from the air. We get "forums" instead.

One of the results of having a vision of the whole is that Mr. White is forced to see the part for exactly what it is. If it is part of something big he sees that. (Remember the comment on college fraternities.) If it is part of something little he sees that. If the part is so small as to be almost nothing he cannot help seeing that too.

In July, 1938, he wrote, "It must have been two years ago that I attended a television demonstration at which it was shown beyond reasonable doubt that a person sitting in one room could observe the nonsense in another." Now this too is more than a witty and perfectly constructed sentence. It actually is a complete summary of all that is fundamentally important about television. Note that Mr. White does not say that it is not pleasant to observe nonsense. On the contrary, he knows, as we all do, that nonsense may be very pleasant, indeed, and interesting and even mildly necessary. But nonsense is small. The implication of the sentence is that television is small. It is small when it relays the contortions of a blues singer twenty feet into another room. It is exactly as small (though vastly more dreadful) when it relays the antics of diplomats ten thousand miles if the antics say no more than does the blues singer. Mr. White has his eye on the ends; the big network giants have their eye on the means. This is quite proper, because the size of the eyes involved is exactly proportioned to what they are interested in observing.

Television is only a small part of our national activity; but it is part of the mainspring of that activity, which is accumulation. Mr. White, even in his very early days, never lost sight of the design of that mainspring and of the basic fact that the accumulator, living under whatever system of government, is a slave. I offer two diverting samples (but all Mr. White's diversions, remember, seek rather than escape the center). Way back in the New Yorker of May 26, 1928, he printed this small quip:

A life insurance man told us of a remarkable business migration which took place in Madison Square recently. He said that one division of the Metropolitan Life moved en masse from one building to another, across the connecting bridge. At 2:30 the one hundred clerks ceased work and got up from their desks. At 2:41 the first desk was upended by a porter. At 3:45 the whole works had been transferred to the other building and electricians were installing the telephones. At 3:36 the clerks sat down and took up their duties. "And didn't any of the clerks escape?" we asked. But it was the wrong question.

It was of course the right question. It is we who have been giving the wrong answers.

Which leads to another brief entry, of May 13, 1933:

Mr. Edward A. Filene, the merchant of New England, told the alumni of Columbia University that we all want the same thing. "We all want some arrangement by which more people will be enabled to buy more things." Do we? That is a fair question to ask because the cumulative goal of "more things" has remained most unchallenged in all the long palaver of industrial recovery. A little research among the writings of another New Englander, who long ago turned out a passable essay on economy, reveals a more amusing, possibly a more sound, ideal. "The mass of men," he wrote, "lead lives of quiet desperation." And then, you will recall, he told of being present at the auction of a deacon's effects and of noticing, among the innumerable odds and ends representing the accumulation of a lifetime of endeavor, a dried tapeworm.

Thoreau remembered the tapeworm; White remembers the tapeworm; most of the rest of us merely manufacture the tapeworm.

He who remembers the tapeworm is the only crucially valuable commentator on American life. When Knute Rockne died, for instance, the nation gave away to an orgasm of grief, and President Hoover sent a eulogistic message. Mr. White (this was in 1931) uttered the one piercing comment on this national event. He said of it that Knute Rockne "was in the big money, and that was why Hoover happened to know about him." He then said the proper and human thing: "We see nothing wrong in the President's expressing grief over the loss of a beloved football coach," but he went on, finally giving us the insight that marks the thinker and the critic of civilization, "from a diplomatic angle it seems to leave out certain other deceased members of college faculties, men who worked with undergraduates in groups other than groups of eleven. In our official capacity, therefore, we take this opportunity to express the nation's grief in the death of all the other upright members of college faculties who died during the past year. We are sorry we don't know their names."

The point I should like to make about Mr. White's attitude is that it is not the attitude of an amiable, educated young man with high ideals. It is the attitude of a realist. His whimsical remarks are not sweet, though they are sweetly put; each one grasps a truth, holds it fast, exhibits it for all to see. That is why I have called this advertisement "E. B. White, Realist." His wit is realistic, his humor is realistic and of course, his fantasy is realistic. It is, for example, the stock market reports that are fantastic, whereas it is Mr. White who is realistic in saying, "If a man wants to buy wheat, let him buy wheat and let the wheat be delivered to his door."

The spur of Mr. White's realism is the fact that he has the eye of a poet, a poet being a man who sees through things. Having the eye of a poet he is intensely aware of the unreality of our taken-for-granted environment. He is aware of the millions of substitutes for things, the millions of substitutes for emotions, the millions of substitutes for human beings. Out of this awareness the sweet and bitter of his prose continually wells.

Perhaps I can make this clear by a personal reminiscence. About two weeks ago I passed an average American day. In the course of it the following minor things occurred:

1. I received a bill for my quarterly dues—which I gladly paid—from the American Federation of Radio Artists. But I am not a radio "artist," and neither are 99.9 per cent of my colleagues "artists." I am a radio worker, my status being that of employe.

2. I lunched with an amiable publisher, a valued friend, who suggested

to me four ideas for books which he said would prove popular.
They would have, too; but it never once occurred to him that a book
should come out of a writer's mind and heart rather than out of
a publisher's inventive powers.

3. I noticed an advertisement for toffee showing two American soldiers,
candy bar in hand, riding hell-for-leather in a jeep. The caption read:
"When the going gets tough, it's Blank's Toffee." The writer of the
advertisement and the readers of it were apparently quite unaware that the
statement is pure madness.

4. A placard in a hotel lobby attracted my attention. It informed me that
a well known band was returning to entertain the hotel's clientele
"by command." It is obvious that nobody at all commanded the
engagement of the band, and even if anybody did, the band would
not play better or worse for that reason.

5. Returning home, I found a well-written letter from the alumni
committee of my alma mater, urging me to contribute money.
The money was to be used for seven clearly listed purposes. Not one
of these purposes had anything whatsoever to do with the proper
education of young men, although my college was founded for that
purpose and, so far as I can see, should not be used for any other.

I have drawn up this list of items (selecting these five from a much larger
day's bag) to indicate that, for the most part, we live in a world whose
connection with reality is of the frailest. The average man, one of whom is
speaking to you, functions on a level, observes on a level, entertains himself
on a level, noticeably remote from what is real. It is not that we lie to each
other; it is that we think we are speaking truth. This is the essence of lunacy.

It is this accepted, conventional, respectable lunacy that Mr. White sees
and writes about, as did Swift and every other important satirist that ever
lived. But he has more opportunity than Swift, and vaster scope, because our
lunacy is more extensive, more ramified and more attractively disguised.

The greatest of our lunacies can, however, be put with extreme simplicity.
It is that humankind is fairly well determined to commit suicide. (We are
doing it gradually of course, the two German Wars against Mankind being
merely the first steps.) This is the larger lunacy that has engaged the attention
of E. B. White, realist, during the last two or three years and has impelled
him to write the words which I for one believe entitle him to be called one
of the most useful political thinkers in this country.

If you will write the New Yorker, 25 West Forty-third Street, New York
City, and ask for a reprint of certain editorials, they will probably send you
one. It is called "World Government and Peace" and is the work of a humorous
writer and paragrapher, E. B. White. Perhaps I can give you the gist of it.

Mr. White grasped his central idea some time ago, long before Wendell
Willkie gave it so dramatic an elaboration. On May 2, 1931, meditating on
the popularity of Father Coughlin, he wrote:

We happen to be in a small way on the other side of the fence from Father Coughlin on all his points; but we must confess, after reading the statistics about his audience, that being on the other side of the fence from him is like standing all alone in the middle of a million-acre field. What an impressive thing it is! Talking against internationalism over the radio is like talking against rain in a rainstorm; the radio has made internationalism a fact, it has made boundaries look so silly that we wonder how mapmakers can draw maps without laughing; yet there stands Father Coughlin in front of the microphone, his voice reaching well up into Canada, his voice reaching well down into Mexico, his voice leaping national boundaries as lightly as a rabbit—there he stands, saying that internationalism will be our ruin, and getting millions of letters saying he is right.

That was fourteen years ago. Since then, by dint of using his mind Mr. White has come a long way. He is now the most persuasive (I do not say systematic or exhaustive) American analyst of the lunacy that is nationalism and the sanity that is world law. Mind you, he is no "idealist"; he knows what the product (peace) is, he knows how much we must pay for it, and he knows what will happen if we do not buy.

Let's take a concrete problem that is bothering many of us, the problem of an international police force. Here are one long and one short White paragraph on the subject, dated May 15, 1943:

Dr. Gallup, the asker, has asked people whether they favor an international police force, and three out of four have said they do. That is very nice. It is also quite misleading. Asking a man whether he wants an international police force is like asking him whether he wants the Rockettes. Of course he does, but the question is not whether he thinks the Rockettes are a good idea but whether he knows what is in back of them, making them effective; in short, whether he is in earnest about the girls and willing to give up time and money to build a stage big enough to hold them, hire an orchestra loud enough to accompany them, buy costumes rich enough to adorn them, and in general sustain an organization orderly enough to give them meaning and make them click. Dr. Gallup should ask his question again, this time adding, "And you people realize, of course, that a police force is no good if simply used as a threat to strengthen agreements between independent powers, that to have meaning it must be the certified agent of the law, that to have law we must first have a constitutional world society. and that to achieve that each nation must say good-by to its own freedom of action and to its long-established custom of doing as it damn well pleases. Now how many of you want an international police force?"
Here's one hand up, Dr. Gallup.

In other words, the disease is sovereignty; the cure is justice based on world law. As Mr. White puts it, "We are informed, almost hourly, that a new world order is in the making, yet most of the talk is of policy and almost none of the talk is of law." The law must be planetary, thinks White (echoing, by the way, a large number of other thinkers, including Jesus) and our devotion to it must be planetary also. As the realist puts it, "If somebody were to discover rubber plantations on Mars, a world government would not only be a prime necessity. It would be a damn clinch."

Apparently we are waiting for the discovery of those rubber plantations on Mars, and to pass the time while waiting we are killing each other noisily, torturing each other insanely, and, worst of all, fooling ourselves fatuously. We talk of joint action but we do not know what the term means. History (perhaps we can remember some quite recent history such as Trieste and Poland) shrieks at us that as long as the world is run on the principle of national sovereignty, there will never be any tendency toward joint action until it is too late. "Therefore, the problem is not how to make force available for joint action, but how to make world government available so that action won't have to be joint."

I offer a final quotation from Mr. White, realist. The date is Feb. 24 of this year [1945].

> The delegates to San Francisco have the most astonishing job that has ever been dumped into the laps of a few individuals. On what sort of rabbit they pull from the hat hang the lives of most of us, and of our sons and daughters. If they put on their spectacles and look down their noses and come up with the same old bunny, we shall very likely all hang separately—nation against nation, power against power, defense against defense, people (reluctantly) against people (reluctantly). If they manage to bring the United Nations out of the bag, full blown, with constitutional authority and a federal structure having popular meaning, popular backing, and an overall authority greater than the authority of any one member or any combination of members, we might well be started up a new road.
>
> The pattern of life is plain enough. The world shrinks. It will eventually be unified. What remains to be seen (through eyes that now bug out with mortal terror) is whether the last chapter will be written in blood or in Quink.

Who's crazy? Mr. White, a quiet, rather unimposing man, a mere writer, a humorist who makes a living writing for a small local magazine? Or the diplomats who are going through exactly the same motions that have produced wars for four thousand years? Is it possible that Mr. White and those like him are correct—and the big, busy men with their big, teeming, idea-empty portfolios are wrong? Is it possible that Willkie was right—and that Eden and Molotoff and Stettinius are wrong? Is it possible that T. V. Soong (as Mr. White reported) said the only truly realistic thing at San Francisco when he announced flatly that in the cause of world peace China was willing to give up some of her sovereignty?

Of course, Mr. White is not a practical man. He doesn't make much money and he will never be a Senator. He is—let's be brutal—just a poet. But I seem to remember a sentence he once wrote that stays with me: "A despot doesn't fear eloquent writers preaching freedom—he fears a drunken poet who may crack a joke that will take hold."

Mr. White is now engaged in cracking some remarkable jokes. Who knows? Perhaps they will take hold. If not, we have a choice before us. We may choose war, or slavery. Being a strong, courageous, energetic people we will choose war. But the odd part of it is that after we have done so, we will find that we have chosen slavery.

Read Mr. White and see why.

E. B. White

Warren Beck

Discussing the American blend of humor, Max Eastman once speculated "about what might be done by a mind trained in fact and true to it, equipped as such a mind must be with humor, and yet not ill-at-ease in deeps of feeling and among fervent adventures of imagination, not ill-at-ease among revolutionary ideas, not condemned to make a final resting place of fact and laughter." If such a writer has not yet appeared fullfledged, at least America has his prototype in E. B. White. Some will think White is it, the man himself. Some may think he is better than that, is more than anyone would have known how to specify, a truly original writer, with the unique fusion of basic traits and idiosyncrasies which makes an artist's work freshly representative.

A who's-who glance at E. B. White shows a middle-aged man, migratory between New York City and Maine, a graduate of Cornell University, husband of one wife and father of one son, an editor, a magazine contributor, and the author of a few volumes of prose pieces and verse, together with a story for children. Gradually emergent as a journalist in the tradition of Addison and Hazlitt, White has always been a writing man, having done time in reporting and advertising. He has reaped from his Maine farm, besides its indigenous produce, a number of fresh experiences and well-ripened opinions, regularly brought to market in *Harper's* under the gracious label "One Man's Meat." In the decade preceding his *Harper's* engagement he supplied the *New Yorker* with the "Notes and Comments" which contributed so greatly to that magazine's brilliance. For a professional nearing fifty, his output is comparatively slim and casual, but there are good and honorable reasons for this. White has never allowed himself the commercial advantages of being slick, obvious, and grossly prolific. He is an intellectually fastidious man, who has practiced letters as a vocation, not a racket; and his laconic, critically humorous writing is an honest product. It is to the credit of not altogether creditable times that such a writer has not lacked appreciation.

Editors of pedagogical anthologies have increasingly exhibited White's work. Well they might, for he aids teachers in marking out a continuing stream of literature, a present momentum aware of historic culture and expressive, in modern terms, of those immortal longings, large and small,

Reprinted from *College English*, 35 (April 1946): 175–81.

which beget art. Here is a plain contemporary who has brought back substance as well as polish to the journalistic paragraph, and who can also stand consideration along with the Augustan and Romantic essayists, in such pieces as "Sabbath Morn," "The World of Tomorrow," "Walden," "Camp Meeting," "Freedom," "On a Florida Key," "Once More to the Lake," "Aunt Poo," and "Morningtime and Eveningtime"; and for younger students there is easier access in essays like "Movies" and "Motor Cars." Two qualities above all earn E. B. White high academic regard. One is his prose style, which for a combined ease, scope, and incisiveness is perhaps the best American expository writing in a personal vein since Thoreau. Another of White's achievements is the rehabilitation of the informal essay, which in recent times has often ailed, either of a hectic preciosity or a boisterous madness. White is never precious, never boisterous; and he is always sane, though most characteristically it is with the poet's transcendent sanity, an imaginative bent, paralleling sublime relativities.

Since the haunting dictum that the style is the man himself is often superstitiously interpreted by students to mean a fine frenzy of untrammeled effusion, teachers have special use for any successful contemporary whose style demonstrates the broad, stern meaning inherent in that apparently inescapable definition. White's prose not only shows facets of the matter, it embodies the whole truth. It has a nice diction ranging from the naturally colloquial to an intellectual aptness as juicily tart as a plum. He hears "The Indian Love Call" over loudspeakers at a fair "bathing heaven and earth in jumbo tenderness." He sees a retriever come into the house "full of greetings on a grand scale." When he learns that San Quentin's inmates deluge their prison paper with verse, his leaning toward similitudes identifies all poetry as "the hopeful wing-sprouting of the incarcerated spirit." With that sharp perception of the grotesque which humorists so often reveal by incongruous juxtaposition, White notes that "last week the Forhan toothpaste people put Evangeline Adams on the air . . . Miss Adams being the famous astrologer, versed in the signs of Cancer, Sagittarius, Virgo, and, more recently, Pyorrhea." His is the quick, pinioning phrase, as in naming Hitler's crowd "opportunists in bullet-proof vests." When he characterizes Thoreau's "tale of individual simplicity" as "the best written and the cockiest," he shows a twofold familiarity, doubly pleasing. In the firm context there is no unpleasant jar, but only a rich dissonance, between the word "cockiest" and such phrases as "a document of increasing pertinence." This easy range is seen in the fused allusions of an April item that "the frogs have begun their song of songs, deep in the heart of wetness."

White's prose nears the ideal style defined by Hazlitt, except that White makes freer use of words which have not taken out their final papers with the lexicographer. His colloquialism, an aspect of his independence and informality, can give students of English a model, too, in that it is always a precise diction, and never trite. Actually he is a purist in the best sense, and not least in that he is helping to fix meanings of words that will appear in future editions of dictionaries. Moreover, it is all done without flourish or groaning; White has the true artisan's unaffected dexterity. His sentences are as sure-footed and lightly vigorous as an athletic youth in sneakers. However, if style is the man himself, it is more than a matter of diction and construction, it inheres in the largest possible sense of the thing said, and must be discerned in the whole body of a writer's work, as it projects his temperament and outlook. Such a concept of style is especially important in judging White, whose pieces often have a deceptively cursory look.

The integration of his essays is both subtle and tough. Unimaginative reading would miss, for instance, the reflective sinuosity of such a composition as "On a Florida Key," and might even call it inconsequentially rambling. Nothing could be more erroneous; it is vibrant with thematic tensions. In the rainy weather the Florida Chamber of Commerce writes publicity behind drawn blinds. There is the vacationer's choice concerning the gas heater, whether "to congeal in a well-ventilated room or suffocate in comfort." White's struggle to catch up with the fresh milk contrasts with a news-story centenarian's coming out just right on half a gallon of whiskey a day. The Flag and the motto "Liberty for all" are applauded at the theater from which Negroes are excluded, in a South which seeks to enhance the orange by "Color added." The woman next door tracks in sand bringing pamphlets to prove that America (at least) should mind its own business. (White decides against removing the sand, since "this is the way keys form, apparently," and he has "no particular reason to interfere.") He archeologizes the grass-grown paving of Florida's "unfinished cities. . . . conceived in haste and greed" in "real estate's purple hour" with "orchestras playing gently to prepare the soul of the wanderer for the mysteries of subdivision"; now on the adjacent beaches he hears the sea's eternal murmur, "So soon?" The essay itself is like a series of breaking waves, repeatedly propounding a skepticism confronting human folly. Yet, it also implies White's belief, which he seems to find applicable not only to gas stoves, that "after a little practice a nice balance can be established—enough oxygen left to sustain life, yet enough heat generated to prevent death from exposure."

Out of his work emerges a spare but striking profile. It is that of the ironic spectator, the minority report personified, the man with eyebrows raised but never harshly supercilious, the uncompromising individualist who would as lief split a hair with himself as with anybody else, and a still, small, humane voice through two troublesome decades, when to be at the same time a sensitive, serene, incorruptible, polite, rugged, and charitable person has been the rarest of achievements. White's geniality and fancy, detectable in his briefest jottings, are more generally recognized than his penetration and virility. The worst mistake to make about him is to assume, as the hyper-solemn may, that he is a light-weight, a trifler and escapist. Intellectually and morally he is hard as nails, and he is as unpretentiously functional as a snow fence. His informal and whimsical manner is no theatric quaintness; he is above egotistic or self-promotional airs. He is a proud realist, too, and soberly conscious of the intellectual's obligations. His integrity makes it possible of him to speak of serious matters quietly and conversationally, with frequent quips and smiles, and yet with no deviation from good sense. Thus he describes shingling a barn roof while the Munich conference proceeded: "In my trancelike condition, waiting for the negotiations to end, I added a cupola to the roof," he says implicatively, "to hold a vane which would show which way the wind blew." He defends this "sitting out a dance with a prime minister and a demigod," inquiring, "Who has the longer view of things, anyway, a prime minister in a closet or a man on a barn roof?" Calling it England's "ugliest peace," he winds up with a judgment emphasized by its handy blending of figure, frolic, and irony. Chamberlain's sacrifice to preserve peace reminded White of "the strange case of Ada Leonard, the strip artist of superb proportion," who, rather than have her appendix out, "risked her life in order to preserve, in unbroken loveliness, the smooth white groin the men of Chicago loved so well." "But," he goes on, "there comes a point beyond which you can't push Beauty, on account of the lines it leaves in the face."

White's basic seriousness is the more remarkable in that it outran the tendency of its time, the inclination to rest cynically in fact and laughter. He came to his work when the pantaloon humorists of the twenties were at their height, peddling the anodyne of nonsense as raw as the era's gin, or busy at what Lamb called "wringing out coy sprightliness." White never joined that sad assembly line, despite its bonuses, or got his bread by literary preening. No man has written more wittily of our time than he, but he has had no truck with inanity. Neither can his excursion into the pastoral life be judged escapist. Indeed, in 1938, the critical year of his retirement to Maine, he at once began to express in *Harper's* a realistic internationalism well ahead of the *New Yorker* and of lagging public opinion generally. (It seems likely that White is responsible, too, for recent *New Yorker* "Notes and Comments" which have argued, with such logical and ethical force, the cause of a genuinely dedicated and empowered world order.)

Even more revealing than White's prompt, right stand on the war and world peace is his earlier position as the deftly humorous but never merely playful satirist of the incredible twenties, which could not wring either acquiescence or cynicism from him. Hearing a businessman's boast of how an entire clerical department was moved, desks and all, from one building to another so expeditiously that the hundred employees sat down to work again in about an hour, he asked, "And didn't any of the clerks escape?" "But," White concludes, "it was the wrong question." Apparently the inquirer remained unabashed; he went on asking just the right wrong questions. White's probings have gone a long way beyond Sinclair Lewis's crude satires of crudity and puerile escapist reactions against conventionality, just as they rose above such typical sophistications as Benchley's short-winded jesting or Woollcott's capsuled sentiment and morbid fascination with the decadence of his own age and kind. At times such a fascination has seemed to sway the *New Yorker*, crazing its polish, as if it really navigated under its jibing slogan, "Not for the old lady from Dubuque," and meant to take up where Lewis and Mencken might well have left off. The acquisition of White's services and influence probably has been the fortunate *New Yorker's* greatest single piece of luck with personnel, in helping it transcend the snobberies and seasonal enervation of a locale and a period. Certainly White never evinced the twenties' faddish hatreds of the sticks and everything therein. He has not conceived of culture or felicity bounded by fences geographical, economic, or formally intellectual. He escaped the lure of the Left Bank and the addictions of the Village. When asked, on his removal to Maine, whether he was not afraid of becoming provincial, he retorted with another question. "Aren't you afraid of becoming metropolitan?" Neither does White belong to that stylishly nauseated group of demi-metropolitans who escaped to Connecticut cottages, wherein to deplore the city, whence cometh their sports clothing. White often writes of Manhattan with a zest as keen as Morley's, though with a more detached humor and without any laureate arpeggios. Whether at the typewriter or in the henhouse, White is ingenuously himself, cool but appreciative, at once fanciful and sensible. When he lives on the land, he is no ruddy country gentleman posed in riding boots, nor does he try to enact the flinty rustic. His neighbors expectantly ask, "You going to get your deer?" But, says he, "I can't seem to work up a decent feeling of enmity toward a deer. Toward my deer, I mean." And of his appearance on his own acres he writes, "I have fitted myself out with standard equipment, dungarees and a cap; but I should think twice before I dared stand still in a field of new corn." (It must be remembered, though, that Farmer White—phone Waterlot 40 Ring 3—brought a lot of hen's eggs to market during the war years.)

Neither is White's history one of discreet abstention from sticking his neck out. In courageous and consistent assertion he has surpassed both the cynical humorists who aped the mode of a Neronian frivolity and a whole decade of angry ideologists marching in cadence with a prescribed social consciousness. And White has not only spoken out, he has made it stick. He has never been caught napping intellectually; he has not had to beat his breast publicly and read himself out of a previous folly, or still more shamefully, to sneak down from a flat-tired band wagon; he is not yet dated. Many of his winded and backtracking contemporaries must ruefully envy his record, which in a generation's lengthening perspectives is seen to have resulted not from temporizing or cautious aloofness, but from force of judgement, faith, and conscience. Humorously White had blamed his hay fever for a "tendency toward the spineless middle ground. . . . in time of political strain," charging himself with "the compromising nature of a man who from early childhood has found himself without a pocket handkerchief in a moment of defluxion," but here he is only elaborating a wry essay on Webster's summer catarrh. There is nothing spineless about White's serious comment on a litterateur who in the same days of political strain pledged himself never to write anything that wasn't socially significant. "A writer must believe in something, obviously," says White, "but he shouldn't join a club . . . Even in evil times, a writer should cultivate only what naturally absorbs his fancy, whether it be freedom or cinch bugs. . . . Only under a dictatorship is literature expected to exhibit an harmonious design or an inspirational tone." To write that in the late thirties required pluck. White has achieved his place by moving across professional currents, not drifting with them. The abnormal thing about him has been that he has quietly maintained a humanistic norm in a period of noisy aberratons, naturalistic or dogmatic. In a double sense, he has stood up well.

Politically White seems to be a sweat-of-brow, easy-does-it, lower-case democrat. While condemning the system of free enterprise for having been "predatory and unfair," he thinks that "in essence it was a good thing, which might have fitted people like a glove" had it chosen to recognize that "what the common man wanted really was a sense of participation," had the bonus at Christmas, "season of generosity and remorse," been "given a ring and a name and made into an honest woman." White thus differs not only from the rival zealots of laissez faire or Marxism, but from intermediate pessimists, for he evidently believes that there is in men a cultivable and rightful human quality (neglected by extremists, denied by cynics), a potentiality of independent conduct both provident and reciprocally considerate. To this ideal, slowly emergent in men's most generous experience, and basic to the theory of democracy, White seems firmly committed. It is this faith which enabled him to refute Mrs. Lindbergh's *Wave of the Future* so devastatingly. "Is my own intellectual resistance," he asks, ". . . any less promising that the force of nazism itself, merely because mine does not spring from human misery but from human sympathy? I don't see why. And I do not regard it as a sin to hang fast to principles which I approve of and believe are still applicable." Here, as in many similar passages, White seems to voice something comparatively inarticulate but fundamental and staunch in American life. It is his special honor to have kept this value in sight during a time when the writers with the simpler answers, or despairing of answers, were clouding the air with slung mud, custard pies, and good red brick.

The gold medal of the Limited Editions Club has gone to *One Man's Meat* as "the book which is considered most nearly to attain the stature of a classic." Though enthusiasts are prone to count classics still unhatched, it is not impossible to pick a winner in his own time. Landor gave the essayist Elia a verbal gold medal and a passkey to immortality; a century has approved the judgement. Lamb, too, was an informal, ironic, fanciful and humane writer whose quietly conversational remarks got heard in an era of big bow-wowing. How do they do it, Elia and E. B. White and the other rare writers of quiet-voiced, casual, classic paragraphs? Certainly not by being mousy or childish or inconsequential. Those who see them in any such light are describing shadows cast by their own stuffy postures. Hearing Lamb blandly tell off a Southey for religious hypocrisy, hearing White politely put down Mrs. Lindbergh for impercipience, one recognizes a firmness that quite suffices without any pulpit-thumping, a conviction resting not on a prefabricated ideology but on the writer's own humanity, that constant which he verifies in his fellowmen, and in the whole pitiable and joyful history of man.

Thus in his classic discussion of freedom, White can report his awareness that he "traveled with secret papers pertaining to a divine conspiracy," which had begun in childhood with "the haunting intimation. . . . of nature publishing herself through the 'I'." This, he says, is the feel of freedom in a planetary sense; "to be free, in a social sense, is to feel at home in a democratic framework." In Hitler, White pointed out, "we do not detect either type of sensibility," for he has "no sense of communion but rather an urge to prevail," and "his feeling for men is not that they co-exist, but that they are capable of being arranged and standardized." White holds his nose at the "adaptable natures" who compromise such a fundamental distinction. Resenting "the patronizing air" of such persons, he declares that "if it is boyish to believe that a human being should live free, then I'll gladly arrest my development." White's position is boyish only in the Wordsworthian sense that "the Child is father of the Man." The basing of democratic sympathies in his personal-planetary sense of freedom interestingly parallels the Hartleyan element in Wordsworth, as White's fanciful confusion of himself with his own son in "Once More to The Lake" resembles Wordsworth's sense of life's resounding cycle, with its potent recollections.

Such a deep-flowing, intense existence, romantic in the fundamental and best sense of the word, is what gives White's writing not only its humane integrity but its great charm. That charm involves the sincerity and gusto of a capable writer genuinely concerned with his subject. It employs the understatement by which an independent and civil personality would allow others also the inalienable right to taking or leaving it. It plays gracefully with the heterogeneous and discrepant, in that most disarming and endearing judiciousness which is humor. Aesthetically it adds to an intellectual comprehensiveness the candor, lively allusion, tactful implication, and the cordial pauses of sympathetic conversation. White is an eudaemonist, whose mind is his kingdom, in which he is a benevolent monarch, blessed with good genius, diligent in the regulation of internal affairs and the conduct of free trade and genial diplomacy with the world. He has gone beyond sad fact and cynical laughter to prove the humane value he once defined as "gaiety, or truth in sheep's clothing."

In art as well as in conduct, individualism needs the regulative ingredient of common kindness. On this score White surpasses Thoreau, whom he admires, and with whom he is often admiringly compared. Thoreau's independence sometimes stooped to spiritual parsimony; his transcending was often a deliberate skipping, so that he failed to read the whole text of life. Conversely,

White's expense account on a visit to Walden includes a baseball bat and glove, "gift to take back to a boy"; and he remarks that Thoreau "never had to cope with a shortstop." White has had to, and apparently the compulsion is not just of circumstance but of temperament. Empathy has moved him to cope with much that a self-centered individualist would overlook, or that a Levite would pass by. Egoistic preoccupation sometimes makes the informal essay inhuman; but White's writings, however personal, abound in that wide-ranging awareness and response essential to an achievement of literature's fullest dimensions.

E. B. White, "Farmer/Other"

Norris W. Yates

A brief biography of Elwyn Brooks White before he joined the New Yorker staff reads like that of many upper-middle-class Americans in his generation. He was the youngest of eight children at a time when large families were still common among the solid citizens. His birthplace was Mt. Vernon, New York, a "carefully zoned suburb," and his father was "a God-fearing man" who "never missed a copy of the New York *Times* either." White entered Cornell University, but as soon as he was old enough he dropped out to join the Army during World War I. Eventually he returned to the campus, where in his senior year he edited the Cornell *Daily Sun*.

REPORTER AND WANDERER

In 1921 White got his A.B. and took off for the West Coast, guiding westward the Model T Ford which he and Richard Lee Strout later depicted as a symbol of adventure in the pioneer years of the auto age. The young pioneer, like Milt Daggett, the mechanic in Sinclair Lewis' *Free Air*, wound up in Seattle, where he worked on the *Times* of that city, discovered he was of little use as a mere reporter, and was soon put to writing features in which some quaint or colorful detail gave the budding stylist a chance to display his highly personal approach, a chance not offered by the reporting of straight news. Before long, he left the *Times* and sailed to Alaska, working part of his passage as a mess boy. After this adventure he came back to New York and lapsed into advertising—with an occasional stab, he confesses, at ghostwriting. In this suburban background, university education, uneventful military service, and mild wanderlust, there was little thus far to set White apart from large numbers of his fellow men, and in later years an important feature of his life and thought has been his sustained attempt to recapture and retain a sense of connection with as large a number of Americans as possible. Despite his cultural equipment and polished prose style, he has not intended to appeal only to an elite.

Reprinted from Norris W. Yates, *The American Humorist: Conscience of the Twentieth Century*, 2nd ed. Ames, IA: Iowa University Press, 1964, 299–330. Reprinted with permission.

Like Don Marquis, Ring Lardner, Dorothy Parker, and James Thurber, White placed a few early contributions in F.P.A.'s column, "The Conning Tower." In 1925 he began to sell poems and short prose pieces to the *New Yorker*. Two books of verse, *The Lady Is Cold* (1929) and *The Fox of Peapack* (1938) were in the so-called "light" vein, but some of this verse is explicitly as well as implicitly serious. Thirteen volumes of prose and verse now bear his name. None of them is large but he has written over a million words for the "Talk of the Town" department in the New Yorker, most of it anonymously.

In 1926 Katharine Sergeant Angell, one of Harold Ross's most valued assistants on the New Yorker, hired White for Ross at a salary of thirty dollars a week. She eventually became White's wife, and his collaborator in editing an anthology, *A Subtreasury of American Humor*. Twenty-one years later, Thurber said that White had been the "number one wheel horse" of the magazine.[1] Among the jobs White did for the *New Yorker* in the early years were these:

(1) He edited the "Talk of the Town" and for many years wrote the first page of that section, subtitled "Notes & Comment."[2] Thurber says that "'Notes and Comment' . . . did more than anything else to set the tone and cadence of the *New Yorker* and to shape its turns of thought . . ." If this is true, White has been one of the most influential prose stylists in the twentieth century. Thurber also pays tribute to "White's skill in bringing this page to the kind of perfection Ross had dreamed of . . ."[3]

(2) He played a part in getting Ross to hire Thurber.

(3) He encouraged Thurber to publish his drawings and to keep on drawing in his unique, deceptively simple style.[4]

(4) He wrote most of the one-line captions for the column "Slips That Pass in the Type," having shown a knack for making quips about slips that no one else has consistently duplicated.

(5) From the first months of the magazine's life he contributed poems and "casuals" (pieces not written on assignment). The first number of the *New Yorker* appeared February 22, 1925, and White's initial contribution appeared on May 9, 1925, nearly a year and a half before he joined Ross's staff.

CITIZEN OF THE CITY

White's first casual in the *New Yorker* was an exercise in quaintness entitled "Defense of the Bronx River." His second was "Child's Play," a brief essay in which he describes how a waitress spilled buttermilk over him in a Child's restaurant and how rattled she got. White here selected an episode from his real life in which he could appear with only slight distortion as the Little Man to whom miniature disasters happen, a role in which he consciously resembled Benchley. White's early sketches were the kind of thing Benchley and his other imitators (including Thurber at that time) were doing for *Vanity Fair, Life, Judge*, and the *Bookman*; Dale Kramer says that most of the early pieces by White and others in the *New Yorker* owed something to the style of *Life* and *Judge*. Kramer thus documents the view taken in this book that the *New Yorker* style was not a mutant or "sport," but a direct outgrowth of its journalistic and humorous milieu. In Kramer's view, White differed from Benchley "in that, beneath the whimsy, he had tried to insert beauty." With his buttermilk piece "White had made a dent in the contemporary *Life* and *Judge* pattern of the 'funny' writer."[5] White added a touch of the poet to prose humor, a lyric note to the style of Benchley and his followers. Because of White's lyricism and his interest in nature, Warren Beck is probably right in suggesting that White did much to keep the *New Yorker* from merely baiting the booboisie as Mencken and Sinclair Lewis were doing.[6]

Certainly White often took pains to resemble in print the ordinary literate citizen rather than Mencken's illiterates. The Lardner type of character, with an idiom that suggested incomplete servitude in a small-town grade school, was still numerous in the early nineteen-twenties, but the number of citizens with some college or university background was on the increase. These were the readers White was aiming for.

However, the *New Yorker* assumption of "a reasonable degree of enlightment on the part of its readers" did not prevent White from making frequent use of the technique so often employed by Dunne (a crackerbox humorist) and Benchley (another university man) of reducing broad problems to their effect on any humble citizen. In *Alice Through the Cellophane* (1933), a collection of "Notes & Comment" material, White said of the New Deal plan to cut production and raise farm prices: "The farmers are to be asked to withdraw some of their land from cultivation, to save their own skins. This is a toothsome paradox ... I have been thinking about the allotment idea particularly in relation to my own agricultural life, which has found expression in the burgeoning of a rubber plant's acreage, and I doubt if farmers will be happy in their restrictions either." That there was no excess acreage of rubber plants in most homes and that the analogy with commercial crops was faulty anyway, merely lent a wise-foolish tinge to White's comment. What he stressed was the *feeling* that anyone who keeps even a single house plant may experience if he identifies himself with those commercial farmers whose rights may be violated by economic planners. Moreover, such a feeling would tend to bridge the gap between the metropolitan reader of the *New Yorker* and his country cousin.

In other ways too, White kept insinuating that he was just an ordinary fellow trying to puzzle things out. In *Every Day Is Saturday* (1934), another collection from "Notes & Comment," he remarked that "in a small way" he was against the isolationism of Father Coughlin, a radio commentator with a sizable following in the thirties. White said, ". . . there stands Father Coughlin in front of the microphone, his voice reaching well up into Canada, his voice reaching well down into Mexico, his voice leaping national boundaries as lightly as a rabbit—there he stands, saying that internationalism will be our ruin, and getting millions of letters saying that he is right. Will somebody please write us one letter saying he is wrong—if only so that we can employ a secretary?" White here sets himself in opposition to millions of plain people who he feels have been misled, but he also suggests that he himself is somewhat absurd despite his sensible ideology. Mencken and Benchley used the same technique, often with even more abrupt switches from good sense to absurdity. The views of the solid citizen and the Little Man are valid, but their authors are primarily writing humor, not sermons or moral essays.

In "Notes & Comment," White tried to be less often a political or economic oracle than a commentator on quaint, colorful trivia about life in New York City. In some of his paragraphs he reminds one of what George Ade had done for Chicago in "Stories of the Streets and of the Town," although White showed a delicate intensity in drawing large implications from these trivia, whereas Ade used cruder strokes. In making the small momentous, White used exactly the reverse of his political technique of reducing the momentous to the small, but in either method his spotlight usually focused on himself as Little Man:

> Coming out into Eighth Avenue from the Rodeo, fresh from the joust and the great scenes of prowess, with the noise of the hooves of death still in our ears and in our head the respect for the strong-kneed of the world and the lean-hipped and stilt-legged; coming out we got caught alone in the middle of the charging hordes of cars from the north and the stampede of cars from the south, and as we stood there, firm, never yielding, never flinching, letting them brush the nap right off our coat, we realized how special an Eastern feat that was; and for a second we were blood brother to a bronc-rider, and his nerves of steel were our nerves of chromium, one and the same.

Into this one graceful sentence about an experience duplicated by millions of people every day, White packs implications about technology, the East, the "wild" West, and the integrity as well as the role-playing tendencies of the Little Man.

White's narrator tried to cope with a world in which the harmony and order of nature contrasted with the confusion and discord of the man-made environment. While living in New York City, White searched constantly for evidence that even here nature was the abiding reality, and he delighted in his discoveries of that reality. On spotting a thrush near Turtle Bay, he declared, "There is a special satisfaction to a city person in such a visitation; we took twice the pleasure in this thrush that we would have felt had we discovered him in the country." There were instances when the blend of natural and man-made beauty stimulated White to prose-poetry:

Sometimes, just before nightfall, the buildings and roofs and chimneys come to rest in a calm bath of light which makes them seem suddenly clear and good. The sun being gone, there is no glare, no distortion of shadow; the city is touched with a clarity which gives it a feeling of direction, almost of serenity. There is no moment in the day quite like it—the terraces stand firm in flat colors against a west in which quiet clouds are moored. Dogs and children cry out, distinctly, crisply, then cease—the sounds sharp as country sounds. Windows stand open and curtains stir in the imperceptible air; and when the "L" goes by, the murmur it makes down the street is as significant, as mysterious in its own right, as the bucolic dialogues of katydids.

That White put many such lyrical bulletins from nature into "Notes & Comment" indicates his judgment that city readers were as eager to re-establish their contracts with trees and grass and birds as he was. Paragraphs like this also reveal that long before White moved to Maine, he was striving to banish his sense of alienation from the natural cosmos, in contrast to the wistful resignation of Don Marquis and the distrust of or indifference to nature shown by Benchley and Thurber.

It is not surprising, then, that the first collection of White's longer essays, *Quo Vadimus? or the Case for the Bicycle* (1939), is partially unified by the incongruous contrast between natural harmony and man-made discord. Caught between these two worlds, the average man, says White—and this includes himself—struggles half blindly, but he does struggle. Though often absurd, he becomes strong whenever he recaptures for a moment the mystic oneness with the universe that is his if he wills to feel it. In the title piece of this volume, the narrator asks a man in the crowd where the hell he is going— "Quo vadis?" He gets this answer: " 'I'm on my way to the Crowbar Building, Forty-first and Park, in Pershing Square, named after General Pershing in the Grand Central zone, zone as in Zonite, because I forgot to tell Miss Cortright to leave a note for Mr. Josefson when he comes in, telling him he should tell the engraver to vignette the halftone on page forty-three of the salesmen's instruction book that Irwain, Weasey, Weasey, & Button are getting out for the Fretherby-Quigley Company, which is to go to all their salesmen on the road.' " The narrator says, "All you really want is a decent meal when it comes to mealtime, isn't it?" The man adds, "And a warm place to sleep when it comes night." These needs are "natural" in their simplicity, but this white-collar unhero has been caught in the same welter of commercial and mechanical trivia that entrapped Benchley's man. White as narrator sounds a note of cosmic doom with a characteristically light touch—"Paths of glory, leading to the engravers, my man."

The narrator gets his answer to the main question only after he has amended "Quo vadis?" to "Quo Vadimus?" (Where are *we* going?). It turns out that the narrator (and the reader, *hypocrite lecteur!*) is in the same fix; he too is bound on a trivial errand that has nothing to do with his need of a decent meal and a warm place to sleep. However, the mutual recognition of each other's plight is not enough to release either of them from that plight; the moment of communion dissolves, and they continue on their "lonely and imponderable ways."

Elsewhere in *Quo Vadimus?* White is again the bemused but thoughtful citizen among citizens as he ponders on "How to Tell a Major Poet From a Minor Poet"; is moderately confused by the meaningless overuse of "Thank you," "Please," and other polite mouth-noises; lingers over the problem of how to pronounce word-coinages in *Time* magazine such as "cinemaddict" and RFChairman"; listens skeptically to his thirteen-year-old nephew's account of the Chicago World's Fair and its evidence of a "Century of Progress"; ponders the problem of choosing an Arthur Murray dance instructor on the basis of the glowing ads; writes an angry letter to the "Association of National Advertisers"; admits he can't get along with women; doubts that a certain pretentious writer in *Harper's* gets along any better; makes pithy pronouncements on public affairs ("The Economics of Abundance means that there is an abundance of economists."); exults, Benchley-fashion, over having survived a visit to the dentist, and squirms when nurses and dental nurses try to sooth him with false phrases.

In his struggles with environment this man sometimes loses, sometimes wins. With the help of "Baby," his pet bird, he vanquishes a life-insurance salesman, but he is victimized by the craze for "organization" of one's work, "being happily disorganized by nature." Doilies are among the trivia of an unnecessarily complex age that bother him. He makes the Benchleyish mistake of carrying his ice skates into a model home on exhibit, under the impression that he is entering a public rink; he sympathizes wordlessly with a man whose wife has led him into the trials of building a house. He shares the exuberance of nature as manifested in his child, who has "a certain intensity," and in his dog with its "idiot love of life," but he reacts coldly to the comments of the boy's teacher at a "progressive" school. In brief, the author-citizen of these pieces is often befuddled by practical problems but never confused for long in his sense of values, and whenever he feels that some event or observed detail is right and good, it is likely to be in some way associated with natural phenomena rather than with phenomena perpetrated by men.

Thus, in "Irtnog," the narrator describes how the mass production and consumption of printed matter resulted first in reader's digests, then in digests of these digests, and so on until all printed matter was condensed into one (nonsense) "Word of the Day." People, he observes, then quit reading, with the result that nature's harmony was restored and man's life regained the goodness it had lost through his correlated abuse of nature and of himself: "Forests, which had been plundered for newsprint, grew tall again; droughts were unheard of; and people dwelt in slow comfort, in a green world."

Citizen of the Township

White's friend, the humorist and scholar Morris Bishop, says that "In 1938, E. B. White went through some sort of inward upheaval."[7] As his favorite writer Thoreau had done, White left the city and went to the woods and pastures in search of reality. Having found it, partly on a salt-water farm near Brooklin, Maine, and partly in the perpetual search itself, he quietly examined the march of the world into war. *One Man's Meat*, a series of essays most of which appeared in *Harper's* magazine from July, 1938, to January, 1943, contains the fruits of that examination.

Perhaps intensification is a better word than upheaval, insofar as White's intellectual life is concerned. The essays in *One Man's Meat* show a concentration of elements that had been important in his work long before his removal to the Maine coast. One was his presentation of himself as citizen-writer, a role changed only in that this Little Man was now attempting to gain inward stature by working a small farm. Another was White's method of discussing public affairs by showing how they affected this man. A third was his continued urging that all men need communion with nature.

White was aware that the "back to the land" movement was not free from affectation. In earlier pieces he had satirized well-to-do urbanites who "take up" farming, remodel old farmhouses, and clutter them with all the modern gimcrackery these remodelers are supposedly escaping from. In *One Man's Meat* therefore, White continued to present himself as a Little Man tainted by absurdity. By means of this role he conducted a semidetached, public examination of himself and his experiment. In the first essay he told of his efforts to get rid of a large, ugly, gold mirror, "a sort of symbol of what I was trying to escape from." He couldn't even give it away, and finally he had to slip it into a doorway and just leave it. On the farm, he was plunged into comic chagrin because his hens produced so many eggs that ". . . we now had a first-rate farm surplus problem on our hands." He mused ruefully over how the profit motive lured him into unloading the extra eggs "on a storekeeper who used to be my friend." He pooh-poohs those who claim that farm life is simple and relaxed—"Pressure! I've been on the trot now for a long time, and don't know whether I'll ever get slowed down." He makes no pretense at living the simple life—the Whites have an electric pump, heater, lights, and refrigerator—or even to being a good farmer: "I have been fooling around this place for a couple of years, but nobody calls my activity agriculture. I simply like to play with animals." In a "letter" to Thoreau he lists the expenses of his own visit to Walden Pond and apologizes to the Concord apostle of simplicity for spending so much on shoes, shelter, and food; however, he defends the purchase of a baseball bat and glove for his son—"You never had to cope with a short-stop." White writes as a family man, not as a loner. The good life must be achieved without the sacrifice of normal, healthy domesticity.

White's relations with his immediate neighbors were evidently good, and his sense of having become part of the community was one of the rewards of his changed life. "The Flocks We Watch by Night," written in November, 1939, three months after the Nazis had rumbled into Poland, is a low-pitched account of how he and a neighboring farmer handled a sick sheep and afterwards talked a bit. "Town Meeting" is an account of that ancient and honorable New England phenomenon from the point of view of E. B. White, participant. Possibly White overstresses the degree of his acceptance by the local citizenry. Yet his satisfaction at being accepted by Charles the farmer, Dameron the lobster fisherman, and other blunt Maine folk does not prevent him from reporting evidence that he was not thus accepted by everybody in the township. When a rumor got around that White was running for the school board, the author gleefully quoted Dameron's comment, "You would have been murdered." White implies that suspicion is the normal reaction for many years of the community as a whole to the outlander in a Maine township.

On the other hand, the average man is above as well as below some of the people. After all, White was a university man writing for *Harper's* and the *New Yorker*. He pokes fun at the illiteracy of the folks who compose letters to the *Rural New Yorker*, his favorite farm journal—fun that is tempered by his admiration of that periodical's ability to interpret modern scientific farming and yet "to preserve and transmit a feeling for the land . . ." Under the wise-foolish mask of "a middle-aged hack," he shows the solid citizen's suspicion of Dr. Francis E. Townsend's old-age pension plan as presented at a Methodist camp-meeting—". . . he wanted to keep the Plan simple and beautiful, like young love before sex has reared its head." Mencken did not damn the fundamentalists in Dayton, Tennessee, more effectively with abuse than White does the Townsendites through faint praise and ironic metaphors. And although White in certain moods admires farmers' "healthy suspicion of book learning," his choice of the following quotation as an example of "practical" folk wisdom is surely satiric: "'The time to cut hay,' he [a neighbor] said firmly, 'is in hayin' time.'"

Politically, White insisted that his own tendency in times of strain was "toward the spineless middle ground." He has never been a party man, but neither has he been a drifter. In *One Man's Meat* his standard for judging any public event or proposal continued to be: how will it affect me, the ordinary citizen, in my day-to-day experience? The battle of France moved him to imitate Don Marquis' The Almost Perfect State and present in dialogue form some propositions on democracy and freedom. One comment was:

VOICE: How do you know what's good for the people?
STINGING REPLY: I know what's good for me.

In essay after essay White brought great public affairs down to the level of his average narrator. The question of how far the Government can go in aiding farmers or anyone else without undermining self-reliance vexed White when he received his allotment of free limestone fertilizer under a provision of the Agricultural Adjustment Act. "Thus the New Deal came home to me in powdered form." He heard someone admire the "fine alert faces" of the young German soldiers, and fascism came to him as the disturbance in the stomach which he felt on hearing this remark. America's participation in the war became real to him when he got his occupational questionnaire from Selective Service headquarters—he proudly put himself down as "Farmer/other," the only farm classification on the blank besides "Farmer dairy." The war also became real when he took the post of airraid warden and raced through the blacked-out countryside, blowing his horn to warn his neighbors of the "at-tack." Some essays in this book are wholly devoted to the foreground of daily matters, with no reference to the shattering events in the outside world, but more often White's pictures of daily life include carefully interspersed comment on these events: "At 8:55 exactly the Russians resume their withdrawal, the Germans resume their advance, the Japs resume their position along the Siberian border, and it's time to shut the pullets up . . ." White felt that the war was being fought so that individuals could go on doing such tasks and experiencing the elemental as manifested in the simple cycle of the day's activities and the grand cycle of nature's year:

> I sit and feel again the matchless circle of the hours, the endless circle Porgy meant when he sang to Bess: "Mornin' time and evenin' time." . . . It's almost midnight now. Nothing has meaning except the immediate moment, which is precious and indisputable. . . . This gate is dewy on a man's behind. . . . The tenderness of March, the brutality of August. . . . In the west, from the other side of town, the church bell rings, so far away that I can barely make it out, yet there it is. Give me to hold the beloved sound, the enormous sky, the church bell in the night beyond the fields and woods, the same white church near which I stood my watch this afternoon. That was before the sky had cleared. The sky is now intemperately clear. Ring bell. . . .[8] forever ring!

Global war, White felt, tended to make men forget that "the land, and the creatures that go with it, are what is left that is good." Throughout *One Man's Meat* White was trying to stimulate the ordinary man's awareness of world-wide social problems (as the Progressives had tried to do) and to reawaken his sense of relationship with the earth as part of the cosmos. White was also trying to make him feel the interrelatedness of the social and natural realms and the significance of that relatedness for the average man's fate: ". . . a man's free condition is of two parts: the instinctive freedoms he experiences as an animal dweller on a planet, and the practical liberties he enjoys as a privileged member of human society . . ." Without either, true freedom is impossible. The need for stressing freedom through harmony with nature at a time when the admittedly important struggle for political freedom was getting all the headlines was the justification White offered for writing mostly about farm and household chores while "Countries are ransacked, valleys drenched with blood."

Even so, in 1943 White returned to the city in order to participate more directly in the war effort. In *Here Is New York* (1949), written after the war for *Holiday* magazine, he showed that his ability to find dignity, color, and humor in the city as well as in the country had not waned. He did not, however, abandon his farm or his agrarian philosophy, nor did he abandon another view, to which he had gradually come in the closing months of his stay on the farm. This view may be extracted by implication from his early writings, but it is one of the few major ideas "produced" by White on the farm in the sense of first finding overt expression during his years there.

"The earth is common ground," he wrote in *One Man's Meat*, "and we are all overlords, whether we hold title or not; gradually the idea is taking form that the land must be held in safekeeping, that one generation is to some extent responsible to the next. . . ." Paradoxically, White's individualism had led him to an agrarian collectivism of a traditional American sort. A hundred years earlier, the United States had been dotted with experimental colonies that included in their ideologies the common right of all men to all the land, from the Fourieristic "consociations" to the "United Orders" among the Mormons. Among writers, Thoreau had held the surprisingly anti-individualistic view that the State must protect forests and wildlife by regulating trappers and loggers, and that townships should preserve some wild land as public property.[9] Henry George had maintained that ". . . the common right to land has everywhere been primarily recognized. . . ."[10] William Faulkner was not interested in George's single-tax theory, but through Uncle Ike's cogitations in *Go Down Moses*, Faulkner too has suggested that individuals can only hold the land in trust, not really own it, because it belongs to all men in common. The roots of White's agrarian communalism reach far back, and into some odd corners.

CITIZEN OF THE WORLD

Despite his distrust of Father Coughlin's isolationism, White during the early thirties could himself be described as moderately isolationist. An early poem, "Statement of the Foreign Policy of One Citizen of the United States," expressed a view held by Will Rogers and much of the public of both humorists in the late nineteen-twenties and early thirties. White's little citizen says,

> I have no plan
> Involving Japan.
>
> I do not wish to crush
> Soviet Rush . . .

Germany, as far as I am concerned,
Can consider the other cheek turned . . .

But White did not consider the problem of world peace solved by such passivity. In the same volume (*The Fox of Peapack*, 1928–1938), he prophesied that war would yet take many lives. Any confusion in his mind vanished before World War II was very old. During the battle of France, in June, 1940, White suggested in *One Man's Meat* that planning a "perfect state" would involve designing an all-inclusive world society. Later he hinted that isolationism died when the Japanese attacked on December 7, 1941, and internationalism would have to be its replacement. He warned that, "Before you can be an internationalist you have first to be a naturalist and feel the ground under you making a whole circle," but from a feeling of unity with nature one might progress to a sound interest in the unity of man. Thus White's urging that world government was the possible redeeming force in global politics was closely related to his belief in nature as the source of personal redemption.

Beginning on April 19, 1943, White intermittently used his "Notes & Comment" section in the *New Yorker* as a blackboard for essays of usually no more than three or four paragraphs encouraging "a federation of democratic countries, which differs from a league in that it has a legislature that can legislate, a judiciary that can judge, and an executive that can execute." These essays were collected in book form in *The Wild Flag* (1946). In these pieces he supported the budding United Nations, though he believed it fell short in not requiring any nation to get rid of the great stumbling block to global unity: national sovereignty.

How far White was ahead of the average reader of the *New Yorker* it would be hard to say, especially as White had no blueprint for achieving a workable world government and mainly confined himself to general principles. He rejected the old-style nationalism of one newpaper of mass circulation, Hearst's New York *Daily Mirror*, but he liked to feel that he spoke for "Pfc. Herbert Weintraub" and other millions of people who "are groping toward something which still has no name but which keeps turning up . . . the yet unclaimed triumph: justice among men of all races, a world in which children (of whatever country) are warm and unafraid." White tried to make this groping articulate.

In his role of spokesman for the ordinary man, White did not flatter the man's capacity for "supernationalism," rather, he cited Thurber's "The Day the Dam Broke" as an example of how liable the people are to panic, and he warned that "World government is an appalling prospect . . . Certainly the world is not ready for government on a planetary scale. In our opinion, it will never be ready. The test is whether the people will chance it anyway, like children who hear the familiar cry, 'Coming, whether ready or not!' " Man might make a botch of world federation and so perish, but without trying it he would certainly perish. One course was risky, but the other was fatal.

In voicing what he hoped the people felt, White usually spoke as an insignificant fellow who, however sure of his values, was bewildered by the facts. He portrayed himself as "just a nervous little homebody in a sack suit, trying to unravel supply lines, spearheads, flank movements . . . and the whole impossible mystery of modern tactical warfare." Once in a while he dropped the mask of meekness and hurled political epigrams with cracker-barrel deftness:

> One nation's common sense is another nation's high blood pressure.
> Bear in mind always that foreign policy is domestic policy with its hat on.
> Remember, an intelligence service is, in fact, a stupidity service.

Had they been White's contemporaries, Ade, Dunne, and their fellow wits of the Whitechapel Club would have applauded their colleague on the *New Yorker*.

THE MAZE, AND THE WAY OUT

White showed his feeling for rural ways in two narratives for children that are probably read more often by adults, *Stuart Little* (1945), and *Charlotte's Web* (1952). After *The Wild Flag*, the fullest and most forthright statements of White's main ideas appeared in *The Second Tree From The Corner* (1954).[11] This collection included short stories, essays, prefaces, parodies, poems, and extracts from "Notes & Comment." White's concern with the acceleration of change in our time shows in his choice of titles for the first two groups of pieces in this book. Group I is headed "Time Past, Time Future," and the second group is labeled "Time Present." The choice of these phrases from T. S. Eliot's "Burnt Norton" does not, however, imply any special interest on White's part in the intellectual as a superior being. White's basic theme is still the common citizen trying to preserve his integrity, and he still believes that the chief anchor for that citizen must be nature in all its regularity and mystery.

In "A Weekend With the Angels," the troubles of the narrator are largely those of Irvin S. Cobb in "Speaking of Operations—" i.e., hospital troubles. In "The Door," a man is making arrangements for his own commitment to a mental institution and possibly for a lobotomy. Unlike Walter Mitty, White's man in "The Door," though disturbed, is still sane ethically; it is environment that has taken leave of reason and integrity:

> Everything (he kept saying) is something it isn't. And everybody is always somewhere else. Maybe it was the city, being in the city, that made him feel how queer everything was and that it was something else. Maybe (he kept

thinking) it was the names of the things. The names were tex and frequently koid. Or they were flex and oid or they were duroid (sani) or flexsan (duro), but everything was glass (but not quite glass) and the thing that you touched (the surface washable, crease-resistant) was rubber, only it wasn't quite rubber and you didn't quite touch it but almost. The wall, which was glass but thrutex, turned out on being approached not to be a wall, it was something else, it was an opening or doorway—and the doorway (through which he saw himself approaching) turned out to be something else, it was a wall.

To thus abandon reality as this man's environment has done is to become, in the words of the cartoonist Jules Feiffer, "Sick, sick, sick." Religion, science, and sex have all offered "doors" out of this sick society—doors that turned out to be blank walls. The man feels like a rat trapped in a maze and deliberately tricked by a high priest of this society—a scientist—for some end known only to that scientist, if to him.

Even the reader is thrown into a daze by "The Hour of Letdown," in which a man carries a mechanical "brain" into a bar and buys drinks for it.[12] In contrast, the alleged psychoneurotic in "The Second Tree From the Corner" suddenly discovers what Walt Whitman, an author whom White has parodied but respects, once called the "primal sanities" of nature. Paradoxically but not surprisingly, what touches off Trexler's revelation is his sudden awareness that his analyst too is on the ragged edge. When Trexler throws the analyst's own question, "What do you want?" right back at him, the doctor says, "I want a wing on the small house I own in Westport. I want more money, and more leisure to do the things I want to do." At this expression of commonplace and mutually contradictory aims, Trexler's self-absorption and fear is suddenly replaced by pity. "Poor, scared, overworked bastard," he thinks. With this rush of feeling comes a restoration of his solidarity with nature. He catches sight of a small tree in the twilight, and ". . . his sickness seemed health, his dizziness stability." He announces, "I want the second tree from the corner, just as it stands," and the renewed communion restores his courage.

Trexler's rediscovery of nature is part of a personal revolt, but man in the mass can revolt too. "The Decline of Sport" is a satiric parable in which radio, television, and sky-writing have made each passive mass of spectators emotionally the prey of several sporting events at once. The result is catastrophic and then a rediscovery of simpler, more contemplative pleasures like "old, twisty roads that led through main streets and past barnyards, with their mild congestions and pleasant smells." Here, as in "Irtnog," the New-Citizen-as-consumer of whom Walter Weyl spoke in 1912 has finally expressed his resentment in a boycott. The difference between the optimism of the first Progressives and the more cautious, less political outlook of White some forty years later is seen in that mass catastrophe is needed to provoke the consumers' revolt, and nature, not politics, turns out to be the chief restorative.

In "The Morning of the Day They Did It," White warns of what may happen should man go too far in manipulating nature through technology. At a time perhaps not so far in the future, toxic disinfectants like "Tri-D" (a name suggested, no doubt, by DDT)[13] have rendered the earth dangerous for human habitation. Two average Americans, from Brooklyn and from Iowa, who happen to be U.S. Army officers flying with a secret weapon, suddenly experience the intoxicating detachment induced by stratospheric flight. They feel like "doing a little shooting," and civilization is thereby destroyed. The few survivors move to another planet where the people do only what genuinely holds their interest and where the unsprayed apples are often wormy but have "a most wonderful flavor." The narrator, just another white-collar man who in this case happens to be a video newscaster, had been fed up with the scientific nightmare of life on earth, but White reminds us of the confusion that often blurs the average man's insight: the fellow says nostalgically, "I would be lying if I said I didn't miss that other life, I loved it so." White believes that the ordinary man can, if pushed, discover nature and its harmonies, but the insight that leads to this discovery isn't permanent; it must be perpetually renewed.

The third group of sketches in *The Second Tree From the Corner* is entitled "The Wonderful World of Letters" and includes some provocative remarks on humor and a discussion of Don Marquis, whom White admired as a satirist and as a poet, and of whose idealism White had more than a touch (the protagonist in "The Door" quotes from Marquis' *Dreams and Dust*, "My heart has followed all my days something I cannot name," and suggests that disappointment in this quest killed Marquis).[14] White, as seen, does not share the complete disillusion of this protagonist or of Marquis. Nine poems comprise the fourth group in this book. The magic of nature in both city and country is the main subject of "The City and the Land," the fifth and last group of sketches in this volume. In this group appears the mock-epic "Death of a Pig," in which E. B. White, farmer, copes with the cosmic mysteries of life and death as they disrupt his works and days through the sickness and demise of an animal. As usual, White draws a sweeping moral from a small incident: ". . . I knew that what could be true of my pig could be true also of the rest of my tidy world." The writer-farmer is moved, though not upset, by the basic insecurity of all things.

Moved but not upset—this is true of White whether he is dissecting the follies of an age of gadgetry or pondering on the butchery of a lamb or the death of a pig. For all his interest in nature, White was not a pessimistic Darwinian like Dreiser, Dos Passos, or Hemingway, or like Marquis or Thurber, despite his agreement with Thurber on so many other matters. Despite his realism about nature's brutality to farm animals, White's over-all view is more like that of the great romantic writers than like the Darwinians'. Blake with his ability to see eternity in a grain of sand, Wordsworth recalling the glimpses of immortality he had had as a child, Thoreau hearing "an Iliad and Odyssey in the air" when a mosquito hummed, Whitman inviting his soul by observing a spear of summer grass, Frost finding in the use of an ax "My avocation and my vocation"—these are among White's spiritual predecessors. He belongs also with the eloquent naturalists who, in spite of Darwinism, felt that man must achieve a oneness with nature beyond merely scientific understanding, and with present-day ecologists like Aldo Leopold and Paul Errington who feel, as Joseph Wood Krutch has put it, that "conservation is not enough."[15] In an early poem White had asked "The God I half believe in" to

> Keep most carefully alive in me
> Something of the expectancy
> That is somehow likeliest to be
> In a child waking,
> A day breaking,
> A robin singing,
> Or a telephone ringing . . .

The last item suggests that White will find intensity in the man-made environment if given half a chance (Wordsworth had found it on Westminster bridge as well as among the Cumberland lakes), but he looks more hopefully to a cosmic order of which man could be a harmonious part if only he would. White denies the premise of the literary Darwinians that nature is indifferent to man. It could be so only if man remains indifferent to it. The view of Wordsworth and Emerson that as a child man felt his unity with nature but lost it as he grew older was strongly felt by White. In *One Man's Meat* he declared of his "love affair" with freedom: "It began with the haunting intimation (which I presume every child receives) of his mystical inner life; of God in man; of nature publishing herself through the 'I.' " White's two books for children amplify this view. One of the chief ends of man, he felt, was to recapture this unity and in a sense, to put it to work straightening out the inevitably "unnatural" confusions of civilization.

At home in both the country and the city, E. B. White helped the *New Yorker* to combine small-town informality with cosmopolitan breath and refinement. The prose and some of the poetry of this Cornell graduate suggest a neighbor leaning on the fire escape to talk to another neighbor. His main *persona* is the urban white-collar man attempting to recapture the "sanity and repose of nature,"[16] and this character is yet another version of one met with among White's humorous predecessors and colleagues, particularly Finley Peter Dunne, Clarence Day, Jr., Donald Ogden Stewart, Robert Benchley, Frank Sullivan, Wolcott Gibbs, John McNulty, and James Thurber—the Little Man who, even in his deteriorated condition, represents the closest we can get to the ideal, rational citizen.

Notes

1. Thurber, *The Years With Ross*, p. 92.
2. In 1912, before he started "The Sun Dial" column, Don Marquis wrote a section of the editorial page for the New York *Evening Sun*, entitled "Notes and Comment," which seems to have been similar in character to the "Notes and Comment" section of "Talk of the Town" in the *New Yorker*. See Anthony, *O Rare Don Marquis*, pp. 137, 355–356.
3. Thurber, *The Years With Ross*, pp. 95–96.
4. *Ibid.*, p. 56.
5. Kramer, *Ross and the New Yorker*, p. 153.
6. Warren Beck, "E. B. White," *College English*, VII (April 1946), 367–373.
7. Morris Bishop, "Introduction" to E. B. White, *One Man's Meat*, Harper (New York, 1950), p. viii. The first edition of this book was published in 1942 and contained fewer essays than the 1944 edition. Bishop's introduction was written for the 1950 edition.
8. The period and ellipses in this instance and the second instance are White's.
9. John C. Broderick, "Thoreau's Proposals for Legislation," *American Quarterly*, VII (Fall, 1955), 285–290.
10. Henry George, *Progress and Poverty*, [first published 1879] Robert Schalkenbach Foundation (New York, 1946), p. 369.
11. A later collection of White's work is *The Points of My Compass*, Harper and Row (New York and Evanston, 1962).
12. This story has faint overtones of an article by Poe, "Maelzel's Chess-Player," concerning a mechanical "man" that was attracting much attention in the eighteen-thirties.
13. Ironically, an article sympathetic to the continued widespread use of DDT appeared in the *New Yorker* in the same year that *The Second Tree from the Corner* was published. See Robert Rice, "DDT," *New Yorker*, XXX (July 17, 1954), 31–56.
14. I am indebted to my colleague, Professor John F. Speer, for tracing the source of this quotation after I had overlooked White's use of it.
15. Joseph Wood Krutch, *The Voice of the Desert*, Sloane (New York, 1954), pp. 186ff. Cf. Aldo Leopold, *A Sand County Almanac*, Oxford University Press (New York, 1949), pp. 201–226, and Paul L. Errington, *Of Men and Marshes*, Macmillan (New York, 1957), pp. 116, 124, 125–139.
16. John Burroughs, *Whitman: A Study*, Houghton Mifflin (Boston and New York, 1904), p. 5. If White is a "naturalist," he is in the mode of Burroughs rather than of Dreiser. In addition to his scientific observations, Burroughs became a farmer, and in work with his hands on the land he found a stimulation that he had not previously got from nature. See *Literary Values and Other Papers*, Houghton Mifflin (Boston and New York, 1902), pp. 244–256.

The Designs of E. B. White

Gerald Weales

Back in 1938, with his tongue in his cheek, E. B. White wrote, "Close physical contact with the field of juvenile literature leads me to the conclusion that it must be a lot of fun to write for children—reasonably easy work, perhaps even important work." He had just been sampling the children's books which flooded his house in those days jostling for a place in his wife's annual New Yorker column, and he had come away "gibbering." Yet even then, as he later admitted, he had tucked away in his desk drawer a dozen episodes in the continuing story of a boy named Stuart, who was only two inches high and looked like a mouse. The character had come to him in a dream back in the 1920's, he said, and had been committed to paper for an audience no larger than any favorite uncle might command.

Finally, in 1945, the chapters were taken out the desk drawer for good; the mouse went public; "Stuart Little" was published. Seven years later came "Charlotte's Web." "I am not a fast worker, as you can see," he wrote in an all-purpose letter which his publisher, Harper & Row, sends to the fans who write him. He has just won the 1970 Laura Ingalls Wilder Medal for a lasting contribution to children's literature ("It is deeply satisfying to win a prize in front of a lot of people," he wrote in "Charlotte's Web,") and has been named a runner-up for the Hans Christian Andersen Medal for authors. His new book, "The Trumpet of the Swan," is scheduled for publication in June.

Although I doubt that writing the books has been particularly easy, surely White's tongue has come out of his cheek as far as the rest of the opening quotation is concerned. Yet, it is not the author's fun nor the books' importance that concern me here. I have been considering how the books are made.

When White revised "The Elements of Style," the writer's manual by William Strunk Jr., he introduced a new Rule 8: "Choose a suitable design and hold to it." Taken at face value, without the qualifications that follows, that sounds rather like Stuart Little's method for winning a boat race: "I'll sail the Wasp straight and true, and let the Lillian B. Womrath go yawing all over the pond." But writing a book is a boat race of a very special kind;

Reprinted from *New York Times Book Review*, 24 May 1970: 2, 40. Copyright © 1945/5462/1970/77 by the New York Times Company. Reprinted by permission.

sometimes, as White says, "the best design is no design," and, in any case, "The writer will in part follow this design, in part deviate from it."

Deviation is the art of "Stuart Little." The way the story grew is probably partly responsible for this. White's word *episode*, is the key method. The book is really a series of self-contained incidents, designed to be read to a child (or by a child) whenever the occasion arises. Although White is quite capable of using a cliff-hanger when an incident spans two chapters (for the best suspense, close the book on "Stuart's down the mousehole" at the end of Chapter IV) and although many a family has read the book in the traditional chapter-a-night way, a week or two could pass between readings with no disturbing disruption of the story and episodes need not be taken in sequence. Having once heard the story, any child is likely to ask over and over again, "read me about the sailboat race."

Yet, "Stuart Little" is not a collection of short stories, as "Winnie-the-Pooh." When White sat down to write or re-write or redact or whatever one does to a twenty-year accumulation of episodes, he found the perfect genre to encompass his separate passages. White has called the book "my innocent tale of the quest for beauty," and so it is. In quest literature, whether it be picaresque novel or Grail romance, the search is only the string on which the beads of incident hang. In "Stuart Little," the quest does not begin until the book is more than half finished, and even then it is interrupted by apparently peripheral adventures: Stuart's day as a substitute teacher; his courtship of Harriet Ames, who, being two inches tall, might have been just the right girl for him.

In emphasizing the separate units in "Stuart Little," I do not intend to deny the design, for the quest requires a continuing hero and it usually resorts to recurring figures and verbal or thematic echoes. Stuart's bravery is established when he goes down the drain to get his mother's ring. His sense of adventure, his resourcefulness, even that touch of dandified pompousness which recalls Lancelot, are all dramatized before beauty—in the person of Margalo, the fugitive bird,—flies in and out of his life. There is a nice thematic line from Katharine's souvenir pillow in the schoolroom chapter to the canoe with which Stuart hopes to impress Harriet. The pillow was the gift of a boy Katharine met at summer camp and the canoe, also a souvenir, is labeled "Summer Memories." But the little girl will not let Stuart have the pillow and the canoe is smashed before he can use it—and rightly so. They represent the comfort of settling for less and are not for Stuart; after all, he, like Cuchulain, is a hero. But, despite these thematic lines, the book has no real ending. The quest for beauty is necessarily open-ended; we can always cheerfully pick up our hero at any point on his journey.

The design of "Charlotte's Web" is more intricate, a fact that would surely please Charlotte. In 1948, White wrote "Death of a Pig" which appeared in Atlantic Monthly, an oddly affecting account of how he failed to save the life of a sick pig, made ironic by the fact that the pig had been bought to act its part in the "tragedy" of the spring pig fattened for winter butchering. Since literature is not life, White set out in "Charlotte's Web" to save his pig in retrospect, this time not from an unexpected illness but from its presumably fated "tragedy." The main plot, then, is that staple of adventure literature—the rescue of the innocent. The hero, however, is neither Jack Dalton nor a Knight disguised as a wandering bard; it is a committee of sorts, consisting of a little girl, a rather wordy spider and a rat named Templeton. Nor is there a villain; Wilbur has to be saved from the inevitable course of events. Fern rescues Wilbur in the first chapter, pleading with her father not to kill him because he is a runt, only to learn that he must grow up to be bacon in any case. Then Charlotte, out of love and friendship, and Templeton, out of greed, join forces and save the pig again. If the natural processes cannot be disrupted now and then, what is fantasy for?

Yet, E. B. White tells the story of Wilbur's escape within a context that embraces the natural world, the process of growth and change. The sub-plot is Fern's story, her growing up and out of the barn where she feels at one with the animals into the world of men. One of the loveliest things in the book is that White chooses the scene of Wilbur's triumph, the prize-giving that saves his life, when all the formerly indifferent humans dance around him, to let Fern break away, to let her think not of Wilbur and Charlotte but of Henry Fussy and a ride on the Ferris wheel. Allied to the rescue story is the plot implicit in Charlotte's methods, the advertising slogans in her web ("Some Pig!"), a comment on self-delusion which in this book at least is life-giving. Finally, from the opening threat to Wilbur to Charlotte's lonely death toward the end, the book holds to the idea of death as a fact of life, but the last chapter brings new spiders, new lambs, new goslings, another spring. The book is not about the charmed life of Wilbur, but about real life and all that implies.

"Charlotte's Web" is probably a better book than "Stuart Little," a more complicated one, a deeper one. Yet I confess a fondness for that boy who looks like a mouse. "If I had been very small at birth, would you have killed me?" cries Fern in "Charlotte's Web." If E. B. White had followed all the conventionally wise advice that saw his mouse child as a runt that would do his reputation no good, he would have killed Stuart at birth. Thank God, he didn't. As Charlotte would say, SOME MOUSE!

Remarks on the Occasion of E. B. White's Receiving the 1971 National Medal for Literature on December 2, 1971

JOHN UPDIKE

A good writer is hard to talk about, since he has already, directly or by implication, said everything about himself that should be said. In the case of E. B. White, a consummate literary tact and a powerful capacity for reticence further intimidate the would-be eulogist. And indeed where would eulogy begin? E. B. White's *oeuvre*, though not very wide on the shelf, is far-flung in its variety; it is a nation gaily built on scattered islands, and the mind moves retrospectively through it as if sailing in a flirtatious wind. Letters arrive from all points of the compass; peaks glisten in unexpected places; sunny slopes conceal tunnels of anonymity; a graceful giddiness alternates as swiftly as cloud shadows with sombre sense; darkness threatens; and but for the North Star of the writer's voice, his unflickering tone of truth, we would not know where we are. White's works range from some of the noblest essays of the century to the most famous cartoon caption of the Thirties, the one that goes,

"'It's broccoli, dear.'

'I say it's spinach and I say to hell with it.'"

He broke into print as a poet and has most recently triumphed, for the third time, as the author of a novel for children. Along the line he edited and augmented what has become a standard college textbook on English style and usage. He has been associated with *The New Yorker* for almost all of the magazine's life, and indeed he has demonstrated mastery of every kind of thing *The New Yorker* prints, from poetry to fiction to the quips that cap other publications' typographical errors. But also he wrote the grave and graceful essays of *One Man's Meat* for Harper's Magazine, and *Holiday* elicited from him his beautiful tribute, *Here is New York*. Daunted, then, by this body of work so polymorphously expressing concern, wit, and love, I will, as writers tend to when confronted with a subject too big for them, take refuge in the more manageable topic of myself. My life and E. B. White.

After reading White's essays in *Harper's* throughout World War II, my mother in 1945 bought a farm and moved her family to it. It is one of the few authenticated cases of literature influencing life. White's adventures in Maine, rather than Thoreau's recourse to the Concord woods or Louis Bromfields's *Malabar Farm* (a book White reviewed in the last verse review I have seen anywhere), gave my mother the necessary courage to buy eighty rundown acres of Pennsylvania loam and turned me overnight into a rural creature, clad in muddy shoes, a cloak of loneliness, and a clinging aura of apples.

Oddly, I sought the antidote for my plight in the poison that had produced it, and devoured the work of White, of Thurber, Benchley, Perelman, Sullivan, and all those other names evocative of the urban romance that not so long ago attached to New York City, the innocent longing for sophistication that focussed here. When, infrequently, my parents brought me to New York, I always imagined I would see E. B. White in Grand Central Station. I never did, but the wish in its intensity gouged a distant memory imprint, delicate as a leaf sedimentized in limestone, of White's dapper, crinkled-haired, rather heavy-lidded countenance, that I had studied on book flaps and in caricatures, superimposed upon those carmel-colored walls. I still never enter the station without looking for him. For me, he was the city, and I wonder, will anybody ever again love this city, and poeticize it, as he did, when, to quote one of his poems,

> In the days of my youth, in the days of my youth,
> I lay in West Twelfth street, writhing with Truth.
> I died in Jones Street, dallying with pain,
> And flashed up Sixth Avenue, risen again.

I did at last meet White, an ocean away, in Oxford. He and his wife Katharine came through the door of our basement flat on Iffley Road. E. B. White himself! It was an experience that had all the qualities of a nightmare, except that it was not unpleasant. He spoke; he actually uttered words, and they were so appropriate, so neutral and natural yet—in that unique way of his—so trim, so well designed to put me at ease, that I have quite forgotten what they were.

A consequence of that awesome visit was employment of sorts; while working on West 43rd Street, I would see White in the halls and what struck me in his walk, in the encouraging memos he once or twice sent me, and in the editorial notes that in lucky weeks headed up the magazine, was how much more fun he had in him than us younger residents of those halls. Not loud or obvious fun, but contained, inturning fun, shaped like a main spring. I dealt mainly with Mrs. White, I want to add, and what a fine warm mentor she was!—a formidable woman, an editor of the magazine before White was a contributor, gifted with that terrible clear vision some women have—the difference between a good story and a bad one loomed like a canyon in her vision—yet not burned by it, rather, rejoicing in it, and modest and humorous in her firmness, so that she makes her appearances in White's accounts as a comic heroine, a good sport helping him dispose of their surplus eggs by hurling them against the barn wall.

After I quit my job and the city, my encounters with White became purely those of a reader—a reader to myself, and a reader aloud, to my children. When I asked my ten-year-old girl if I could say today that *Charlotte's Web* was her favorite book, she said, "No, tell them *Stuart Little* is."

Eulogy is disarmed. White has figured in my life the way an author should figure, coming at me from different directions with a nudge, a reminder, a good example. I am not alone in feeling grateful, or he would not be winning this prize. For three generations he has reinforced our hopeful sense that the kingdom of letters is a fiefdom of the kingdom of man. He writes as one among us, not above us, a man pulling his mortal weight while keeping a level head and now and then letting loose with a song.

Magic in the Web:
Time, Pigs, and E. B. White

HELENE SOLHEIM

Though few twentieth-century Americans need to be introduced to the work of E. B. White, this essay is a kind of a preface to his work, having in mind Dryden, that it is in the nature of a preface to ramble, "never wholly out of the way, nor in it." My purpose is to show that in *Charlotte's Web* are brought together the concerns and the methods that are consistent in White. It is too often true that critics discussing the work of a writer who produces children's books as well as grown-up writing toss off rather as an addendum, "He also writes children's stories," as though it were a hobby, or a bad habit. In White, and particularly in *Charlotte's Web*, there is nothing in his children's stories inconsistent with or unlike the substance of his articles or essays or poems for adults. White's only sustained fictions are in his three children's books (*Stuart Little*, 1945, *Charlotte's Web*, 1952, and *Trumpet of the Swan*, 1970).[1] *Charlotte's Web* is the best of the three, and it seems to me that the best of White is there: rather than being incidental, *Charlotte's Web* is central to White's work. I begin with an essay that has much in common, both its theme and its source, with *Charlotte's Web*.

"Death of a Pig," says E. B. White, was written at "a curious interlude in my life when comedy and tragedy seemed to cohere."[2] The cycles and circles which are important thematically in White's work, as in *Charlotte's Web*, are manifest, too, in his style, as in "Death of a Pig." One critic observes, "with a technique he has often used, White summarizes the events first . . . and then turns back and relates the whole matter in more leisurely detail."[3] White's essay begins:

> I spent several days and nights in mid-September with an ailing pig and I feel driven to account for this stretch of time, more particularly since the pig died at last, and I lived, and things might easily have gone the other way round and none left to do the accounting. . . .
>
> The scheme of buying a spring pig in blossomtime, feeding it through summer and fall, and butchering it when the solid cold weather arrives, is a

"Magic in the Web: Time, Pigs, and E. B. White," Helene Solheim, *South Atlantic Quarterly* 80: 4 (Autumn 1981): 390–405, published by Duke University Press, Durham. Reprinted with permission of the publisher.

familiar scheme to me and follows an antique pattern. It is a tragedy enacted on most farms with perfect fidelity to the original script. . . . The classic outline of the tragedy was lost. I found myself cast suddenly in the role of pig's friend and physician—a farcical character with an enema bag for a prop. I had a presentiment. . . . that the play would never regain its balance and that my sympathies were now wholly with the pig. This was slapstick—the sort of dramatic treatment that instantly appealed to my old dachsund, Fred, who joined the vigil, held the bag, and, when all was over, presided at the interment. When we slid the body into the grave, we both were shaken to the core. The loss we felt was not the loss of ham but the loss of pig. He had evidently become precious to me, not that he represented a distant nourishment in a hungry time, but that he had suffered in a suffering world. But I'm running ahead of my story and shall have to go back.[4]

White goes back, and he examines not only the event, but also his response, now from another perspective: "From the lustiness of a healthy pig a man derives a feeling of personal lustiness; the stuff that goes into the trough and is received with such enthusiasm is an earnest of some later feast of his own, and when this suddenly comes to an end and the food lies stale and untouched, souring in the sun, the pig's imbalance becomes the man's vicariously, and life seems insecure, displaced, transitory" (p. 247). The veterinarian advises by telephone that the pig should have an enema, and after every semi-legitimate excuse not to, White administers it, aided eagerly by Fred. "The pig, curiously enough, stood rather quietly through this colonic carnival, and the enema, though ineffective, was not as difficult as I had anticipated.

"I discovered, though, that once having given a pig an enema there is no turning back, no chance of resuming one of life's more stereotyped roles. The pig's lot and mine were inextricably bound now, as though the rubber tube were the silver cord (p. 248)." White circles again, and as the pig's death becomes a nearer inevitability, he averts his glance, apparently deriving the larger issue from the effort to avoid the one at hand: "I had assumed that there could be nothing much wrong with a pig during the months it was being groomed for murder. . . . The awakening had been violent and I minded it all the more because I knew that what could be true of my pig could be true also of the rest of my tidy world (p. 249)." As the pig is laid to rest for the second time in the essay, so at last is White's part in the event. "The news of the death of my pig travelled fast and far, and I received many expressions of sympathy from friends and neighbors, for no one took the event lightly and the premature expiration of a pig is, I soon discovered, a departure which the community marks solemnly on its calendar, a sorrow in which it feels fully involved. I have written this account in penitence and in grief, as a man who failed to raise his pig, and to explain my deviation from the classic course of so many raised pigs" (p. 253).

In "Death of a Pig," as in White's other essays, his poetry, and *Charlotte's Web*, his tenor is often almost humorlessly intense; at the same time his vehicle is light and informal and filled with humor. White's essays often express "a deadly seriousness that may be richly compounded with humor,"[5] and that compound seriousness is at work in "Death of a Pig." "Contrast is at the heart of White's style," Edward C. Sampson rightly notes, though he also finds a "tonal dualism" that works against rather than for White. "And just as there is a dualism in White about the city and the country—his love for Maine and his love for New York City—so there is a tonal dualism in White. If he found it hard to write anything long or sustained, he seems also to have found it hard to maintain a consistent tone of seriousness or of lightheartedness."[6]

But it is exactly this constant contrast of tone—not the inability to sustain one, but the agility to maintain two—that enables White in "Death of a Pig" first to see the event as farce and then to pull meaning from farce. "I discovered, though, that once having given a pig an enema"; this is ridiculous, and one expects the sentence to continue so. Instead, it shifts: "there is no turning back, no chance of resuming one of life's more stereotyped roles." The shift is abrupt but not disruptive; it is compelling. The reader is compelled to share White's perspective, and his dualism. Paying attention to the untimely death of a pig is absurd, a colonic carnival, but we come to see it is the untimely death itself, rather that its victim, which occasions a greater loss—a disruption in the community of things.

In earlier times and different perspectives man's rhythms are analogues of God's. In a finely concise expression of the medieval view, "since earthly things are joined to celestial things, the cycles of their times join together in an harmonious succession as if in universal song."[7] But White muses to a different calliope, and what leads to immortality in the work of other writers is in his vision a sequential mortality, as in his poem "Subway People," which was first published in the *New Yorker* December 5, 1925,

> Sitters, waiters,—riders to eternity,
> Shuffling in the shadow world, all day long;
> Standers, thinkers,—joggers to eternity,
> Swaying to the rhythm of the sad loud song,[8]

Sampson finds its rhythm "strongly suggestive of Vachel Lindsay and Stephen Vincent Benet," and that "White captures in this poem something of the aimlessness of life, and something of its pathos."[9] There is pathos, though it is the everyday, pre-nine, post-five pathos of the quiet desperation crowd. Rather than aimlessness, I see the repetitive sameness of the trip, and the hint of the theme of the circularity of time which White later develops in "The Ring of Time" and in *Charlotte's Web*. The poem's rhythm echoes the rhythm of the ride, and while the identical rhyme is weak, it echoes commuter boredom. Here, eternity is no more than your stop, and that caesura is—of course—somebody else's.

To say "Subway People" is like Lindsay or Benet is to allude also to Walt

Whitman, and there is in White's poem something of the joggingly insistent train rhythm evoked in "When Lilacs Last in the Dooryard Bloom'd," especially in Whitman's fifth stanza.

> Over the breast of the spring, the land, amid cities,
> Amid lanes and through old woods, where lately the violets peep'd
>   from the ground, spotting the gray debris,
> Amid the grass in the fields each side of the lanes, passing the
>   endless grass,
> Passing the yellow-spear'd wheat, every grain from its shroud in
>   the dark-brown fields uprisen,
> Passing the apple-tree blows of white and pink, in the orchards,
> Carrying a corpse to where it shall rest in the grave,
> Night and day journeys a coffin.

But Whitman's death train bears a national figure (as do those later caravans which have made the train the harbinger of death in our public life that the telegram has been in our private lives), and White's riders are an anonymous unembraced multitude. And besides, White's short poem is light verse.

In a whimsical essay, "How to Tell a Major Poet from a Minor Poet," White once and for all defines the difference between serious poetry and light verse. "Any poem starting with 'And when' is a serious poem written by a major poet. Any poem, on the other hand, ending with 'And how' comes under the head of light verse, written by a minor poet."[10] He implies, too, that light verse is that which is suitable not only for publication but also for sale. Light verse like White's leads me, tentatively, to another opinion: that light verse is not, or not much, less "serious," but that it has a more tenuous web of meaning, mood, and form than that which doesn't sell. What this means in "Subway People" is that there is White's familiar tonal dualism in the tenor of a statement like that of Ecclesiastes borne in the vehicle of a round-trip subway ride, with both those things cast in the rhythm of a cheerleaderish doggerel. And, finally, light verse makes its own critical statement, in the "And how." Most critical statements come to that, but seldom in so few letters.

(I am alarmed, and it is a topic for some essayist like White, that the little volume *Quo Vadimus?* in which I read "How to Tell a Major Poet from a Minor Poet," reprinted in 1946, the year I was born, is rotting, and bits of the brittle edges of pages fall off. Though the losses are as yet marginal, they imperil print. This is a painfully literal example of the confluence and inseparability of the themes of continuity and mutability that interlace the stories of Fern, Wilbur, and Charlotte. That same short-sighted year that optimistically began the post-war baby boom gave us its words on paper that lives little longer than our hope. Maybe it doesn't matter in White's case, since his essays are often reprinted, but if we lose words like White's we lose a part of the future as well as the past.)

White's first children's book is *Stuart Little* (1945), and its hero is a mouse born into an otherwise normal human family. The book is episodic, and the episodes of unequal weight or motivation: it is curiously unresolved and unsatisfying. Comparing Stuart with Huck Finn, however, gives the book added interest—both of them light out for the territory in a particularly American picaresque way. At the end Stuart is advised, "'A person who is heading north is not making any mistake, in my opinion.' 'That's the way I look at it,' said Stuart. 'I rather expect that from now on I shall be traveling north until the end of my days.'"[11]

The most amusing vignette in *Stuart Little* is Stuart substitute teaching in small-town School Number Seven for Miss Gunderson, who the doctor says, may have rhinestones (pp. 88–93). White's model for Stuart's unwavering pedagogism in the episode seems to have been his old Cornell English professor, Will Strunk, Jr. His 1957 sketch of Strunk was the occasion of the request for White to edit Strunk's "little book" for republication, resulting in the 1959 edition of *The Elements of Style*. The description of Strunk in White's introduction comes from the earlier essay, though they both look remarkably like Stuart Little in the schoolroom:

> "Omit needless words!" cries the author on page 23, and into that imperative Will Strunk really put his heart and soul. In the days when I was sitting in his class, he omitted so many needless words, and omitted them so forcibly and with such eagerness and obvious relish, that he often seemed in the position of having shortchanged himself—a man left with nothing more to say yet with time to fill, a radio prophet who had outdistanced the clock. Will Strunk got out of this predicament by a simple trick: he uttered every sentence three times. When he delivered his oration on brevity to the class, he leaned forward over his desk, grasped his coat lapels in his hands, and, in a husky, conspiratorial voice, said, "Rule Seventeen. Omit needless words! Omit needless words! Omit needless words!"[12]

White examines character and event from all points of his compass, and Strunk seems to be recalled also in the repetition and imperative mood of the goose and gander of *Charlotte's Web*; for example, when the goose "takes command" in Wilbur's escape (pp. 20–23) and in the goose family's machine-gun response to roll call (p. 86). In such similarities among apparently unrelated characters in his works are the permutations of aspects of character which are a part of his control of content, just as variation in repetition is a part of his mastery of form. Though there may be as much White as Strunk in the description, the memory of Strunk's classroom manner seems to have influenced, intentionally or not, the 1945 Stuart, and that portrait influenced the 1957 sketch of Strunk.

There is no "*New Yorker* style," but what is meant by that term is E. B. White; his pervasive influence on what is said and how it is said in the *New*

Yorker in their long association (and the same style seems part, too, of White's other work, as in *Charlotte's Web*). That style, it seems to me, is composed of these things. The first element is Strunk's rule: Omit needless words. The second element is a juxtaposition, perhaps derived from the exigencies of twentieth-century advertising,[13] of beauty and the mundane, and a neutrality and apparent randomness in that juxtaposition, like the random inventory of "important things" in Miss Gunderson's classroom.[14] Lastly, from this accumulation of closely observed things, it is typical of this style to move to larger contexts—that meaning comes from the assortment of things.

This style is not limited to White, nor for that matter to the *New Yorker*, but White's style is still intrinsic, especially to the "Notes and Comment" section, although he no longer regularly contributes. In the issue for 6 February 1978, "a New England correspondent" writes of southern Rhode Island after a heavy snow, in a description which bears an uncanny resemblance to the winter observations of Maine which occur from time to time in White's letters.

I started floundering out to the stable, breaking through the thin crust. Looking down at the glittering whiteness beneath my feet, I could see that I was not the first abroad. Where the wind had blown the snow to lesser depths, the roofs of mouse-made tunnels were visible, forming wandering patterns like veins. I paused to wonder about the vista inside the tunnels from the point of view of the mice. Is there icy-blue light when the sun shines through, or is the light golden? I imagine that the walls of snow tunnels look a bit like the white tile in the Holland Tunnel, but that, unlike the Holland Tunnel, a mouse tunnel is filled with clean white air. There is no engine roar, and only an occasional squeak at traffic intersections.

Floundering on to the stable, I rounded a corner and surprised a fox snoozing on the manure pile. This, I realized, must be the warmest spot in town. Its internal heat, plus its steep slope and the sun on its dark surface, had melted the snow, creating a sort of Red Fox Riviera. It seems foxes have known about alternate energy sources all along. Reluctantly, the fox got up, shook himself, and trotted off lightly on the delicate crust of the snow.

Content aside, all those elements which result from White's half-century with the *New Yorker* culminate in the style of such an article, and it has its fellows—some as good, some not—in almost every issue. This immediate and seemingly random association of ideas and trivia occurs in White's essays, as in the excerpts from "Death of a Pig" above, or "Will Strunk," which begins, "Mosquitoes have arrived with the warm nights, and our bedchamber is their theater under the stars,"[15] and in *Stuart Little* and *Charlotte's Web*, too.

Brendan Gill quotes Harold Ross, the founder and first editor of the *New Yorker*: "Don't worry about White! White was the runt of the litter! Runts live forever!" Gill responds: "If it was sufficiently startling for me to hear him describe the most exquisite of his writers in barnyard terms, what was still more startling was the fact that there was something to it—something in

White that coincided with Ross's view of him, for he later wrote a book called *Stuart Little*, about a mouse who was indeed the unexpected runt of a litter of human children. And *Stuart Little* is a masterpiece because, like *Alice in Wonderland*, it is one of the least guarded of autobiographical fantasies."[16] Gill is careless on several counts here. If *Alice* is autobiographical fantasy, it is guarded beyond recognition. *Stuart Little* is not a masterpiece, nor is Stuart a runt—just an odd offspring for a human family. And it shouldn't be a surprise to hear an allusion to country matters in reference to someone who for most of his adult life has had one foot on his Maine farm while the other remained firmly planted in Manhattan; he writes equally well from both places, despite the precarious equipose.

But the most egregious oversight is to be unaware of *Charlotte's Web* and Wilbur, who *is* a runt. Stuart appears to be, in part, a memory of Strunk; if pressed to find autobiographical fantasy in White's children's stories, it would more likely be in Wilbur, who outgrows the accidents of birth size and order to become, at last, Some Pig. There is, in fact, a hint of an association of himself with Wilbur in White's 1971 letter to the man who had been removed as director from the production of the animated film of *Charlotte's Web*. "At age 71, there's one thing I understand fully: the creative life is hell more than half the time, riddled with trials and terrors, and paved with woe. I know what it is like to try to bring something into being, as you've been doing the last few months. I know what an unhatched egg does to the spirit."[17]

White carried in his pocket, he says, for many years a copy of Thoreau's *Walden*; he read it often, quoted from it almost involuntarily, and wrote about it in several essays. In his centenary essay "Walden—1954," he says that *Walden*, "encountered" at the proper time (a similar time to that of its writing in Thoreau's life) of one's life, can be like "an invitation to life's dance."[18] (And for a spirit as capable of "new, radiant action" and remarkable feats as Wilbur's, *Walden's* different drummer plays a catchy, syncopated beat.) In an earlier letter about the animated film project, White wanted to make very clear that the animals on Zuckerman's farm not appear to live in "community"; that they be seen as an aggregation of "rugged individualists," each out foremost for its own interests, and working together in compromise only when pushed to the wall. "Interdependence? I agree that the film should be a paean to life, a hymn to the barn, an acceptance of dung. But I think it would be quite untrue to suggest that barnyard creatures are dependent on each other. The barn is a community of rugged individualists, everybody mildly suspicious of everybody else, including me. Friendships sometimes develop, as between a goat and a horse, but there is no sense of true community or cooperation. Heaven forfend!! Joy of life, yes. Tolerance of other cultures, yes. Community, no."[19] But White isn't quite right about the farm, or about communities— the best kind of community is that made up of rugged individualists. In a sense, Stuart Little shares the snobbish individual anarchism Thoreau has, and though he is too urban and urbane (and too dependently small) to be a rugged individualist, in heading north at the end of the book, Stuart is avoiding the commitment and responsibility that participation in community demands. It is those who, like Wilbur, seek to retain individualism while staying in one place, who become, finally, the most solid citizens—if that term means full participants in the life of the community. Beginning with his brutely selfish instincts to stay alive despite the usual routine, Wilbur grows and, with more than a little help from his friends, learns to enjoy his unique, exceptional nature, and at last can drop back to the supporting role of foster parent to newer, shinier lives. And in that he has achieved some resolution of individual expression and community welfare.

"I at least have so much to do in unravelling certain human lots, and seeing how they were woven and interwoven, that all the light I can command must be concentrated on this particular web, and not dispersed over that tempting range of relevancies called the universe," George Eliot writes in 1871, comparing her *Middlemarch* to the more "spacious" time and work of Henry Fielding. But her universe is clearly as large as Fielding's, and we see in writers like Fielding and Eliot and White (different as they are) that a range of relevancies is indeed a web, and that light which is attracted and reflected by the threads of some particular web can illuminate a little universe—like a circus.

That voice of experience and wisdom in *Charlotte's Web*, the old sheep, tempts Templeton: "A fair is a rat's paradise" (p. 124). Though fairs have linear competitive goals, and circuses are overlapping circles of entertainment, they are, for the most part, pretty much the same thing. And a circus, like a web, weaves a magic spell. White sees it this way, in "The Ring of Time":

> The circus comes as close to being the world in microcosm as anything I know; in a way, it puts all the rest of show business in the shade. Its magic is universal and complex. Out of its wild disorder comes order; from its rank smell rises the good aroma of courage and daring; out of its preliminary shabbiness comes the final splendor. And buried in the familiar boasts of its advance agents lies the modesty of most of its people. For me the circus is at its best before it has been put together. It is at its best at certain moments when it comes to a point, as through a burning glass, in the activity and destiny of a single performer out of so many. One ring is always bigger than three. One rider, one aerialist, is always greater than six. In short, a man has to catch the circus unawares to experience its full impact and share its gaudy dream.[20]

"The Ring of Time" is dated March 22, 1956, four years after the publication of *Charlotte's Web*. Like many of White's essays, it has two topics. The first is personal, small in the world sense, and thereby universal: White's observations while watching the circus rehearse in Sarasota, Florida. Written two years after the Supreme Court's separate-but-equal segregation decision, the essay's second topic is the effect—or apparent lack of effect—on Florida of that decision. This is topical and public, and thereby locked into its time. White establishes his perspective by keeping a distance: "Here in Florida I am a guest in two houses—the house of the sun, the house of the State of Florida. As a guest, I mind my manners and do not criticize the customs of my hosts" (p. 57). This distance keeps him from commitment and substantial comment on the second topic, but in the house of the sun no shade keeps White's observations from being sharp and focused and intimately involved.

He stands with other observers watching rehearsals of the Ringling Brothers circus at their winter quarters. He observes a young bareback rider, whose mother (White assumes) is an older version of the same, though it is apparent, if not explicitly stated, that this daughter and mother are separated by far more than a generation.

> The richness of the scene was in its plainness, its natural condition—of horse, of ring, of girl, even to the girl's bare feet that gripped the bare back of her proud and ridiculous mount. The enchantment grew not out of anything that happened or was performed but out of something that seemed to go round and round and round with the girl, attending her, a steady gleam in the shape of a circle—a ring of ambition, of happiness, of youth. (And the positive pleasures of equilibrium under difficulties.) In a week or two, all would be changed, all (or almost all) lost. . . .
>
> As I watched with the others, our jaws adroop, our eyes alight, I became painfully conscious of the element of time. Everything in the hideous old building seemed to take the shape of a circle, conforming to the course of the horse. The rider's gaze, as she peered straight ahead, seemed to be circular, as though bent by force of circumstance; then time itself began running in circles, and so the beginning was where the end was, and the two were the same, and one thing ran into the next and time went round and around and got nowhere. The girl wasn't so young that she did not know the delicious satisfaction of having a perfectly behaved body and the fun of using it to do a trick most people can't do, but she was too young to know that time does not really move in a circle at all. I thought: "She will never be as beautiful as this again"—a thought which made me acutely unhappy—and in a flash my mind (which is too much of a busybody to suit me) had projected her twenty-five years ahead, and she was now in the center of the ring, on foot, wearing a conical hat and high-heeled shoes, the image of the older woman, holding the long rein, caught in the treadmill of an afternoon long in the future. "She is at that enviable moment in life (I thought) when she believes she can go once around the ring, make one complete circuit, and at the end be exactly the same age as at the start." Everything in her movements, her expression, told you that for her the ring of time was perfectly formed, changeless, predictable, without beginning or end, like the ring in which she was travelling at this moment with the horse that wallowed under her. And then I slipped back into my trance, and time was circular again—time, pausing quietly with the rest of us, so as not to disturb the balance of a performer. (pp. 54–55)

White's prose in this passage jogs and wallows like the circus horse, and though its gaze is straight ahead, what falls within its compass is rhythmically and syntactically circular. Beginning with the linear paradox of richness in plainness, the prose seems to move out, pick up speed, and hit its stride, as the horse and the girl (and time) do. Repeatedly, we are caught up by a series of parallel additives—"of horse, of ring, of girl"—and then White lets out the line with a virtually endless string of "and"—"and so the beginning was where the end was, and the two were the same, and one thing ran into the next and time went round and around and got nowhere." In the sentence which follows—"The girl wasn't so young that she did not know the delicious satisfaction of having a perfectly behaved body and the fun of using it to do a trick most people can't do, but she was too young to know that time does not really move in a circle at all"—the force of the multiple negatives is emphatic, but more than that, the sentence not only encourages but almost requires a circular reading—it is nearly impossible to get it "straight" the first time. With White, then, we must pause to observe. White has defined his position as observer, and as the rider approaches him and recedes, his self-awareness varies directly with the size of her image. That is, the narrator's intrusions in this description—"I thought," quotations, parenthetical expressions—seem to come when the rider has completed one circle, having reached the point on its circumference nearest White, and is beginning another circle. There is an eroticism here, though rather than being pursued by time's winged chariot, the circus rider drives it. The lure the maid holds out is time itself. The point at which she comes nearest White is the point at which she begins to recede (and *carpe diem* becomes an impossible calculus of reach and grasp). As she approaches White he becomes engaged, too, and the "I" becomes as active a participant as the "she." But the ring she commands also confines, and as she begins a new circle, White slips back from participant to observer. In the first paragraph it is "something" that goes "round and around and around," but in the echo in the paragraph that follows, the something is identified as time; then time is identified as the ring—not the tangible circus ring, but the one circumscribed by the rider—and finally time becomes another observer, pausing with White in awe of the performer. But he said "*a* performer," and in the economically ambigious "a," we see that White, like Charlotte, has been the performer, too. Here again, as in "Subway People," tenor far outweighs vehicle, relying on motion to maintain balance. From this kaleidoscopically circular image of a circus rehearsal, White pulls one of the silver cords of meaning from life's web. If time *were* a circle, Coleridge might have had such passages of White's in mind, as much as he had Donne and Dryden when he wrote in *Biographia Literaria*, "The vividness of the descriptions or declamations . . . is as much and as often derived from the force and fervor of the describer, as from the reflections, forms or incidents, which constitute their subject and materials. The wheels take fire from the mere rapidity of their motion."

Of the traditional "classics" for children, of which *Charlotte's Web* may be the last, there are, of course, girls' books and boys' books. I don't believe the

difference I see in the girl and boy protagonists need be sex-related, but it falls
that way in the books. The girls are dreamy and existential things, and
observers, knowing the rules but waiting for time to give them the apparatus
to take part in the game. Like George MacDonald's Princess Irene, they pursue
the thread of life. The boys, on the other hand, are having adventures (and a
surprising number of them playing at pirates). It would be simplistic to say
the boys are active and the girls passive (Alice, after all, is awfully busy, and
rather aggressive, too), and equally simplistic to call the girls thoughtful and
the boys rash (Tom Sawyer plots childhood like chess). Instead, the boys learn
to be adults by initiating adult (if fantastic) action—"as if his whole vocation/
were endless imitation," Wordsworth says—while the girls try to figure out
what is going on. It is only after time, and some loss, that the girls are able
to participate in adult activity. And, traditionally, these options for boys and
limits for girls have been sex-related.

Avery and Fern Arable demonstrate this difference clearly (and it is
suggested in their names). "That morning, just as Wilbur fell asleep, Avery
Arable wandered into Zuckerman's front yard, followed by Fern. Avery carried
a live frog in his hand. Fern had a crown of daisies in her hair" (pp. 67–68).
Avery is timely and insensitive. Fern, for some moment, is timeless, and
hypersensitive. She is all eyes and ears, and as we see in the violent fight
against the injustice of killing the runt piglet Wilbur with which the book
opens, even her emotions are a sense.

The addition of Fern to the story of life in the barnyard was an after-
thought,[21] and it makes all the difference. Fern is an observer of life in the
barn, rather than a participant, and in fact she is not mentioned at all from
page 16 through page 43. As in so many children's books, the little girl Fern
is the character who makes the trip from the real world in the fantasy world,
but unlike many other heroines, Fern takes the fantasy world back into the
real one.

She grows up a great deal during the year of this story and puts away
"childish" concerns. At the end, "Fern did not come regularly to the barn any
more. She was growing up, and was careful to avoid childish things, like sitting
on a milk stool near a pigpen" (p. 183). After Wilbur's life is saved Fern's
interest turns, as though her vision were altered by confinement in the ring
of time, to another future promise in Henry Fussy. What she remembers from
the fair is not Wilbur's glory or Charlotte's death, but Henry, and the Ferris
wheel. Parenthetically, Avery is a bit of a clown and a performer himself, and
as Wilbur becomes more of a celebrity, Avery spends more time with him:
rather than observing from outside the ring, Avery climbs right in to share
the limelight. Though the reader begins *Charlotte's Web* with great sympathy
for Fern and her cause, when Fern's concern shifts, the reader's sympathy stays
with Wilbur. She forfeits our sympathy when she ceases to care.

It might well be asked how White gets away with devoting so much of
Charlotte's Web, a children's book, to death. Somehow, it is not enough to say

that death is a part of life—or life's dance. Art makes its own demands, and in this case the issue is the audience, and decorum. It seems to me White gets there, and gets the reader there, by a sequence of images, and by "image" here I mean an object which is at the center of an action. After White's fashion, I will summarize, and then look to the detail. The first image is the rope swing (pp. 68–69), then Charlotte's painstakingly constructed web (pp. 92–94), next the Ferris wheel, and finally Charlotte's last web.

We are prepared for the pleasure of the barn swing, if not by memory, by Wilbur's expectation that, if he wants to and tries to spin a web, he will have a filament like Charlotte's strand extruding from his rear (p. 56). He is wrong, but we begin to see possibilities. Then, in the rope swing passage, we are virtually forced to become imaginatively involved in swinging through the insistent second-person address (twelve "you's," in fact). As Charlotte plans and constructs her "Terrific" web (Wilbur's hoped-for filament having become the child's rope, and that in turn become Charlotte's rope-like web strands), we see her enthusiasm and effort and determination in a creation which is only transitory and briefly functional. (It is, of course, Wilbur whom the web advertises as "Terrific." But what is confusion and disagreement among the characters becomes the critic's ambiguity: the web and Charlotte are terrific, too.) The same roundish shape of the web recurs in the Ferris wheel—another childish joy, and Fern's happiest memory—and the wheel, too, is a passing pleasure. On the day the Ferris wheel is taken down, Charlotte dies, having begun the renewal of life by planting her egg sac and her last, wheel-shaped web.

I have laboriously connected what rests easily independent in the book. But if we can see that Wilbur's hoped-for filament is like the rope swing, and the rope swing like the elements of Charlotte's web, and the shape of that web like that of the Ferris wheel (that other symbol of child-like, if temporal, joy), and that the Ferris wheel—never for long a closed circle—is like Charlotte's last life-nurturing web, then we can see that the magic of the web of this story encompasses both what is permanent—death, and the memory of joy—and what passes—life, and sorrow. "The song sparrow, who knows how brief and lovely life is, says, sweet, sweet, sweet interlude; sweet, sweet, sweet interlude'" (p. 43).

The spring is Fern's season: the book opens with her story, in that time. The summer, radiantly, belongs to Wilbur, though his growth and development are a motif, if not more, throughout the whole. In the fall and the harvest fair, our attention, though not the crowd's, turns to Charlotte: autumn is, to borrow a metaphor from another part of the kingdom, Charlotte's swan song. In winter Fern has outgrown her interest in the barnyard, and so we lose interest in her. Wilbur is mature now and is taking on the uninteresting manners of parents. Charlotte is gone. And so, as the year comes full circle we see here, too, that time is not circular at all. It is the time for new heroes, and for a new story. The final chapter is, really, an epilogue. Perspective draws back to take the larger view—life, rather than lives—and to celebrate life in the barn, and the glory of everything. There are three stories in *Charlotte's Web*: Fern's, Wilbur's, and Charlotte's. The three are joined in the miracle of the web, which, like time and like comedy, bring renewal and new life. *Charlotte's Web*, like *Walden*, is an invitation to life's dance.

Sampson says, "Except for his three children's stories, White has been above all a writer of his times, an interpreter of the contemporary scene; and, as such, it has seemed not only wise but necessary to consider his writing against the changing background of his times."[22] The contemporary scene, the changing background of the times, are a reason to except them. "Fiction," says Virginia Woolf in *A Room of One's Own*, "is like a spider's web, attached ever so lightly perhaps, but still attached to life at all four corners." My aim has been to show that *Charlotte's Web* is not on the periphery of White's work but at its center. And when we see in *Charlotte's Web* how White weaves together the themes, the tone, the style that recur in his work, we see it is a winter's tale, a romance, a curious interlude when comedy and tragedy seem to cohere. And how.

Notes

1. All three books published in New York by Harper & Row; quotations from *Stuart Little* and *Charlotte's Web* are from these editions.
2. Dorothy Lobrano Guth, ed., *Letters of E. B. White* (New York, 1976), pp. 289, 375.
3. Edward C. Sampson, *E. B. White* (New York, 1974), p. 123.
4. E. B. White, "Death of a Pig," *The Second Tree from the Corner* (New York, 1954), pp. 243–44.
5. Louis Halsey, "The Talk of the Town and the Country: E. B. White," *Connecticut Review* 5(1971): 37–45.
6. Sampson, pp. 44, 156.
7. D. W. Robertson, Jr., *A Preface to Chaucer* (Princeton, 1962), p. 117. Robertson quotes St. Augustine's *De musica* (6,11,29).
8. As quoted in Sampson, p. 39. Copyright © 1929 by Harper & Row, Publishers, Inc. From the book *The Lady is Cold*; reprinted by arrangement with the *New Yorker* and Harper & Row, Publishers, Inc.
9. Sampson, p. 39.
10. E. B. White, *Quo Vadimus?* or *The Case for the Bicycle* (Garden City, 1946), pp. 68–69. The book is dedicated to "Walt Whitman, of Paumanok; Grover Whalen, of Flushing Bay; and the openers of time capsules in the world of tomorrow."
11. E. B. White, *Stuart Little* (New York, 1945), p. 129.
12. William Strunk, Jr., and E. B. White, *The Elements of Style*, third ed. (New York, 1979), p. xiii.
13. In the mid–1920's, before he began to work at the *New Yorker*, White spent a year in advertising. He writes in "Noontime of an Advertising Man" (*New Yorker*, 25 July 1949, pp. 25–26) of his dualistic response to that experience: "I, too, was unhappy in the advertising world, because I couldn't seem to make myself care whether a product got moved or not. . . . I did not want to overthrow the world of advertising—actually, I believed that the world of advertising was essentially a good thing, and I still believe that—but I did long to slip quietly

away from it." In Charlotte's web, too, advertising is essentially a good thing: it saves Wilbur, and in his transformations to fit his praise, advertising might even be seen to work small miracles. But Wilbur, too, is sometimes unhappy in the advertising (or advertised) world, and finally slips quietly away from it.

14.　Stuart Little grows as quickly tired of the usual "drills" in spelling and arithmetic as the class, and engages them, perhaps only for lack of something better to do, in some consciousness raising. " 'Instead of taking up any special subject this morning, why wouldn't it be a good idea if we just talked about something.' The scholars glanced around at each other in expectancy. . . . 'Henry Rackmeyer, you tell us what is important.' 'A shaft of sunlight at the end of a dark afternoon, a note in music, and the way the back of a baby's neck smells if its mother keeps it tidy,' answered Henry. 'Correct,' said Stuart. 'Those are the important things. You forgot one thing, though. Mary Bendix, what did Henry Rackmeyer forget?' 'He forgot ice cream with chocolate sauce on it,' said Mary quickly. 'Exactly,' said Stuart. 'Ice cream is important' " (pp. 92–93).

15.　E. B. White, "Will Strunk," *The Points of My Compass* (New York, 1962), p. 115.

16.　Brendan Gill, *Here at The New Yorker* (New York, 1975), p. 296.

17.　*Letters*, p. 621.

18.　E. B. White, "Walden—1954," *Yale Review* 44 (1954): 13. The essay is sometimes reprinted as "A Slight Sound at Evening."

19.　*Letters*, p. 614.

20.　E. B. White, "The Ring of Time," *The Points of My Compass* (New York, 1962), pp. 52–53.

21.　Sampson, p. 100.

22.　Ibid., preface.

The Sparrow on the Ledge:
E. B. White in New York

Thomas Grant

E. B. White, like his friend James Thurber, was especially fond of dogs—and I suppose still is since, at this writing, he is still alive. One of the most memorable to him was Fred, a feisty dachshund who used to poke his nose into everything—until he got poked back.[1] He was not as arrogant as Thurber's dog, "The Scotty Who Knew Too Much," who belligerently sought out larger adversaries and ended up "knifed" by a porcupine. Fred took easily to the city and later to the country, where, White once recalled, "his interest in every phase of farming remains undiminished . . . but his passion for details is a kind of obsession. . . . He wants to be present in a managerial capacity at every event, no matter how trifling or routine."[2] Like Fred, White liked to poke around in any urban corner or alley, but always with caution, out of respect for what might poke back, and as an essayist, his own modest size. He liked to sniff out a subject and get its scent, size up the experience and pass on. He didn't want to pick fights lest, like Thurber's scotty, he'd have to offer excuses the next day. He, too, felt equally at home in the city as in the country, so long as the environment (for an essayist) was congenial and he was well fed (with material). And, like Fred, White assumed the unofficial manager's role, becoming the *New Yorker*'s best detail man, most prolific staffer and, over the years, just about the magazine's most versatile contributor.

While both dog and master possessed sensitive noses for news, White's close-to-the-ground view, particularly towards the city, actually ranged wider and a little higher, probably closest to that of the New York denizen who most frequently turns up in his essays: the bird, most notably *passer domesticus*— the sparrow. In a *New Yorker* piece called "Interview with a Sparrow" (April 9, 1927), White wondered why birds struggle to live in the city when they have the country open to them. The sparrow answers unhesitatingly: "here in town I get everything that the country offers plus the drama and the stimulus of interesting contacts" (p. 31). So the sparrow takes to the city for the same reasons writers of magazines like the *New Yorker* do—or, rather, the reverse, for surely the sparrow nested first. The sparrow ranges far and wide, but not

Reprinted from *Studies in American Humor*, Spring 1984: 24–33. Reprinted by permission.

very high, preferring to feed on or near the ground. It will settle on any low-lying crevice. The interviewee found, in fact, a penthouse of a ledge, at the Metropolitan Museum of Art, which offered him, he boasts, "an extraordinary outlook on Greek statuary" (p. 31). "A sparrow," says the narrator of White's parable, "The Wings of Orville" (August 8, 1931), "will gape at anything queer."

White, too, liked to range far and wide, yet feed on or near the ground, searching out the odd or extraordinary amid the inexhaustible variety in New York, that most inexhaustible of American cities. Any ledge or perch in town provided a point of departure, or he could take flight from his regular "nest," a drab office at the New Yorker's West Side mid-town headquarters, with its liberating view of a solid brick wall. He might have identified with the sparrow's dull coloring, which allowed him to blend into the city scape. As an essayist, White liked to flit about unnoticed, savoring his anonymity. "Place yourself in the background," he urged writers in *The Elements of Style*, and keep in the foreground, "the sense and substance of the writing." Indeed, White spoke of style itself as a kind of flight, where "we leave the ground" of rules and, once air borne, the writer "will often find himself steering by stars that are disturbingly in motion."[4] A White essay takes the sparrow's path, meandering about sentence by sentence, allowing the cross-currents of thought and insight to set direction and determine destination, with meaning something not entirely known until found. An essay was a way of traveling light, "a ramble," as he said of the essay Thoreau conceived at Walden Pond,[5] but more uniquely like a flight, and one fraught with its own kind of risk. White celebrated one in "The Wings of Orville," in which a sparrow is determined to "prove the feasibility of towing a wren" from Madison Park to 110th street (p. 8). The small sparrow insists on doing what hasn't been done before, as does the essayist, and nothing less than taking wing will suffice.

Manhattan's building boom of the 1920s and 30s provided many a ledge or capital for adventurous low-flyers, bird or man, thanks to the Beaux Arts tradition in architecture and the subsequent emergence of art deco styles. But during the 40s and 50s the signature style in American architecture gradually gave way to the stark anonymity of Bauhaus-influenced modernism, hard architecture which White found symptomatic of a civilization's decline and a culture's decay. One consequence of sheath steel and plate glass was a shortage of ledges for the city birds—and vantages open to inquisitive essayists. White linked the birds' fate with his own and worried about their extinction in the contemporary city of glass. The great White way to New York lies open to us if we will, so to speak, play the wren and string along on some of the writer's flights of fancy around town.

In the summer of 1948, White wrote a paean to the city for *Holiday* magazine called *Here is New York*. He said there were actually three New Yorks: "There is, first, the New York of the man or woman who was born here, who takes the city for granted and accepts its size and its turbulence as natural and inevitable. Second, there is the New York of the commuter—the city that is devoured by locusts each day and spat out each night. Third, there is the New York of the person who was born somewhere else and came to New York in quest of something." Of these three, the greater is the last, "the city of final destination, the city that is a goal. It is the third city that accounts for New York's high-strung disposition, its poetical deportment, its dedication to the arts, and its uncomparable achievements. Commuters give the city its tidal restlessness; natives give it solidity and continuity; but the settlers give it passion."[6] No contributor to the *New Yorker* felt that passion more than he who so succinctly defines it here. Unlike many New York "settlers" in quest of something, who came from afar, White was born and raised just beyond the shadow of mid-town skyscrapers rising in the building boom, in Mount Vernon, New York. Thus, he early felt the dynamism of a tripartite city. He was something of a native, and hence disposed to accept the city's inevitable turbulence; he became a commuter, and hence understood how schedules deaden the spirit; and both roles made the quester in him more flexible, more compassionate and, hence, more humane. He might even have been the youngest of the *New Yorker* "settlers" of his generation, having journeyed into the city often with his father; and, in his early teens, he attended tea dances held in mid-town hotels. In "Afternoon of an American Boy" (November 29, 1947), he recounted one of these held at the Plaza, calling it an "expedition of unparalleled worldliness": "Dancing or no dancing, this was certainly high life, and I knew I was witnessing a scene miles and miles ahead of anything that took place in Mount Vernon. I had never seen anything like it, and a ferment must have begun working in me that afternoon."[7]

A decade later, after he sated his wanderlust by motoring across the country to Seattle and shipping off to Alaska, White returned to New York, and, in 1923, began working as a layout man in an ad agency. He spent his leisure absorbing the city, allowing that "ferment" to work in him; and he gave lyrical form to his passions in brief poems published in Franklin P. Adams's influential column, "The Conning Tower." Success meant being perfectly placed, in the quintessential American city, ready to be touched by revelation. As he recalled in *Here is New York*: "New York hardly gave me a living at that period, but it sustained me. I used to walk quickly past the house in West 13th Street between Sixth and Seventh where F. P. A. lived, and the block seemed to tremble under my feet—the way Park Avenue trembles when a train leaves Grand Central" (p. 32).

White's precocious sensitivity to the city's growing pains suffuses his earliest contributions to Ross's fledgling magazine. To establish the *New Yorker*'s identity among hoped-for subscribers and the classier advertisers, contributors touted the magazine relentlessly. Ross wanted particularly to reach "the person who knows his way about, or wants to."[8] White was the *New Yorker*'s most unabashed chauvinist. He had a street vendor's savvy of the neighborhoods and a cabbie's feel for the streets; and his unique grasp of New

York detail gave, as Gerald Weales has noticed, reportorial substance to what was essentially fantasy.[9] In his earliest "Notes and Comments" he liked to chide complaisant suburbanites for their neglect and badger ladies who sail for Crete but who have not looked at Rivington Street or Tompkins Square, who come to the "phantom city" from grassy suburbs to confess their woes to psychoanalysts.[10] In his first *New Yorker* piece, "Defense of the Bronx River" (May, 1925), White sought to awaken the even somnulent commuter to what the sparrow liked about New York, the "drama" that lies just beyond the train window. He concluded by seeing himself as one of a reborn race of nature enthusiasts: "here is one commuter who wouldn't trade this elegant little river, with its ducks and rapids for the Amazon or the Snohomish or the La Platee" (p. 14). In "Lower Level" (May 22, 1926), White sought to awaken commuters to touch one another, by imagining a typsy commuter as a protagonist—his soul "made articulate by wine"—who creates a fellowship with his quirky, unexpected greetings: "They liked simple homage paid by a humble soul in an age of inexpressible marvels" (p. 20). In "Hey Day Labor" (August 7, 1926), White found a fraternity of men himself when, mistaken for a pier laborer, he climbs aboard a coal truck and enjoys a bird's eye view as it careens through the streets, all traffic giving way: "taxicabs, once held invulnerable, bend double to honor your passage" (p. 21).

In these early chauvinistic pieces, White presents himself as a modern-day Whitman, a common man, one of the roughs, a man who was there and thus so shall be the reader. "I celebrate myself, and sing myself/And what I assume you shall assume, For every atom belonging to me as good belongs to you." White is also kin to Thoreau, long before he wrote about him, the ambling amateur naturalist with notebook in hand, eager to make a good account of himself on his sojourns. The two poets blend into the one uniquely urban singer. "New York provides not only a continuing excitation," he observed in *Here is New York*, "but also a spectacle that is continuing. I wander around, re-examining the spectacle, hoping that I can put it on paper" (p. 32). The solitary singer's convenient anonymity could also estrange him, when the surging city refused to open him to what the sparrow in White's interview called "interesting contacts." In "Evening on Ice" (March 19, 1927), a lonely protagonist goes to Madison Square Garden's public skating rink seeking the company of other skaters, only to find everyone crowding around a home show exhibit (p. 30). One cure for isolation in the city White found was to immerse himself in his favorite landmarks, to take imaginative possession of cherished monuments, so as to keep that old childlike "ferment" working in him. In "It's a 'ome" (January 5, 1929), "Baedeker Jones" ambles through the Grand Central district and into the terminal's "catacombs," when all the commuters are home sleeping peacefully. Commercial enterprises are suddenly disengaged from daily profit-making as the traveler liberates the building to serve instead a moment of exhilarating play: "I would buy a toboggan and a decoy duck at Van Lengerke and Detmolds and coast, late at night, down the ramps and bannisters until apprehended. When apprehended, I would hand the officer the duck, so he would know I was fooling" (p. 19). Robert Benchley would have converted such a nighttime triumph into a daytime disaster, in a farcical "casual" about the harassed "little man" upended by a few steps—and missing his train. Frank Sullivan would have plunged the tobogganer down into a cool sewer, there to meet a ghostly tribe of Mohawks. White was never an ambulance chaser, on the lookout for collisions to turn into funny copy, or an armchair folklorist in the genteel manner of Irving. He thought, again like Thoreau, that daily life was sufficiently fantastic to occupy the attentive observer. Alone in Grand Central, White showed how a mere pedestrian could, in imagination, accomplish what the city itself, building ever upward, was doing—control gravity and defy nature.

By the late 1930s, after more than a decade exploring New York vantages and flitting about in search of the city's "drama," White made the first of several departures. He provided a whimsical account in a "Talk of the Town" piece called "The Departure of Eustace Tilley" (August 7, 1937). "My departure was in part a matter of temper, in part of expediency," he noted, with deliberate evasions.[11] The reasons were many, both personal and professional, and included White's longing for freedom from magazine deadlines. The following year, after he had decided to relocate in Maine, he tried to explain his departure, confessing to be ill-at-ease with developments in his own profession: "A certain easy virtue in everyone, myself included, and a willingness to accept the manner and speech of the promoter and the gossip writer. A certain timbre of journalism and the stepping up of the news with the implication that the first duty of man is to discover everything that has just happened everywhere in the world a certain idiocy of the newsreel and the glorification of acrobatic eccentricity." He added: "there is a decivilizing bug somewhere at work"—without naming it.[12] Certainly, the city itself, central generator of the nation's commerce and communication, magnified the decivilizing weaknesses in the culture he disliked and whose consequences he most feared. In fact, the changing cityscape itself began to show disturbing signs of rot; and one of the "bugs" was modernist architecture. In the article critical of the new flashy journalism, White also said he was worried by "a hardness and brightness of the materials from which the world about me was being constructed: the steel that tarnished not, neither does it rust, but simply hits you in the eye twenty-four hours of the day with hollow splendor."[13] He recounted a visit to the 1939 World's Fair in "The World of Tomorrow," published in the May 1939 of *Harper's*, in which he seems vaguely apprehensive and tries to hide his uneasiness by pleading a sinus infection. He is ready to endorse the future—if it could cure the common cold. But the old chauvinism is conspicuously missing: "The architecture is amusing enough, the buildings are big enough, to give the visitor that temporary and exalted feeling of being in the presence of something pretty special, something full of aspiration, something which at times is even exciting."[14] He finds the exhibit itself oppressively commercial and the cityscape sterilized, artificially-lighted—all of it comprising a future programmed to elicit only canned responses. "There is a great deal of electrically transmitted joy, but very little spontaneous joy," he laments.[15] The phrase itself lacks White's former verve.

Earlier that year, White imagined himself literally trapped inside the "future." His *New Yorker* sketch, "The Door" (March 25, 1939), was provoked by a visit to a model home exhibit in Rockefeller Center. White's youthful persona, the Whitmanesque enthusiast, has become a tense, neurotic skeptic, lost in a modern labyrinth like a rat in a maze. Surfaces are hard and plastic, and even the once magical names of things now lack identity, reduced to a bloodless collection of amputated prefixes and suffixes: "The names were tex and frequently koid. Or they were flex and olid or they were duroid (sani) or flexsam (duro), but everything was glass (but not quite glass)." "The Door" is a parable about an increasingly alienating environment, the city of glass that New York has since become. It is all the more disturbing for being promoted in a crippled English expropriated by pseudoscientific entrepreneurs. One can imagine the ultramodern home, incongruously lodged inside one of the monuments of 30s era art deco, as the rough beast of Bauhaus modernism slouches towards the suburbs to be born. White's parable also warns against urban renewal as the lobotomization of culture: "The doctors know where the trouble is, only they don't like to tell you about the prefrontal lobe because that means making a hole in your skull and removing the work of centuries." "Maybe it was the city," the beseiged visitor keeps repeating as he struggles to escape the exhibit, "being in the city that made you feel how queer everything was."[16]

The transformation of the "phantom city" of inexhaustible delight into the "hollow splendor" of hard architecture became an objective correlative of White's disaffection for "progress" on nearly all fronts. His skepticism about the future of life in cities grew during the 1940s, after he had found a more tranquil home on a salt farm on the coast of Maine. He established a half-life in the city in 1943; but the inevitable estrangement between the sensitive soul and the human community in dense urban environment subjected to relentless modernization made him cling all the more tenaciously to the species of nature still alive in town. White's search for some root in a forest of steel and glass took parable form in the *New Yorker* sketch, "The Second Tree from the Corner" (May 31, 1947), prompted by his unsuccessful treatment for a nervous breakdown. Its narrator is the protagonist of "The Door," ten years older and now truly neurotic. Even his name suggests that he is a child of the new hard and plastic era—"Trexler"—built, as it seems, from the new "scientific" jargon. The canyoned city has reduced poor Trexler to total indecisiveness, as opposed to the apparently untroubled psychiatrist who is treating him, who wants only more leisure and wing on his house in Westport. The materialistic doctor's disinvestment in the city proves to be a kind of sickness that prompts Trexler to reinvest in the city, to see urban life with fresh eyes. His restored enthusiasm, even his sensitivity for the older city details, sounds like White himself of earlier New York excursions: "It was an evening of clearing weather, the Park showing green and desirable, the last daylight applying a high lacquer to the brick and brownstone walls and giving the street scene a luminous and intoxicating splendor." Trexler finds a genuine fraternity among "the unregenerate ranks" in dimlit saloons on Third Avenue, far from the professional comforters on the fashionable upper East Side. There, he finds what alone can revive the spirit, another living species: "'I want the second tree from the corner, just as it stands,' he said, answering an imaginary question from an imaginary physician. And he felt a slow pride in realizing that what he wanted none could bestow, and that what he had none could take away."[17]

During the cold war period of the late 40s and early 50s, White became increasingly worried about the fate of mankind itself, threatened with nuclear annihilation. He was living on the East Side, near United Nations headquarters, which helped to focus his attention on larger, more urgent questions of war and peace. His contributions to "Notes and Comments" during this time tended to be soberer, often extended mediations on national political crises such as nuclear testing. One of the likely first sites targeted for destruction was White's beloved New York, just when the city was, architecturally, leaping recklessly into the ultramodern future—an irony that shadows many of his contributions at the time to the *New Yorker* and other magazines. White described the city's terrifying fate at the end of *Here is New York*. But first he conjured up memories of beloved monuments—other "trees" that rooted him to the city of his youth. He recalls nostalgically the old elevated railways, Greenwich Village of the 20s and the open, airy places undarkened by skyscrapers. He regrets changes that have cheapened the city. Grand Central, where he once fantasized a wild toboggan ride, has become "honky-tonk": "the great hall seemed to me one of the more inspiring interiors in New York, until Lastex and Coca-Cola got into the temple" (p. 45). Many of the great mansions are gone and that second (or third) tree from a corner that might mark one's kinship with the living is going too: "rich men nowadays don't live in houses; they live in the attics of big apartment buildings and plant trees on the setback, hundreds of feet above the street" (p. 46). Such a city may excite new "settlers" but the "passion" it requires is lost to White. He sees instead a city that is "destructible," and at the end envisions the citizen sparrow of earlier parables transformed into a murderous flock. "A single flight of planes no bigger than a wedge of geese can quickly end this island fantasy. . . . The intimation of mortality is part of New York now" (p. 51). He links the survival of the city, if the UN succeeds in its mission, to the survival of another solitary tree, one standing in Turtle Bay Gardens, where he was living at the time, on East 48th Street: "It is a battered tree, long suffering and much climbed, held together by strands of wire but beloved of those who know it. In a way it symbolizes the city: life under difficulties, and the steady reaching for the sun. Whenever I look at it nowadays, and feel the cold shadow of the planes, I think: 'This must be saved, this mischievous and marvelous monument which not to look upon would be like death' " (p. 53).

By the mid 1950's, White's boom-threatened "monument" had lost nearly every trace of the "marvelous," becoming instead a temple devoted only to getting and spending. In his contributions to "Notes and Comments" at this time, White became unusually acerbic at moments, for example, on the subject of "the function lunch in New York, how drastic and purposeful, everyone there for some reason of business or intrigue: salesmen, applicants, supplicants, agents provocateurs, contact executives, actresses gaming with managers, writers taking the temperature of editors, lovers sparring for the strange vantage, everywhere a sprig of personal increase garnishing the cold salmon."[18] Here was the sort of living "deliberately" that was the very opposite of the kind advocated by Thoreau and once practiced by White in the city. Now, everyone is seeking advantages, not savoring vantages. The new city fosters the first by preventing the second, as White explained in "The Rock Dove" (April 20, 1957), where he took once again the bird's eye view, wondering anew why birds live in cities: "Because a city offers cliffs and ledges. . . . What a pigeon needs is just what a city provides in abundance: a nook, a ledge, a recess, a niche, a capital." But modern glass towers offer no vantages and White felt, like the birds, dispossessed: "Because of the trend toward plainer facades, the city of the future may hold no charm for pigeons. Lever House offers little inducement to a nesting pair. The city of the future may be inhospitable to men and doves alike."[19] In a letter written six years later, White was more direct in criticizing the city in which the plainer facades had multiplied alarmingly: "New York is becoming lost among the enormous glass boxes that are its new buildings. With one or two exceptions there is nothing intrinsically good looking about them, and in clusters they are overpowering and debilitating. I suppose they look quite splashy if you are on the deck of an incoming liner, but I'm not. There's something about these immaculate stone and glass surfaces that destroys all the street-level detail that used to be so much fun."[20] The vanishing nest thus became a fitting emblem of White's lost city. What remained for him were vivid memories of rich and varied details, some of which were lovingly evoked in the pages of *The Second Tree from the Corner* (1954), one of his essay collections that, he said in the "Foreward," was in stretches "a sentimental journey to the scenes of my crime" (xi). "Hotel of the Total Stranger," first published in *Harper's* in 1947 but reprinted in *Second Tree*, is literally that, in parable form. A Mr. Volente, en route by taxi to the hotel named in the title, passes countless city landmarks that jog his memory:

" 'It was in the doorway . . .

'It was down that side street . . .

'It was in the back room of this cafe that . . .'"

That was the thing about New York, it was always bringing up something out of your past, something ridiculous or lovely or glistening" (p. 200).

The recollections—of success, but also of doubts and embarrassments—are actually White's own, all connected to "the interminable quest for the holy and unnamable grail, looking for it down every street and in every window and in every pair of eyes, following a star always obscured by mists" (p. 203). The "hotel" might stand for the city itself in constant flux and the "stranger" for White the anonymous sojourner—exactly the relation between urban setting and viewer that he had found both liberating and enthralling. The story also illustrates that the real city is, after all, the one we imagine and carry around within us. White himself seems to have reached this partially consoling conclusion as his city of ledges and niches disappeared. He said as much in 1951, conceding: "The only way to dwell in cities these days, whether it be wise or foolish, is in the conviction that the city itself is a monument of one's own making, to which each shall be faithful in his fashion." White's fears for New York were well-grounded, for destruction hasn't waited for a bomb drop. Since the 1970's, Manhattan has been overtaken by a massive gridlock of anonymous glass boxes that threaten to darken all of nature's street-scene creatures. Even the few remaining trees are facing extinction— or, rather, they are being "protected," by being glass-encased in mid-town corporate arboreta. This new city has its connoisseur in Donald Barthelme, in a way White's successor as the *New Yorker*'s reportorial fabulist. He has written a number of "city life" fables about people strung out on the grid coordinates, trapped beneath the futuristic city's flat, hard skin. In Barthelme's dystopia, there are no monuments, no memories and certainly no second trees from the corner. Fortunately, enough ledges and capitals survive to offer protection to the hardier low-flyers. "While they endure," White insisted in "The Rock Dove," "we must note their locations, elevate our gaze about the level of our immediate concerns, imbibe the sweet air and perfect promise: the egg miraculous upon the ledge, the bird compact upon the egg, its generous warmth, its inevitable patience, its natural fortitude and grace" (p. 133). The same might be said of White himself, whose own lyrical flights in words continue to warrant close watching.

Notes

1.   On matters of fact in White's life, I have depended on the recent authorized biography by Scott Elledge, *E. B. White: A Biography* (New York: Norton, 1984). See chapter XIV on Fred, the dachshund.

2.   Quoted in Elledge, p. 277.

3.   White, *Quo Vadimus? Or, The Case for the Bicycle* (New Yorker: Harper and Brothers, 1939), pp. 6–7.

4.   "An Approach to Style" in *The Elements of Style*, Second Edition (New York: Macmillan, 1972), pp. 59–62.

5.   From "A Slight Sound at Evening," in *Essays of E. B. White* (New York: Harper, 1977), p. 230. See also "Mr. Forbush's Friends" for White's passion for ornithology.

6. *Here is New York* (New York: Harper and Brothers, 1949), pp. 17–18. Citations hereafter in the text.

7. Reprinted in The *Second Tree from the Corner* (New York: Harper Perennial Edition, 1965), p. 18.

8. Quoted in Elledge, p. 101.

9. "Not for the Old Lady in Dubuque," in *The Comic Imagination in American Literature*, ed. Louis D. Rubin, Jr. (New Brunswick, N.J.: Rutgers University Press, 1973), p. 239.

10. From "Note and Comments" reprinted in *Every Day is Saturday* (New York: Harper and Brothers, 1934), pp. 5–6.

11. Reprinted in Second Tree, p. 145.

12. *Harper's* (October, 1938), p. 555. Reprinted in Elledge, p. 209.

13. Elledge, p. 209.

14. From "The World of Tomorrow" reprinted in *One Man's Meat* (New York: Harper, 1966), pp. 66, 68.

15. Reprinted in *Second Tree*, pp. 76–81. See William R. Steinhoff, "The Door: 'The Professor,' 'My Friend the Poet (Deceased),' 'The Washable House,' and 'The Man Out in Jersey,'" CE, 23 (December, 1961), 229–232. In "The Retort Transcendental," reprinted in *Second Tree*, White imagined a cavernous house "whose inside is as open and manifest as a bird's nest" (p. 94).

16. Reprinted in *Second Tree*, pp. 95–101.

17. Reprinted in *Second Tree*, p. 206.

18. Reprinted in *The Points of My Compass* (New York: Harper, 1979), pp. 130, 132.

19. *Letters of E. B. White*, ed. Dorothy Lobrane Guth (New York: Harper, 1976), p. 508. See also p. 645.

20. "Life in Bomb Shadow" reprinted in *Second Tree*, p. 217.

E. B. White and the Theory of Humor

Stephen L. Tanner

In his own inimitable way, E. B. White pointedly discounted the value of analyzing humor for the sake of theory. "Humor can be dissected, as a frog can," he said, "but the thing dies in the process and the innards are discouraging to any but the pure scientific mind." Humor, he insisted, "won't stand much blowing up, and it won't stand much poking. It has a certain fragility, an evasiveness, which one had best respect. Essentially it is a complete mystery" (White 1941: xvii, xviii). Elsewhere, he added, "To interpret humor is as futile as explaining a spider's web in terms of geometry" (White 1977: 252). Yet these very disclaimers appear in essays in which he himself has a go at making theoretical pronouncements on humor.

This sort of paradox is not surprising, however, to those familiar with the complex personality of E. B. White, one of the shyest of men, who nevertheless made a reputation writing about himself; a man who was both a spokesman for quiet rural living and the principal creator of the *New Yorker*'s urbane voice; a man much acclaimed as a humorist, who detested the word "humorist." I wish to examine White's remarks on humor, made in essays, interviews, and letters, partly to determine what insight they provide concerning that formidable subject of the nature of humor, but more particularly to determine what they reveal about his own characteristic achievement as a writer employing humor.

White's most extensive treatments of the theory of humor appear in the preface to *A Subtreasury of American Humor*, which he edited with his wife in 1941, and in the introduction to Don Marquis's *the lives and times of archy and mehitabel* in 1950. Both pieces, altered slightly, are included in *Essays of E. B. White* (1977). It is characteristic of White's unassuming manner that he would presume to make pronouncements on the nature of humor only in such introductions and with the disclaimers quoted above. He was a man with a gift for humor and a deep respect for its salutary effects, but, at the same time, he was temperamentally suspicious of grand explanations and pat formulae. He was reluctant to pose as a thinker and particularly modest about being considered an expert on humor. To a solicitation for his views on the subject, he once replied, "I don't know anything about American humor that is fit to

Reprinted from *Humor*, 1989: 43–53. Reprinted by permission of the author.

print . . ." (White 1976: 329). To his friend James Thurber's suggestion that he had the wrong idea about humor in our time, he replied, "I haven't got any idea about humor except that I seldom think of anything funny to write . . ." (White 1976: 337). An interviewer once enticed him to respond to the question, what is humor? He began by saying that humor cannot easily be separated from a writer's whole attitude and approach. He suggested that perhaps humor is "a sense of proportion, a bringing of the specific thing into relation to the general." Then he paused and smiled: "I don't know what it is" (Nordell 1962: 9).

But although he claimed that humor was essentially a complete mystery, it so fascinated him that he could not resist trying to explain it. He said some rather profound things about it, and he said them artfully. Naturally his theory is far from definitive. Humor, like poetry, is much too complex to be encompassed by a single theoretical approach. Just as Poe's poetic theory tells us more about Poe than about poetry, White's humor theory probably tells us more about White than about wit. Nonetheless, both authors present some concepts of universal application. Unlike a Freud or a Bergson, White does not break new ground with systematic theoretical arguments. His observations on the relationship between humor and truth or humor and sadness, for example, are not original in the sense that he was the first to make them. Their originality and value derive from the way they are expressed. They embody humor as well as explaining it. The result is theoretical statements with an added dimension: the manner of expressing insights subtly but significantly colors the matter of the insights. Furthermore, White's theoretical observations acquire resonance from the humor in his own body of writing. No such resonance is present in the arguments of theorists like Freud or Bergson, yet it ought not to be ignored in our attempts to understand something as evasive and impalpable as humor.

At bottom, White's efforts to explain the nature of humor were really not attempts to advance humor theory but rather efforts to justify his own devotion to humor. They are the product of an inner tension between an aspiration to create significant literature and the conviction that humorists are inherently second-rate.

White admits in the first sentence of his preface that *A Subtreasury of American Humor* reveals its collectors' tastes. This is an anthology of "literary" humor that leaves "vast fields of American humor" untouched. Some of that humor simply could not be adequately conveyed in print, but a more important reason for its omission is that White preferred humor that is not simply an end in itself. Literary humor often stimulates reverberations: insights as well as laughter. Consequently, newspaper humor was left out, for with time "the news goes out of it (though some humor may remain), and when the news goes out of it the heart goes out of it" (White 1941: xiii). Likewise, dialect humor is unsatisfactory. Comic spellings add nothing that interests him. Dialect is justified, he says, only where it is used as a necessary tool, not as a humorous effect in itself. Tall stories were included sparingly, he says, because they can be boring—tall without being funny. Moreover, he had no taste for the "genial school" of humor: "Geniality is not, per se, humorous, in spite of the illusion of humor it often gives, and too often geniality turns out to be longwindedness in sheep's clothing" (White 1941: xvi). Thus, both what was included and what was excluded reveal White's theoretical assumptions about humor.

Those assumptions are more explicitly expressed in the preface itself. Chief among them is the notion that humor is inextricably bound up with sadness. Humorists are commonly viewed as sad people, clowns with breaking hearts. The essential truth in this, says White, is badly stated: "It would be more accurate, I think, to say that there is a deep vein of melancholy running through everyone's life and that a humorist, perhaps more sensible of it than some others, compensates for it actively and positively" (White 1941: xviii). When adapting this preface for collection elsewhere, he added, "Humorists fatten on trouble . . . They pour out their sorrow profitably, in a form that is not quite fiction nor quite fact either. Beneath the sparkling surface of these dilemmas flows the strong tide of human woe" (White 1977: 243–44). He once referred to Don Marquis, whose humor he greatly admired, as "one of the saddest people of our generation" (White 1976: 171).

The deep vein of melancholy running through White's own life is often ignored. The obituary in *The New Yorker*, for example, mentions his "inexplicitly sunny inclinations." Reacting to this statement, Joseph Epstein in an essay dwelling upon White's darker side—his despondency, hypochondria, depression—counters that "the one thing that can be unequivocally said about him is that one has to search very sedulously indeed to find a gloomier writer than E. B. White. The gloom is not merely incidental but pervasive in his writing" (1986: 49). Epstein may be overstating his case, but *Letters of E. B. White* and Scott Elledge's biography bear out its essential accuracy. White's linking of laughter and melancholy in his theorizing about humor bears the stamp of insight derived from personal experience.

White recognized that often a thin frontier separates laughing and crying. ". . . and if a humorous piece of writing brings a person to the point where his emotional responses are untrustworthy and seem likely to break over into the opposite realm, it is because humorous writing, like poetical writing, has an extra content. It plays, like an active child, close to the big hot fire which is Truth. And sometimes the reader feels the heat" (White 1941: xviii). It is this notion that humor finds companionship with truth that is most fundamental in White's theory of humor. The best kind of humorist deserves attention because, like Shakespeare's fool, he has "the truth hidden somewhere about his person." "Think of the trouble the world would save itself," says White, "if it would pay some attention to nonsense!" (White 1941: xix). The main idea of the introduction to Don Marquis's book is that Archy and Mehitabel "performed the inestimable service of enabling their boss to be profound without sounding self-important or even self-conscious" (White 1977: 253). Thus Marquis could be funny and wise at the same time. White says of his favorite Marquis piece, it "has the jewel-like perfection of poetry and contains cosmic reverberations along with high comedy. Beautiful to read, beautiful to think about" (White 1977: 254). White himself aimed at and, according to many of his readers, achieved this same blending of comedy and cosmic reverberations. The best of his essays are certainly beautiful both to read and to think about.

From the beginning of his career, White was disposed to blending the comic and serious. While at Cornell he wrote for the college magazine an article about the Manuscript Club he belonged to, stating the club's creed as formulated by a professor Sampson, the advisor, "To be frank, to use one's brains, to write what is in one to write, and never to take oneself too damned seriously or too damned lightly" (Elledge 1984: 22). This guiding statement, particularly its notion of balancing the light and serious, left its imprint throughout his writing. Years later he in turn counseled an aspiring student writer inclined to take herself too seriously, "I should not try to learn to write without learning first to be frivolous" (White 1976: 346). Just out of college and beginning his work in journalism, he confided to a girl friend his distaste for the "knock-down, pie-throwing humor" of other columnists. He wanted to write "whimsy—of a sort that will appeal to persons who can understand words of more than one syllable—a delicate undertaking" (Elledge 1984: 8). Warren Beck (1946) points out that the basic seriousness of White's whimsy was remarkable viewed in light of the tendencies of his time: "He came to his work when the pantaloon humorists of the twenties were at their height, peddling the anodyne of nonsense as raw as the era's gin." But he never joined "that sad assembly line," says Beck, despite its rewards. "No man had written more wittily of our time than he, but he has had no truck with inanity" (1946: 178). His time in the arena of journalism, he said at age 64, had been spent "tilting at the dragons and clowning with the clowns" (White 1976: 510), the tilting and clowning in his case being essentially a single endeavor. The dust jacket of *The Wild Flag*, his book of editorials on world government, contains the statement (written by White himself, suggests Epstein) that the author "regards himself as a clown of average ability whose signals got crossed and who found himself out on the wire with the Wallendas" (Epstein 1986: 54).

White was indeed willing to risk himself on the high wire. "In courageous and consistent assertion," says Warren Beck, "he has surpassed both the cynical humorists who aped the mode of a Neronian frivolity and a whole decade of angry ideologists marching in cadence with a prescribed social consciousness" (1946: 179). White's principal strength was his gift for mediating between preachy earnestness and inane or cynical laughter. His humor is frequently compounded with deadly seriousness. His controlled nonsense often expresses both his sense of the complexity of American culture and his most pessimistic feelings about it. As Clifton Fadiman noted, "His whimsical remarks are not sweet. though they are sweetly put; each one grasps a truth, holds it fast, exhibits it for all to see" (1945: 59). James Thurber fully recognized this strength in White and wrote to him in 1938 that his kind of humor was needed in those bad times and he should provide it as "a point of moral necessity" (White 1976: 207). White's humor is honored in a tense world because it offers more than an easy laugh. As soon as we pin him down as a humorist, he wriggles away and turns up as a philosopher.

Thoreau was an important model for his blending of wit and wisdom, his role as philosopher. *Walden* was obviously the single most important book in his life, and, as Scott Elledge points out, "White recognized himself in Thoreau in a variety of ways" (1984: 314). His statement in the foreword of *One Man's Meat* that "The first person singular is the only grammatical implement I am able to use without cutting myself" echoes this one from the first page of *Walden*: "I should not talk so much about myself if there were anybody else whom I know as well." The two are among the most distinctive and accomplished first-person voices in American literature. It is not surprising that he mentions Thoreau in his analysis of humor in the preface to *A Subtreasury*, even though Thoreau is not (because of the difficulty of extracting short samples) included in the collection. "There is hardly a paragraph of *Walden* which does not seem humorous to me. . . . Thoreau makes me laugh the inaudible, the enduring laugh" (White 1941: xvi). Elsewhere he called Thoreau "the subtlest humorist of the nineteenth century" (Elledge 1984: 314): he is ". . . the most humorous of the New England figures, and *Walden* the most humorous of the books, though its humor is almost continuously subsurface and there is nothing deliberately funny anywhere, except a few jokes and bad puns that rise to the surface like the perch in the pond that rose to the sound of the maestro's flute" (White 1977: 239). These comments clearly suggest what White considered to be the nature and function of humor as the term had meaning for him: humor should be an integral ingredient of delight and perspective in writing whose ulterior aim is truth.

This high estimation of humor prompted within him impatience and some bitterness regarding the condescension usually displayed toward humor and humorists. "The world likes humor, but it treats it patronizingly. It decorates its serious artists with laurel, and its wags with Brussels sprouts" (White 1941: xvii). Rather sardonically he remarks that Americans "cherish the ideal of the 'sense' of humor and at the same time are highly suspicious of anything which is nonserious. Whatever else an American believes or disbelieves about himself, he is absolutely sure he has a sense of humor" (1941: xx). Beneath the surface of White's two essays on the theory of humor is a pervasive if muted bitterness, the bitterness of a skillful and "serious" humorist who feels patronized by an American audience that pays lip service to humor but fails to appreciate it when it has artistic and even moral and philosophical significance. The issue is posed by Archy, Don Marquis's typing cockroach, in reference to that remarkable insect's own poems: "The question is whether the stuff is literature or not." After quoting this statement, White adds, "That question dogged his boss, it dogs us all" (White 1977: 252).

The real question that dogged White is whether humorous writing can be significant art. Humor may play close to "the big fire which is Truth," but is there not still something inferior about it? He replied to a correspondent in 1961, "You are right that no humorist has ever won the Pulitzer prize—there is something not quite first-rate about funny men" (White 1976: 488). To a writer gathering information about humor in 1968, he replied, "But if you're hoping to disabuse people of the notion that there is something vaguely second-rate about humorous expression in literature, I wish you luck. I don't think you have a prayer" (White 1976: 574). Epstein is probably right in attributing some of White's melancholy to a partially frustrated desire "to create something with the 'excellence and delicacy' of true art" (1986: 54). Epstein explains that White, in the late 1930's, "yearned to make something of his life; he yearned to be more than a mere journalist; he yearned—though he never used the word—for significance" (1986: 52). And, as a matter of fact, dissatisfied with the use he was making of his talents, White took a year off from *The New Yorker*, and to some extent from his family, during 1937–1938 to devote himself to "secret" literary projects prompted by his "poetic longings" (White 1976: 154–56). Although he apparently failed to complete his projects, the year was a turning point in his career, for in 1938 he gave up his house in New York and went to live on a farm in Maine, and he switched his primary commitment from *The New Yorker* to *Harper's*, for whom he wrote the reflective pieces later collected in *One Man's Meat*. These events were a stage in what Clifton Fadiman describes as a development "from a paragrapher to a writer, from a light-fingered original humorist to a light-giving original thinker" (1945: 55). White first attracted attention as rather exclusively a humorist, but although he never abandoned his humorous touch, humor was not ultimately his principal strength or concern. It became for him a means rather than an end in itself.

The context described in the preceding paragraph is necessary for a complete appreciation of the theoretical statements of the preface to *A Subtreasury*. Those statements published in 1941 reflect White's personal struggle during the late 1930's to determine the relation of humor to significant literature and map, accordingly, his own career. Consider, for example, his treatment of what he describes as a fundamental conflict between a writer's serious emotion and his sense of humor, a conflict that can determine whether he is viewed as an artist or a mere humorist:

> There constantly exists, for a certain sort of person of high emotional content, at work creatively, the danger of coming to a point where something cracks within himself or within the paragraph under construction—cracks and turns into a snicker. Here, then, is the very nub of the conflict: the careful form of art, and the careless shape of life itself. What a man does with this uninvited

snicker (which may closely resemble a sob, at that) decides his destiny. If he resists it, conceals it, destroys it, he may keep his architectural scheme intact and save his building, and the world will never know. If he gives into it, he becomes a humorist, and the sharp brim of the fool's cap leaves a mark forever on his brow (White 1941: xix).

White felt the pinch and stigma of the fool's cap yet could not suppress the uninvited snicker alloyed with the sob, and his personal conflict in this regard determines the substance and tone of his two essays on the theory of humor. He notes that the day comes for every humorist when someone he loves and respects takes him aside to ask if he is ever going to write something serious. "That day is memorable, for it gives a man pause to realize that the bright star he is following is held to be not of the first magnitude" (1941: xix). This sort of unsettling experience preyed upon his mind for many years and accounts for part of the despondency in his personal life.

In the first paragraph of the essay on Don Marquis, White claims to know at what cost Marquis produced his humorous tales. The claim is justified, for when he mentions that Marquis did not create easily, that he was left gloomy and unsatisfied with what he did create, that he felt the creative juices squeezed out of him by the demands of journalism, and that "he was never quite certified by intellectuals and serious critics of belles lettres," White is listing frustrations that matched his own.

White preferred not to be called a humorist. He wrote to William K. Zinsser in 1968, "I don't like the word 'humorist,' never have. It seems to me misleading. Humor is a by-product that occurs in the serious work of some and not others" (White 1976: 574). When asked about humor in a *Paris Review* interview, he said, "I find difficulty with the word 'humor' and with the word 'humorist' to peg a writer. . . . Writing funny pieces is a legitimate form of activity, but the durable humor in literature, I suspect, is not the contrived humor of a funnyman commenting on the news but the sly and almost imperceptible ingredient that sometimes gets into writing" (Plimpton and Crowther 1969: 80–81). This notion of humor being incidental or complementary to literary significance is the focus of the final and important section of the preface to *A Subtreasury*, which is devoted to Twain. White emphasizes that Twain, one of the few American humorists to become really famous, "was essentially a story teller and his humor was an added attraction" (1941: xxi). He quotes extensively Twain's comments on writers who were merely humorists:

Humorists of the "mere" sort cannot survive. Humor is only a fragrance, a decoration . . . Humor must not professedly teach, and it must not professedly preach, but it must do both if it would live forever. By forever, I mean thirty years . . . I have always preached. That is the reason that I have lasted thirty years. If the humor came of its own accord and uninvited, I have allowed it a place in my sermon, but I was not writing the sermon for the sake of humor. I should have written the sermon just the same, whether any humor applied for admission or not. (1941: xxii)

White concludes the preface by saying, "Well, I didn't intend to get off onto the broad subject of humor, or even to let Mark Twain get off onto it." This, of course, is pure rhetorical self-effacement. He in fact welcomed the excuse provided by the unassuming genre of the preface to air his views on the broad subject of humor, a subject of profound personal concern to him. His final point about the nature of humor is a qualification of Twain's statement: "I don't think I agree that humor must preach in order to live; it need only speak the truth—and I notice it always does" (1941: xxii).

White's practice surpasses his theory, which is to say his practice includes distinctive elements not encompassed by his theory. Perhaps those elements are partly comprised of the "sly and almost imperceptible ingredients" he mentioned in the *Paris Review* interview. They might include his use of slightly incongruous adjectives and adverbs or the arresting figure of speech that is unexpected, perhaps even zany, and at the same time delightfully accurate. They might include his delight in pouncing on the ambiguities resulting from "the broncolike ability of the English language to throw whoever leaps cocksurely into the saddle" (White 1979: 54). These are aspects of style and particularly of diction. A good deal of White's humor is generated by these aspects, but his theoretical statements about humor ignore them. And on the other hand, interestingly enough, his "Approach to Style" section in *Elements of Style* does not recommend humor as an approach to style. Such omissions suggest that much of his ability to generate humor was intuitive, which is probably always the case with the varied achievements of the best artists. He once expressed his own belief "that no writing, by anybody, begins to get good until he gets shed of tricks, devices, and formulae" (White 1976: 514).

Also omitted from his analysis of humor is his own most enduring and characteristic approach: the comic story told on himself. He employed this method in his first column with the *Seattle Times*, and his first piece for the *New Yorker* was a self-mocking story. "The proof of humor," James Thurber once said, "is the ability to put one's self on awkward public record" (Elledge 1984). White (speaking through one of his characters) acknowledges that he made, early in his career, the "enormously important discovery that the world would pay a man for setting down a simple, legible account of his own misfortunes" (Elledge 1984: 7). Yet this method of "profitable confession" found no place in his theory, and neither did his related method of implicating himself in his satire, of conveying a sense of complicity that narrows the line separating the satirist from his target, the humorist from his subject, the teller from the told. Perhaps these approaches are hinted at in the preface to *A*

Subtreasury when he states that humorists' sympathy for their characters is indispensable: "It is sympathy, not contempt or derision, that makes their characters live" (1941: xv).

But even though White's theoretical statements fail to encompass even his own most characteristic methods, they are nevertheless a valuable contribution to our understanding of American humor. And they make clear what he once described as his love affair with Humor, a mistress for whom his affection remained undiminished despite "seeing her blow hot and cold, running her unreasonable errands, taking her lip." He found the perfect description of this mistress in a quotation from Proudhon: "Humor [the Frenchman's word was actually *l'ironie*]—true liberty!—it is you who deliver me from ambition for power, from servitude to party, from respect for routine, from the pedantry of science, from admiration for celebrities, from the mystifications of politics, from the fanaticism of the reformers, from fear of this great universe, and from self-admiration." He reprinted this quote in *The New Yorker* "with pride and embarrassment—the sort of mixed feeling you have when walking with a pretty girl and the girl is whistled at" (Elledge 1984: 27). The quote from Proudhon encapsulates the emphasis of his own theoretical principles, and the playful figurative frame he provides for it epitomizes the deftness of his own practice.

References

Beck, Warren. 1946. E. B. White. *College English* 7, 367–373.
Elledge, Scott. 1984. *E. B. White.* New York: Norton
Epstein, Joseph. 1986. E. B. White, Dark & Lite. *Commentary*, April, 48–56.
Fadiman, Clifton. 1945. In Praise of E. B. White, Realist. *New York Times Book Review*, 10 June, 1, 10, 12, 14–16.
Nordell, Roderick. 1962. The Writer as Private Man. *Christian Science Monitor*, 31 October, 9.
Plimpton, George A., and Frank H. Crowther. 1969. The Art of the Essay I: E. B. White. *Paris Review* 48, 65–88.
White, E. B. 1941. Preface. In White, E. B., and Katharine S. White (eds.). *A Subtreasury of American Humor*. New York: Coward-McCann.
   1950. *One Man's Meat.* New York: Harper & Row.
   1976. *Letters of E. B. White*, Guth, Dorothy Lobrano (ed.). New York: Harper & Row.
   1977. *Essays of E. B. White.* New York: Harper & Row.
   1979. *Points of My Compass.* New York: Harper & Row.

Contesting Discourses
in the Essays of E. B. White

KEN SMITH

As our conceptions of literary style evolve, what do we come to think of E. B. White, who has been called the "prime instigator of the contemporary essay, and a master of modern American prose style"?[1] His style has traditionally been seen as "an expression of himself," and honesty, clarity, and spontaneity have been counted as the basis of its "perfection."[2] But some recent critics look away from familiar expressivist conceptions of style. Mikhail Bakhtin, most often cited as a theorist of the novel, has argued that the essay and other genres are, like the novel, profoundly marked by the presence of contesting discourses. He did not value prose for the achievement of a unified aesthetic effect, but rather for its capacity to represent the social dialogues and contested languages and meanings of modern life. He believed that "diversity of speech, and not the unity of a normative shared language, . . . is the ground of style."[3] This more extravagant, more deeply social and historical conception of prose invites readers to be alert to the divergent speech of different social groups, and to see analogies between contesting speech in an essay and conflict in contemporary society.[4] Other recent critics support Bakhtin's notions of conflicting voices in prose in a more general sense. Geoffrey H. Hartman describes a pull toward "accommodation" in the essay, a tendency to compose within the bounds of the conventional. At the same time, Hartman praises the genre's contrary urge to "make strange," to defamiliarize experience and to expose it to fresh thought.[5] Theodor W. Adorno believed that an ability to commit or compose "heresy" is the essential quality of the essay. For Adorno, the true essay challenges some more or less doctrinal aspect of the social order, some common sense.[6] These theorists see the essay as a form that brings contesting social voices into a written dialogue shaped to reveal the writer's critical perspective. Long recognized as a master stylist of the old type, E. B. White was greatly influenced by the dynamic trait of prose that these theorists have described.

While not a literary theorist himself, White to some degree acknowledges the contesting discourses of essayistic prose in his comments on the genre. In

This essay was written specifically for this volume and is published here by permission of the author.

the Foreword to the *Essays of E. B. White* he remarks on the wide range of
social voices from which he chose the persona of his essays. "The essayist arises
in the morning and, if he has work to do, selects his garb from an unusually
extensive wardrobe: he can pull on any sort of shirt, be any sort of person,
according to his mood or his subject matter—philosopher, scold, jester, racon-
teur, confidant, pundit, devil's advocate, enthusiast."[7] In *The Elements of Style*
White describes the many social voices available to the writer, "the beat of
new vocabularies, the exciting rhythms of special segments of his society, each
speaking a language of its own." But he advises young writers to write
conservatively, noting that "the general rule here is to prefer the standard,"[8]
by which he means the most well-established or authoritative stylistic norms
of the English language. He recognizes the contesting voices that Bakhtin
called heteroglossia, but he does not accept them as a virtue in the prose of
student writers.

But White's own practice was far more intricately textured than his
cautious and teacherly advice for students suggests. Among his short "Notes
and Comment" or editorial essays for the *New Yorker*, "The Age of Dust" is
a wonderful example of the prose of contesting discourses. The essay was
written in 1950, long after works such as John Hersey's *Hiroshima* had
documented the terrible power of nuclear radiation, and far enough into the
cold war for White to see what was later to be called the military-industrial
complex steeling itself for a fight with the Soviet Union. The immediate
impulse for the essay, however, was a 1950 article in the *Bulletin of the Atomic
Scientists* that rather casually or thoughtlessly speculated about the use of
radioactive substances as a weapon of war.[9] In his rebuttal White argues that
the article's "detached" language is, like the weapon it represents, a threat to
innocent citizens. In each paragraph White sets the discourse of its scientist-
author against several other discourses of his day, and against a somewhat
lyrical, sentimental image of a little girl on a swing. The essay offers a contest
between these discourses and images for the right to name or represent the
little girl and the weapon that threatens her and thousands like her. The
conflicting voices are essential to this essay, for each highlights the other's
characteristics, informing readers of White's judgments concerning the shared
beliefs or common sense of each social group involved in the dispute over
radiological weapons. By allying himself with one social voice, the language,
experience, and common sense of his likely audience, White gives his readers
a position, a site of value and knowledge, from which to resist. As a result, he
represents his audience as individuals empowered to make a judgment on this
public issue.

This essay's contesting discourses are expressed in the words of a persona
suited to its magazine audience. White begins, for example, with a cleanly-
written, descriptive sentence in what must have seemed in 1950 a familiar
style to the *New Yorker*'s comfortable readers, an informal or middle range of
diction and image: "On a sunny morning last week, I went out and put up

a swing for a little girl, age three, under an apple tree—the tree being much older than the girl, the sky being blue, the clouds white."[10] I would call this style a sort of prose suburban pastoral, a prose steadily familiar and yet graced with small lyrical touches, such as the decorative images and the gracefully varied parallelism of the sentence's concluding catalog. The first sentence establishes this prose, with its implied middle-American readership and accompanying body of shared beliefs, as the ground for the argument that follows, and we hear the other social voices in the essay more sharply because they differ from this one.

Having sketched this scene from "everyday life," a scene that is "normal" for those who live like White and who speak as he speaks, White walks back to the house and encounters the July 1950, *Bulletin of the Atomic Scientists*: "I pushed the little girl for a few minutes, then returned to the house and settled down to an article on death dust, or radiological warfare, in the July *Bulletin of the Atomic Scientists*, Volume VI, No. 7." This sentence disturbs the essay's grounding style in two ways. Most obviously, the sentence offers a bibliographic reference to the article, indicating that we have changed realms of discourse. Here, in the realm of scientific journals, new rules of evidence, new decorums of conversation, apply, and a socially weightier voice begins to speak. The second disruption takes place around the names for the weapon itself. "Radiological warfare" is the first phrase in the essay actually borrowed from the scientist-author. But White offers a resistant or combative synonym for this technological phrase, "death dust," even before he has used the scientist's term. This might seem "merely" a stylistic quirk of White's, who always makes abstract terms concrete as soon as possible in his writing. But by taking a phrase out of the threatening language of another and "translating it" into a phrase grounded in a more familiar physical reality, White argues against the name the scientist offers. He reclaims the right to name or describe his own experience and world, which is a move for intellectual and emotional sovereignty founded on the words and experiences he thinks of as normal or common, and in a language of his own choosing.

Yet he struggles against powerful social voices, and as he lets them speak more directly in the second paragraph of his essay, they threaten to overwhelm his voice. White takes back a bit of the scientist's authority by criticizing his tone, but the dispassionate talk of poisoning two or three "major cities" still outweighs the little girl's lyrical swing ride, and seems even to steal the "ABC" out of her mouth in order to ally it with radiological warfare. "The world of the child in the swing (the trip to the blue sky and back again) seemed, as I studied the ABC of death dust, more and more a dream world with no true relation to things as they are or to the real world of discouragement over the slow rate of disappearance of cities." The scientist makes White doubt his own conception of reality, as in the third paragraph the very words and values of his everyday life are swept into the nuclear weapons age. White speaks as a "literary man" for a couple of sentences, reading and offering criticism, much as a book reviewer would do. But no protest halts the progress of "man's adjustment" to the violence of the "atom age," as everyday words are lent to the nuclear weapons industry: benign "mothproofing" has mutated into quotidian (and delusional) "bombproofing," in the form of civil defense drills. It takes a powerful detachment for the scientist-author to choose phrases, such as "radiological warfare," that abstract or distance reality, or to bury horrible possibilities with neologisms like "bombproofing," that are made to seem ordinary by analogy. This dangerous detachment suggests to White the broad strategy of his entire essay: to *refuse* detachment, to *attach* the words of the scientist-author to the image of the little girl, to *connect* himself repeatedly with the author by quoting him and speaking back, in other words, to write in a dialogic fashion. He clarifies the character of the scientist's language by the elementary tool of contrast.

The remainder of the essay takes the author very seriously, repeatedly quoting him and connecting his words with images of the girl and the prose of the suburban pastoral. Yet in the last two paragraphs that prose is muted and heavy, as the scientist transforms the meaning of even as basic a word as "humane."

> "This is a novel type of warfare, in that it produces no destruction, except to life." The weapon, said the author, can be regarded as a horrid one, or, on the other hand, it "can be regarded as a remarkably humane one. In a sense, it gives each member of the target population [including each little girl] a choice of whether he will live or die." It turns out that the way to live—if that be your choice—is to leave the city as soon as the dust arrives, holding "a folded, dampened handkerchief" over your nose and mouth. (author's brackets)

By claiming that such warfare produces "no destruction, except to life," that sentence absurdly or unconsciously seeks to transform the common meanings of those words in the human community. The common sense of White's age suggests that if there is "no destruction," there can be no destruction to life, for the fundamental value to be preserved is human life, community, and the fabric of history and tradition. White tries to restore this common sense when the scientist wrenches it from its base. The scientist tears the fabric of White's lived experience because he abandons, in five words, the centrality of human life as a value, without an argument or suggestion for its replacement. He simply asserts, in a buried way, as in an enthymeme, that the weapon is a "remarkably humane one," giving its victims (an illusion of) choice. But only in the cloaked rhetoric of the article, and in the policies of the institutions that would follow its advice, is that really a choice.

"The Age of Dust" accurately reflects the great imbalance of power between its different social voices. White manages to speak for himself and for the girl, who is silent, but most of the paragraphs are dominated by the ominous words of the other author. In what should have been an age of

American triumph, an age of dust settles upon the country and possibly the world. The civil consensus necessary to refute the voices that support this weapon does not exist, as far as White can tell, or exists as the past of the memoirist exists, only slenderly in the minds and bodily reminiscences of those who work to preserve contesting memories. Who will create or discover what needs to be said, White wonders, and how? White turns to the resources of private life for his public voice as a political essayist, even in the face of the great technological changes of his age. Yet his single voice seems so overmatched by voices of change that it is all the more remarkable and moving. He coolly crafts his sentences and trusts them to speak against the values of an emerging technological world that was perfectly happy to speak for him. But in an essay of contesting voices White can temporarily change the society's balance of power, setting one voice much more equally against another. By capitalizing on this trait of the genre White makes the personal political when he wishes it to be.

MORE COMPLEX CASES

"The Age of Dust" shows that Bakhtin's conception of style accounts more fully for aspects of White's literary practice than do his own cautionary remarks for student writers. According to Bakhtin, a writer's "creating consciousness stands, as it were, on the boundary line between languages and styles."[11] Among the longer essays that are most commonly anthologized and addressed by critics—White's canonical works—a complicated yet economically expressed jangle of social voices often mark the center. In the autobiographical essay "The Years of Wonder," for example, White recalls how, in his youth, he learned to negotiate between dozens of social voices that influenced his growth. White portrays his younger self awkwardly forming his consciousness and style as a writer from among these voices, trying them out, even though much of the essay's humor comes from the gangly results of these early efforts. He had yet to find a suitable middle ground among these social influences. "No splendor appeared in the sky without my celebrating it, nothing mean or unjust took place but felt the harmless edge of my wildly swinging sword. I walked in the paths of righteousness, studying girls" (170). Living at the borders of these conflicting social voices, the young man was just learning to make a life. As in this passage, perhaps this essay's greatest accomplishment is its warm and accepting portrait of the as-yet-styleless young man, including the embarrassments of his youthful diary, within the graceful cadences and sharp images of the mature writer's style.

Longer and more complex than "The Age of Dust," "The World of Tomorrow" is composed of successive waves of social voices and related images that are organized around another conflict between a broad new social power and an "everyday" set of values founded in White's past. In this case the antagonists to White's common sense are members of a conglomerate putting on the 1939 World's Fair in New York—a conglomerate allied for the sake of visionary commerce, one might say. While it may seem that the conflict between social voices helps *reveal* White's stance in this essay, on another level that conflict *is* his essential stance in this and other essays. For White the realm of personal experience always stands as the touchstone, the site of the contesting values that sanction his public voice.

"The World of Tomorrow" begins with a gracefully balanced and collo-quial passage that nevertheless announces something unusual about White's visit to the Fair. "I wasn't really prepared for the World's Fair last week, and it certainly wasn't prepared for me. Between the two of us there was consider-able of a mixup" (111). The first clause measures White against the Fair's standards, and the second measures the Fair against White's standards. In its balance the opening sentence announces the contest between the two parties and implies that either set of standards is as valuable as the other. This is a strike against the Fair's sponsors, who touted it for its utopian vision of the future, more important than any individual. But White gives notice that no special favors are to be granted the Fair, or the future, even if they are grand and electronically amplified. No matter how big, both the Fair and the future must master common decencies in order to suit him. The Fair, he notices in the second paragraph, has bungled a detail of its wardrobe: "It couldn't find its collar button." In personifying it, White stands shoulder to shoulder with the Fair, and when the Fair collectively tries to name the future, he turns that name over in his palm and asks a tough question. Rhetorically, he treats the Fair as just another citizen, entitled to no more of a voice than his own in naming the future.

Though many individuals and companies make up the body of the Fair, they are assembled in spirit as a masculine, commercial or industrial, scientific, and romantic voice, drawing from these several sources to make its picture of the future. White is made uncomfortable by the cocky conglomerate of voices, by their certainty and unity, and so he spends a lot of time looking for other voices to break the eerie monotone of the Fair's prophecy. To help accomplish this, White takes on the role of the "memorist of the past," the suburban pastoralist voice we know from "The Age of Dust." He frequently offers images of the ordinary life he prizes, the middle-American life that his memoirist is chartered to preserve. He notes the "delicate pink blossoms on the fruit trees in the ever-hopeful back yards ... the clothes that fly bravely on the line under the trees with the new little green leaves in Queens' incomparable springtime" (111). He notes at greater length the little boy's world of David Wagstaff, the winner of a free long distance phone call at the American Telephone and Telegraph Exhibit, where he prizes especially the boy's story of a train making "a great—big—BUMP!" (116). He notes when the details of the Fair are all wrong, by the standards of the pastoralist's common sense:

the shadows on the fruit trees are on the upper rather than the lower leaves; little boys cannot climb the trees due to their glass canopies; there is no clear path for bees to find the blossoms; the cow's udder is brightly lit, rather than in shadow; the voice of the cow comes "not from the cow but from a small aperture above your head" (115). These mistakes in the everyday workings of the world undercut the Fair's visionary message. The memoirist even notes that there are no dialogues, only monologues, when the voice of the future speaks through its aperture.

When White as memoirist draws on the values common to a class of people through words and images connected to their common experience, he uses a powerful resource not completely within the grasp of social institutions. Individuals do not need social institutions to understand the paths of bees to flowers, for example, and ideological formations like the Fair's utopia, that contradict that common sense may be undermined by any individual's knowledge. White uses this tool when he sets his sinuses against the World's Fair. "The truth is that my ethmoid sinuses broke down on the eve of Fair Day, and this meant that I had to visit the Fair carrying a box of Kleenex concealed in a copy of the *Herald Tribune*. When you can't breathe through your nose, Tomorrow seems strangely like the day before yesterday" (111). The common cold is a symbol of shared human experience in White's work, as in his 1969 editorial on the occasion of the first moon walk. In that essay he proposed that the first flag planted on the moon ought to have been "a limp white handkerchief, perhaps, symbol of the common cold, which, like the moon, affects us all, unites us all!"[12] But the aggregate corporate voice of the Fair speaks against that shared bodily knowledge, by coining words that have no history. As White demonstrates in the third and fourth paragraphs of "The World of Tomorrow," a great deal of name-giving has already occurred. On the way to the Fair White tours the billboards and signposts of Queens, "a long familiar journey, through Mulsified Shampoo and Mobilgas, through Bliss Street, Kix, Astring-O-Sol, and the Majestic Auto Seat Covers" (111). White's catalog of business and product names continues, surrounding his lyrical evocations of spring in Queens. The catalog of new words and product names, with all their promises and hyperboles written into them, blurs in the middle of the third paragraph into a language of the future, the visionary language of the Fair: "man's dream . . . the brave hope of a glimpsed destination." This visionary language slides into another visionary language, borrowed from the romance of Camelot: "the tournament all men wait for, the field of honor" (111–112). As the third paragraph ends, this voice slides again, not into a new voice, but into the old commercial voice he heard again and again on the road through Queens. "A closer inspection, however, on the other side of the turnstile, revealed that it was merely Heinz jousting with Beech-Nut—the same old contest on a somewhat larger field, with accommodations for more spectators, and rather better facilities all around" (112). The fourth paragraph repeats this journey among the voices that hope to account for the future and the Fair.

White journeys toward the sound of "distant choirs," toward the architectural monuments that "still beckoned me on," over "many months of anticipation and after so much of actual travail and suffering," until at last he arrives "at the very threshold of Tomorrow," only to be stopped by a mechanical failure and to hear "a bald contemporary voice say, 'There will be a short wait of a few minutes, please'" (112). By this point White comes to see the Fair as a play of outrageous voices, and he spends much of the rest of the essay teasing them all into speech. (If White's skepticism seems misguided here, remember that the IBM exhibit at the 1939 Fair was housed in a large building resembling a cash register.) The memoirist can hardly keep from thinking that these commercial dreamers have gone insane. Though the touchstone to test their vision remains, their voices are powerful, and White's protest has a wistful quality to it, especially today, when both the Fair's dream year, 1960, and George Orwell's nightmare year, 1984, have passed, and some of their prophecies have come true.

All along the way White searches for the carnival, the favored model of a fair that he trusts from experience. He wants to smell the cows that he sees behind the plastic screens, to see their shadows beneath them, not above, and to hear their sounds emanating from the right place. But he also wishes for the joy of music and carnival, and he gives the Fair's creators advice about how to restore noisy, even chaotic, pleasure to this Fair. A carnival is a productive model for an essayist, for it contains the loud and jangly multitude of society, bumping up against, eyeing and making commerce with each other, telling tall tales and drawing gazes aside with sleight of hand. No utopian, White distrusts the Fair's organizers and trusts the noisy customs that already exist in the United States, or that he remembers when he sits down to his work as memoirist.[13]

While longer and more complex than "The Age of Dust," "The World of Tomorrow" also employs dialogic materials through most of its pages, but closes much more innovatively. As in many of his essays, White ends with a sort of "capsule image," a sentence or short passage describing a scene or sketching some very brief anecdote. Because of experiences and voices that have prepared the way, the closing image encapsulates the tensions and social voices of the piece. It compactly represents the physical beings and the place where the essay's major themes intersect. At that intersection we can hear echoes of different social voices, remember the past and spot trends that may carry us into the future. Because White draws on both socially constructed knowledge expressed through social voices, as well as the more private knowledge of the individual's bodily life, both ideology and body come together in a capsule image, carrying meanings that look outward to society and inward to the individual. This makes the capsule image another contested or dialogic moment in the essay.

In the capsule image that ends "The World of Tomorrow," White describes a robot, a giant man, used together with some dancing girls to attract customers to one of the entertainments:

> At the start of each show, while the barker was drumming up trade, a couple of the girls would come outside and sit in the robot's lap. The effect was peculiarly lascivious—the extra-size man, exploring with his gigantic rubber hands the breasts of the little girls, the girls with their own small hands (by comparison so small, by comparison so terribly real) restrainingly on his, to check the unthinkable impact of his mechanical passion. Here was the Fair, all fairs, in pantomime; and here the strange mixed dream that made the Fair: the heroic man, bloodless and perfect and enormous, created in his own image, and in his hand (rubber, aseptic) the literal desire, the warm and living breast. (117)

The word "pantomime" here is a wonderful touch, for all the common and uncommon senses that have animated White's essay, both his own and those he is struggling against, have been brought into the bodies of these women and the robot. In this capsule image we reread the entire essay's contesting discourses and see again White's judgment against the Fair and its attempt at visionary commerce.[14] In a capsule image the concrete language that White praises and teaches in his old-fashioned way in *The Elements of Style* becomes an essential part of the dialogic form of his best essays.

Once it becomes clear that an essay's contesting discourses can be made to echo in concrete images, and that much of an essay's dialogue is created with and against various bits of a social common sense, then a further innovation appears. In some essays White manages to create capsule images and a dialogic structure even without quoting social voices. In "The Ring of Time," for example, White conjures several common senses of the passing of time—not something an essayist can readily quote—in order to make a political statement about racism.

In this essay White describes a chance encounter at the circus. When he visited the winter training headquarters of the Ringling circus, in Sarasota, Florida, he and other paying spectators came upon a practice session of a young, bareback rider. In this session an enchanting incident took place, and in the first half of the essay White struggles to describe it. In drawing our attention to his struggle as a writer, White sympathizes with the bareback rider's own struggle for artistry. He argues that the richest moments of life, the grace notes of its daily melodies, are personal and elusive, and he sketches some of the ensuing concerns of the artist. He tries to show, by analogy at least, what (he believes) the rider's efforts must mean to her. But he also tries to evoke two very different senses of time, one that White argues is common to the young and one that he holds in his later years. The first of these White believes the bareback rider feels as she takes her practice ride, since she is "too young to know that time does not really move in a circle at all. . . . She is at that enviable moment in life when she believes that she can go once around the ring, make one complete circuit, and at the end be exactly the same age as at the start" (145). In her bodily grace and ease White feels her confidence in time's enduring circuits.

This illusion is sustained by several things: the girl's youthfulness, her common sentiment of youthful immortality; the light generated by her own graceful and casual artistry, which creates the lovely circuit that time follows here; White's own artistry in recreating the circuit; and additionally, the fact that many human experiences are circular rather than linear, or at least they feel that way to us as we experience them in our bodies. As in "Once More to the Lake," the richness of physical experience as the seasons circle and move us through their displays is very seductive. This sense of time is made up of circuits that return each day and year, enveloping the body and teaching the mind what the body has known. But we commonly know time in another way as well, as a linear progression leading us into age. The first half of "The Ring of Time" evokes the charm of the first of these two senses of time and sustains it as long as possible, only to withdraw in the end and admit that the enchanting ride, the seemingly timeless event, has ended and the rider has left the arena. While the artist seeks to make something of her own artistry, to improve the golden moment, the present, and occasionally succeeds, time marches on relentlessly and sweeps away the youth's faith in the ring of time, the protected circle.

In setting one sense of time against another, White prepares readers for the second half of the essay. Not all anthologists publish both halves of the essay, and not all critics discuss the second part.[15] Some editors and critics have ignored the careful artistry of the whole piece by dealing only with the enchanting account of the rider, even though White published the two halves together as a single essay.[16] It is true that the first section about the rider does not at first glance relate to the second section, which is largely about the speed of racial changes in the South. In part two, White eases into his account of the general shape of things in Florida, by describing certain physical sensations and traits of the South: "the softness of its music" against its other "cruel and hard and prickly" traits (146). White chooses as an emblem of the South "a little striped lizard, flattened along the sharp green bayonet of a yucca, [wearing] in its tiny face and watchful eye the pure look of death and violence" (146). With well-publicized and representative events like the lynching of Emmett Till still fresh in White's memory as he wrote in 1956, a level of urgency supports his use of the lizard as a representative figure. Other public events of those years included the 1954 Brown vs. Board of Education decision that states could no longer offer "separate but equal" school systems that divided races, and Jackie Robinson's breaking of the race barrier in major league baseball. White not only alludes to these last two powerful events, but he borrows key words from the political debate surrounding racism to describe them. Though White's language is marked by the uncritical and outdated phrase, "colored people," he carefully notes the customs associated with race that he comes across during his stay in Florida. "Colored people . . . [do] turn up at the ballpark, where they occupy a separate but equal section of the left-field bleachers and watch Negro players on the visiting Braves team using the same bases as the white players, instead of separate (but equal) bases" (147). Similarly, White describes the Florida sunrise as "a triumph of gradualism," alluding to the demands of some conservatives to proceed very slowly with social changes meant to overcome racism. White uses these terms from the status quo and from the gradualist camp to link a sense of Florida's geography and natural history to its social patterns. The sunrise is especially gradual, White says, as is the society, and as a visiting Northerner, he chooses to "do as the Romans do" to the extent that he does not protest or object to anything he witnesses. Yet as he turns toward the end of the essay, at least in the form published before 1962, he challenges the "common sense" of time that he has noted in Florida's nature and culture. Though he is not as bold as his spiritual guide, Henry David Thoreau, who said that "one generation abandons the enterprises of another like stranded vessels,"[17] White claims that "the sense that is common to one generation is uncommon to the next" (148), and he returns to the sense of time that he had promoted, over the rider's enchanting artistry, in part one of the essay: the idea that "the only sense that is common, in the long run, is the sense of change, [though] we all instinctively avoid it, and object to the passage of time, and would rather have none of it" (148). In relating these two sections to each other, and depicting several conceptions of time—the youth's sense of immortality, the artist's illusion of a moment's perfect crystallization, the natural slowness of the sun and tides, the impulses of law and social action, and the urge to resist change, as well as the essayist's own sense of impending transience and change—White rather subtly undoes his earlier claim that he is "doing as the Romans do." Instead of challenging particular racist customs, as a more overtly political writer would do, White undermines a perhaps deeper psychological structure that he may instinctively judge to be a support for racist practices. The white Southern sense of time and its cousins that have appeared elsewhere in the essay are rebuked in the final paragraph: "But there is certainly a great temptation in Florida to duck the passage of time. Lying in warm comfort by the sea, you receive gratefully the gift of the sun, the gift of the South. This is true seduction. The day is a circle—morning, afternoon, and night. After a few days I was clearly enjoying the same delusion as the girl on the horse—that I could ride clear around the ring of day, guarded by wind and sun and sea and sand, and be not a moment older" (148). Here the key words bear the weight of the essay's realization about gradualism: it is a "temptation," then a "seduction," and finally a "delusion" to accept the circular motions of time in the South. One must not be deluded by the body, by Southern culture, or by an artist. Instead, one must accept what the law teaches: one must make over the culture so that gradualism no longer shines down, but law. One must undo the common sense of the whole place, with the help of the powerful voice of law.

But this essay does not rely much on the voice of law for its dialogic force. There are a few quotations, a few paraphrases here and there, but the main dialogic quality comes through the senses of time. In making a reader deal with common senses of time White personalizes the struggle for civil rights, especially for his particular audience. The *New Yorker*'s readership was probably largely white, and perhaps only white readers would need this roundabout approach. Only these readers might feel distant enough from racist events and their urgencies to need their sense of political time and the moral cost of gradualism challenged. White was speaking mainly to members of his own social class, then, as he sounded an alarm about gradualism in his final paragraph.

"The Ring of Time," then, is about two sections that reflect on one another, a point missed by anthologists who ignore the second part. In many different arenas of life, the essay argues implicitly, human beings are beset by their own urge to ignore time's passage, their urge to feel or be static. White urges that we not be fooled by the circle of time, which is an illusion, even though its circuits deepen and enrich our bodily knowledge of days and seasons, creating resources of power and knowledge that White taps in other of his works, such as "Once More to the Lake." Setting one illusion beside another, the rider's artful and youthful image of perfection beside the South's natural and social ritual of stasis, White creates a kind of *carpe diem* in prose. His own urgency at the decay of his body, the slipping away of his life, explicitly the topic of other pieces and present here in the urgent tone, serves as a moral touchstone, directing White through the political language, natural and artistic experience, to make these familiar rituals strange again and recover an outside perspective from which to see them anew. By tapping into the emotional base of *carpe diem*, White finds a point of connection between his undoubtedly somewhat shielded Northern white readers and the seductive Southern ways he reports. It is a masterful stroke of connection, grounding an appeal in one area of common sense at the cost or criticism of another.

Here, then, is the heresy Adorno called for in an essay. In "The Age of Dust," "The World of Tomorrow," and "The Ring of Time," White displays the power of a dialogic essay to represent the multiplicity of social forms, common senses, and individual voices that make up the life he has known. In setting certain voices in the unwanted company of others, White recovers some of the freshness of experience and insight that common sense and institutional voices deaden. When White recovers from common sense, he steps out of culture's unconscious and comes to his own senses, not merely because he is a master concrete stylist and a tough-minded individualist, but also because he understands the social practice of dialogue. He makes his essays sites where he can recover from overpowering social voices, from unexamined common sense, not merely to express himself, but as a way of creating himself. Because his essays are profoundly dialogic, they invite his readers to create themselves as well at the "boundary line between languages and styles,"[18] out of the jangle of society. Now that E. B. White has come to rest, he remains for readers a powerful voice that we must incorporate, with all his blemishes and graceful notes, as we create our own.

Notes

1. Donald Hall, *The Contemporary Essay* (New York: St. Martin's Press, 1984), 14.
2. Edward C. Sampson, *E. B. White* (New York: Twayne Publishers, 1974), 155–58.
3. Mikhail Bakhtin, *The Dialogic Imagination*, Michael Holquist, ed. (Austin: University of Texas Press, 1981), 308.
4. I refer mainly to Bakhtin's discussion, in *Dialogic*, of heteroglossia, the many-voiced characteristic of several genres that he suggests have been shaped by "novelistic prose."
5. Hartman's recent work on the essay is found in *Minor Prophecies: The Literary Essay in the Culture Wars* (Cambridge, Massachusetts: Harvard University Press, 1991). See, for example, 89 and 160.
6. Adorno's "Essay as Form," in *Notes To Literature* (New York: Columbia University Press, 1991), 3–23, contains his extended discussion of the social role of "heresy" in the essay. Other critics have written, in their own terms, of the problem of accommodation and heresy in the essay, including Richard Ohmann, who argued in an essay based on E. B. White's style manual that the uncritical character of some concrete prose styles leads to accommodating the status quo. See "Use Definite, Specific, Concrete Language," in *College English* 41 (1979): 390–97. Isaac Rosenfeld, in a review of White's political book, *The Wild Flag* in *Nation*, 28 Dec. 1946: 762–63), described tone itself as a marker of social class and a source of subtle allegiances that can be difficult for a writer to overcome. James Slevin also addresses the politics of style in "Reading (E. B.) White," in John Clifford and John Schilb, *Writing Theory and Critical Theory* (New York: Modern Language Association, forthcoming).
7. E. B. White, "Foreword," in *Essays of E. B. White* (New York: Harper, 1977), vii. Subsequent references to this volume will be indicated in parentheses in the text.
8. William Strunk, Jr. and E. B. White, *The Elements of Style*, 2nd ed. (New York: Macmillan, 1972), 74, 76.
9. Louis N. Ridenour, "How Effective Are Radioactive Poisons in Warfare," *Bulletin of the Atomic Scientists* 6–7 (June–July 1950), 199–202.
10. E. B. White, "The Age of Dust," *Poems and Sketches of E. B. White* (New York: Harper & Row, 1981). All references to this essay are from pages 187–88.
11. Bakhtin, 60.
12. Scott Elledge, *E. B. White: A Biography* (New York: Norton, 1984), 366.
13. Though Bakhtin also greatly admired the idea or image of the carnivalesque, his critics disagree about how much freedom the carnivalesque spirit actually offers its participants if they do not otherwise hold social power. This fair would also seem to raise that question, since its vision is so thoroughly shaped by its sponsors.
14. It is possible that White was even more disturbed by the image of the mechanical but disembodied voice in the essay's second-to-last paragraph. The mechanical replica of the human speech system hints, in a way that did *not* please White, of a cyborg-like future in which even the motor parts of the human body are subject to utopian construction.
15. This has been noted by other writers as well, including Carl Klaus, Chris Anderson, and Rebecca Blevins Faery, in their recent anthology, *In Depth* (San Diego: Harcourt Brace Jovanovich, 1990), 716.
16. See, for example, Sampson, 147: "The rest of the essay, when White turns to other matters, is not notable."
17. Henry David Thoreau, *Walden* (New York: Signet, 1960), 12.
18. Bakhtin, 60.

Forms of Imposture
in the Essays of E. B. White

RICHARD F. NORDQUIST

The identity of the essayist on the page is always and inevitably a textual construct—a mask, a persona, a rhetorical voice. In the essay, as in all writing, there is no unmediated expression, "no truly artless transfer of inviolable being to violable representation," as Harold Fromm has argued, "no mere sincerity or authenticity."[1] The familiar "I" of the essayist, then, is an artful figure that the reader is invited variously to adopt, complete, or counter. In essays spanning half a century, E. B. White forged a distinctively intimate and conciliatory textual self. Whether describing the ride of a young circus performer or the death of a pig, the exuberance of youth or the decline of a great city, White's persona customarily attempts to establish bonds of identification between self and subject as well as between self and reader. Yet paradoxically, the common bonds imposed by White's sympathetic textual self also signify the inherent disorders and divisions underlying his rhetorical world.

In his brief Foreword to the *Essays*, White comments on the many roles that an essayist may play. Entertaining the familiar metaphor of style as dress, he begins by celebrating the essayist's freedom to adopt "attitudes or poses": "he can pull on any sort of shirt, be any sort of person, according to his mood or his subject matter."[2] Nonetheless, citing Montaigne as a model, White argues in the next paragraph that "the one thing the essayist cannot do . . . [is] indulge himself in deceit or concealment."[3] This last remark echoes his admonishment in *The Elements of Style* to be sincere: to reject all stylistic "mannerisms, tricks, adornments" so that the "spirit" and "identity" of the writer are revealed.[4] In subscribing to such a transparent view of language, White fails to acknowledge that "plainness, simplicity, orderliness, [and] sincerity" are themselves stylistic traits that convey a particular "mood and temper."[5] Even clarity, as Roland Barthes maintains, "is a purely rhetorical attribute, not a quality of language in general, which is possible at all times and in all places, but only the ideal appendage to a certain type of discourse."[6] The essayist's "sincerity," in other words, must be well-practiced, his ingenuousness carefully crafted.

This essay was written specifically for this volume.

At one point in *The Elements of Style*, White does concede that style and meaning are ultimately inseparable: "Style has no such separate entity; it is non-detachable, unfilterable."[7] And yet, as Monroe C. Beardsley has demonstrated in his critique of White's style manual, "the logical implications of this thesis are seldom kept in view."[8] Advice such as "place yourself in the background," "do not inject opinion," and "use figures of speech sparingly" offers, not a way of revealing (or concealing) a "genuine" self, but rather a way of creating the impression of a self on the page.[9] "Taken together," George Roundy concludes, White's contradictory "prescriptions amount to a kind of stylistic recipe for achieving the 'unfilterable quality' that devices are not supposed to mask."[10] Thus, even in his personal correspondence, the writer is not a "nudist," as White once suggested; more accurately, he may be perceived as a rhetorical figure.[11] In fact, White's most perceptive comments on the fictive qualities of an author's persona appear in his response to a librarian who had recommended him as a model for children. "Writing is a form of imposture," he observed. "I'm not at all sure I am anything like the person I seem to a reader."[12]

To a remarkable extent, however, White's critics have generally made a habit of confusing his personal character with his literary persona.[13] In responding to his writing, readers have commended White for his "humanitarianism, gentle humor, and good sense"; his "basic honesty and wisdom"; "his humanity and modesty, the vitality and resilience of his approach to life, his sense of humor and balance, his common sense and uncommon insight."[14] White himself has attempted to explain the impulse behind such encomia: "[T]he man on paper is always a more admirable character than his creator, who is a miserable creature of nose colds, minor compromises, and sudden flights into nobility. . . . I suppose readers who feel friendly toward someone whose work they like seldom realize that they are drawn more toward a set of aspirations than toward a human being."[15] That "set of aspirations"— comparable to what Aristotle calls *ethos*—both forms and informs White's writings, contributing greatly to the coherent rhetorical community that he seeks to establish. A sympathetic narrator, White notes in *The Elements of Style*, helps the writer to "break through the barriers that separate him from other minds, other hearts—which is, of course, the purpose of writing."[16]

The strategies that White relies on to "break through the barriers" and establish a coherent rhetorical community are varied, but his most obvious method of constructing a compelling ethos is through direct self-characterization. By his own determination, he is "a mousy, faintly worried man," "a dreamy-eyed schoolboy," "a nervous little homebody in a sack suit."[17] Such self-deprecating epithets contribute to the image of a timid, idealistic, and mildly neurotic character, "bashful" and socially "backward."[18] Not surprisingly, the author's twin professions of writer and farmer are also his narrator's most common roles, though the writer disparages himself as "a middle-aged hack" and the farmer compares himself to "a little girl playing house."[19] In practice, these two roles are often conflated in White's writings, suggesting a blurring of two American comic types: the nineteenth-century figure of the cracker-barrel philosopher (the sensible and self-sufficient Yankee farmer) and the twentieth-century urban anti-hero (the perpetually frustrated and perplexed writer). As White remarks in the essay "Questionnaire," "Since I now lead a dual existence—half-farmer, half-literary gent—I [find] difficulty in making myself sound like anything but a flibbertigibbet."[20] In short, White customarily projects a version of "the Little Man," the comic type identified by Norris W. Yates as "an insignificant fellow who, however sure of his values, [is] bewildered by the facts."[21]

White's reliance on this bemused and benign comic type puts him in the company of such other literary humorists as James Thurber and Robert Benchley. In the view of Walter Blair and Hamlin Hill, these three writers share a common persona, "caricaturing themselves as ridiculous figures ill at ease in the complex modern world."[22] Like Thurber, White occasionally indulges in fanciful reveries: "There is hardly a waiting room in the East that has not served as my cockpit."[23] Likewise, White at times depicts himself as a comic victim and bumbler in the manner of Benchley: "The fact that my chimney was on fire did not greatly surprise or depress me, as I have been dogged by small and large misadventures for the past ten years, the blows falling around my head day and night, and I have learned to be ready for anything at any hour."[24] One of White's favorite words is "mess," a noun that well captures his recurrent sense of ineffectuality: "Quite aside from the mess my desk is in, everything else here in the east is in a mess, just as it is in other parts of the nation, and in all parts of the world."[25] Yet unlike Benchley, who commonly finds himself alone in a "mess" of his own making, the messiness in White's life is generally projected as symptomatic of disorder in the world at large.

In a number of significant ways, White is not primarily a humorist (a designation he disliked), and his persona is quite distinct from that of either Thurber or Benchley. He is rarely as hapless or neurotic as Thurber's men, never as vain, ponderous, or buffoonish as Benchley. Mild self-deprecation, rather than serving a comic end in itself, is generally a means of establishing rapport with his readers. In one of his final essays, "The Winter of the Great Snows," White sizes himself up as "amiable, honest, and impractical," and it is this combination of traits that invites—in fact, manipulates—an affectionate response from his readers.[26]

White's predominant rhetorical strategy resides in this effort to establish a sense of rapport with both his subjects and his readers. As defined by Kenneth Burke in *A Rhetoric of Motives*, it is the strategy of "identification," an approach that is intended to move an audience "from the factional to the universal": "[W]e might as well keep in mind that a speaker persuades an audience by the use of stylistic identifications; his act of persuasion may be for the purpose of causing the audience to identify itself with the speaker's interests; and the speaker draws on identification of interests to establish rapport between himself and his audience."[27] In White's essays, identification is an explicit strategy. By claiming points of resemblance and correspondence between his self-deprecating persona and his diverse subjects, White attempts to evoke a sense of universality. In general terms, the agonistic nature of classical rhetoric is superseded in White by a Rogerian rhetoric of compromise and cooperation.[28] Put simply, the dynamic of "us" versus "them" gives way to the spirit of community: "We are all in this together."

Nowhere is White more insistent on imposing such overt identifications than in his writings on Henry David Thoreau, his literary mentor and moral "conscience."[29] Thoreau is the subject of one short comic piece, "The Retort Transcendental," and two major essays, "Walden" and "A Slight Sound at Evening." In each of these works, White's effort to establish kinship with Thoreau—to locate a point of common ground—serves as both a key rhetorical strategy and a central theme.

In "The Retort Transcendental," White's persona is almost Thurber-like in his inability to sublimate an urge and contain a fantasy. In this case, the compulsion is to play at being Thoreau, as White illustrates the "danger in rereading a book, or rather in dipping frequently into the same book: the trouble is you begin to learn some of the lines."[30] His replies to a hostess, a headwaiter, his wife, and a pair of young visitors consist wholly of direct quotations from *Walden*. Such intertextual behavior, he suggests, is a result of identifying so closely with his subject: "More and more I find it difficult to distinguish clearly between what I am saying and what I might easily be saying." Yet this confusion arises not from some private neurosis, as would have been likely in a Thurber tale, but from disordered social conditions. "Maybe it's the times," White says vaguely, inviting the reader to participate in his comic dislocation.[31]

Similarly, in the essay "Walden," White implicitly compares his own "escape" to Maine from New York City with Thoreau's two-year retreat to the woods. Throughout his account of a pilgrimage to Concord in 1939, White mingles Thoreau's language with his own: "it appeared to me that the lawn was mowing the lady"; "a chance for some nature lover . . . to live deliberately, fronting only the essential facts of life"; "to improve the nick of time."[32] By this sort of mimicry, the two writers at times become almost indistinguishable in diction and tone. However, at the end of the essay, they are finally divided when White includes in his Thoreauvian expense account a baseball bat and glove for his son—"the kind of impediment with which you were never on even terms."[33]

This general pattern of persistent identification followed by climactic division also underlies the essay "A Slight Sound at Evening," a centenary celebration of the first publication of *Walden*. Characterizing Thoreau's "odd" book as "an invitation to life's dance," White suggests parallels between their occupations ("Even my immediate business is no barrier between us"), their work places (White's boathouse being "the same size and shape as [Thoreau's] own domicile on the pond"), and, most significantly, their central conflicts. "*Walden* is the report of a man torn by two powerful and opposing drives— the desire to enjoy the world (and not to be derailed by a mosquito wing) and the urge to set the world straight. One cannot join these two successfully, but sometimes, in rare cases, something good or even great results from the attempt of the tormented spirit to reconcile them."[34] Interestingly, White's analysis of Thoreau's divided temper closely resembles the self-analysis he offers in a *New Yorker* casual, "Heavier Than Air." "Our own earthbound life, we realize, is schizophrenic. Half the time we feel blissfully wedded to the modern scene, in love with its every mood, . . . bent on enjoying it to the hilt. The other half of the time, we are the fusspot moralist, suspicious of all progress, resentful of change, determined to right wrongs, correct injustices, and save the world. . . . These two characters war incessantly in us, and probably in most men."[35] Clearly, White's inner quarrels, as depicted in his essays, are less profound than Thoreau's. White is customarily perplexed rather than "torn," uneasy rather than "tormented."[36] And yet the sense of inner division to which he lays claim may explain, in part, his persistent urge to establish points of identification with his subjects. In "Heavier Than Air," the incessantly warring characters who represent his own conflicts also serve as tokens of identification with "most men." Invariably, though, the desire for communion is thwarted. In "A Slight Sound at Evening," White must ulti- mately distinguish himself from Thoreau—"a real hairshirt of a man"—even as he remains drawn to "his seductive summons."[37]

More surprising, perhaps, than White's habit of identifying with Thoreau are the personal links that he establishes with less obviously compatible characters. These range from letter-writers in a farm journal ("my brothers and sisters, dwellers in darkness") to a stranger who reportedly interrupted a chain letter and lost all that he had owned: "I felt a curious bond, instantly, with this unfortunate Mr. Nevin. I too am a chain breaker."[38] In the essay "The Summer Catarrh," White "experience[s] an acute identity with one of the major characters" of American history, Daniel Webster. Bound to the nineteenth-century orator through the common burden of hay fever, the narrator shifts back and forth from Webster's trials to his own, stressing connections between their "curiously parallel" lives and ailments. "I feel an extraordinary kinship with this aging statesman, this massive victim of pollino- sis whose declining days sanctioned the sort of compromise that is born of local irritation. There is a fraternity of those who have been tried beyond endurance. I am closer to Daniel Webster, almost, than to my own flesh."[39]

Although White once characterized "The Summer Catarrh" as "pure satire," it might be more aptly described as an extended comic conceit.[40] And yet the humor of this conceit (the equation of hay fever with failure as well as the comparison of White with Webster) is severely tempered—if not undermined—by its lyrical expression, particularly in the concluding paragraph. "Webster, even though he knew very little about the cause of hay fever, must have found, just as I have found, in this strange sensitivity to male dust and earth's fertile attitude a compensatory feeling—a special identification with life's high mystery that in some measure indemnifies us for the violence and humiliation of our comic distress and that makes up for the unfulfillment of our most cherished dream.[41] Rather than ultimately qualifying his identification with Webster, White intensifies this bond at the end so that a further identification—"with life's high mystery"—emerges as a consoling (albeit somewhat vague) theme.

More fanciful, but just as insistent, are the sympathetic bonds that White attempts to establish with animals. He identifies variously with the coon described in the essay "Coon Tree," with the fox in "A Report in January," with the nervous pup in "Coon Hunt," and with the old gander in "The Geese": "I felt very deeply his sorrow and his defeat. As things go in the animal kingdom, he is about my age, and when he lowered himself to creep under the bar, I could feel in my own bones his pain at bending so far."[42] Coming from the author of three books for children, such anthropomorphic identifications may not be surprising, though they can occasion "teeth grinding" in some of his adult readers.[43] Yet as White himself maintains, the "virulent sympathy" that he commonly exhibits toward animals is ultimately self-reflective—"a purely selfish, or turned-in emotion."[44] In one of his most celebrated essays, the mock-tragic "Death of a Pig," he ceremoniously observes that "the pig's lot and mine were inextricably bound." Though "the classic outline of the tragedy" is lost to "slapstick," the narrator ("a farcical character with an enema bag for a prop") is driven by a sense of shared misery and distress to meditate on his own mortality: "the pig's imbalance becomes the man's, vicariously, and life seems insecure, displaced, transitory."[45] In one sense, such identifications are merely a whimsical version of the essayist's traditional task of defining a world through a recognizable persona. In a more important sense, however, White employs the strategy expressly to define the values, beliefs, and anxieties of that persona. Indeed, as he observes in a *Wild Flag* editorial, "Most writers find the world and themselves virtually interchangeable."[46]

Throughout White's essays, therefore, patterns of identification frequently serve to reveal more about the narrator than about his subjects. In fact, one might say that the rhetorical process by which White asserts identification with his subjects mimics the process of self-construction in everyday life. The sense of self, Jacques Lacan maintains, is essentially narcissistic, fashioned through imaginary identifications with persons or objects in the world outside. For Lacan, Terry Eagleton reports, "[T]he ego is just this narcissistic process whereby we bolster up a fictive sense of unitary selfhood by finding something in the world with which we can identify."[47] Paradoxically, then, White's persistent efforts to establish identification foster an illusory unity that ultimately signals the inherent divisions of the narrating self.

Clearly, White's habit of affirming identification with a subject is not merely a whimsical fillip or a structuring device (though often it is both). More importantly, in Burkean terms, it is the dramatistic message of his essays, the rhetorical dance of a fictional narrator and his similarly contrived double—be it an orator, a pig, his son, Soviet Premier Khrushchev, or the New York World's Fair of 1939. And this persistent effort to affirm resemblances and impose a sense of unity finally serves as evidence of inherent differences and division. "Identification is affirmed with earnestness," Kenneth Burke maintains, "precisely because there is division. If men were not apart from one another, there would be no need for the rhetorician to proclaim their unity."[48]

The fragile nature of White's well-ordered textual world is sometimes revealed by the exceedingly facile connections he imposes between the immediate environment of his persona and the affairs of the world at large. In the war-haunted essays of One Man's Meat, for instance, his analogies are at times forced and puerile. In "Second World War," he awkwardly equates an increase in the cost of grain with Hitler's invasion of Poland, and he coolly compares the Third Reich to his own hen house: in each, he observes, "the individual must be sacrificed to the good of the whole."[49] In the essay "Fall," where he describes himself firing a Flit gun at angry flies, White sounds hopelessly adolescent in his effort "to maintain a decent pitch of indignation . . . about the war." Afraid that he "might bust" without an outlet for his "hate," White settles on a local target: "It is a source of relief, after listening to a radio broadcast, to take my .22 and go out to the barn to shoot a rat."[50] Throughout One Man's Meat, in the view of Norris W. Yates, White attempts to make the reader "feel the interrelatedness of the social and natural realms and the significance of that relatedness for the average man's fate."[51] But on occasion that relatedness is simply unconvincing, the significance unclear.

In The Implied Reader, Wolfgang Iser maintains that "'identification' is not an end in itself, but a stratagem by means of which the author stimulates attitudes in the reader."[52] Clearly, White's method of establishing rapport with his subjects through direct and sometimes implausibly forced identifications also fashions a role for his audience. In an essay sharply critical of White, Joseph Epstein observes that one of the "chief services performed by writers who project their own sensitivity . . . is that . . . they make their readers feel that they, too, are sensitive."[53] Although sensitivity (with its tendency to slide into sentimentality) is but one mark of White's persona, Epstein accurately characterizes the subtle process of identification that frequently links the essayist with his audience.

To maintain what he has described as the "invisible friendship" of author and reader, White frequently projects his values and experiences onto others through generalizations that tacitly implicate his readers.[54] At times this method of extension takes the form of a casual observation. "Practically everyone," he notes in "Some Remarks on Humor," "is a manic-depressive of sorts."[55] Likewise, in "The Years of Wonder," he comments that "Youth is almost always in deep trouble—of the mind, the heart, the flesh."[56] Frequently, he climaxes a discussion of a personal ordeal with a remark about "most people" or "all men." After a brief disquisition on the futility of keeping up with his "Incoming Basket," White decides that his experience, "in general, must be true of other people's lives, too. It is the reason lives get so cluttered up—so many things (except money) filtering in, so few things (except strength) draining out."[57] Similarly, in "Afternoon of an American Boy," he concludes his recollection of an awkward teenage date with this lyrical extension: "[T]here must be millions of aging males, now slipping into their anecdotage, who recall their Willie Baxter period with affection, and who remember some similar journey into ineptitude, in that precious, brief moment in life before life's pages, through constant reference, had become dog-eared, and before its narrative, through sheer competence, had lost the first, wild sense of derring-do."[58] This strategy of implicating the reader through extension is simply a way of inviting identification without appearing to impose it. As these illustrations demonstrate, the "universal" experiences that White projects—"depression," "deep trouble," the threat of "clutter," ineptitude—are commonly just the well-established traits of the White persona. One understands, then, White's comment in an interview that he seldom writes with an audience in mind: "It is as though they didn't exist."[59] In one sense, an essayist's readers cannot exist until the author creates a role for them through his persona. George L. Dillon has described this process as "imagining a reader": the essayist does not "attempt to approximate the knowledge and viewpoint of actual persons who might peruse the text"; rather, he "project[s] a self that readers will try on and find agreeable."[60]

The coherent rhetorical community that White attempts to evoke in his essays might be viewed as a literary response to what he believes is a fundamental human need. In the essay "Hot Weather," he characterizes that need by quoting newspaper humorist Don Marquis. "Don always knew how lonely everybody is: 'Always the struggle of the human soul is to break through the barriers of silence and distance into companionship. Friendship, lust, love, art, religion—we rush into them pleading, fighting, clamoring for the touch of spirit laid against our spirit.' "[61]

Therefore, we might view the complementary strategies of identification and extension as responses to this "struggle" as well as expressions of it. Immediately following the quotation from Marquis, in a rare, disruptive aside to his audience, White offers this definition of the reading experience. "Why else would you be reading this fragmentary page—you with the book in your lap? You're not out to learn anything, certainly. You just want the healing action of some chance corroboration, the soporific of spirit laid against spirit. Even if you read only to crab about everything I say, your letter of complaint is a dead give-away: you are unutterably lonely or you wouldn't have taken the trouble to write it."[62] Although surely White simplifies the diverse motives of his readers, this view of the reading process suggests a certain self-consciousness regarding his habitual efforts to evoke a community in his texts.[63] As Kenneth Burke maintains in *Attitudes Toward History*, "*Identification* is hardly other than a name for the function of sociality."[64]

Clearly, White's world is not always as "ordered" and "painless" and "nice" as certain critics have complained.[65] White's persona is commonly a divided figure, his world a disordered, even frightening place. In "The Door," for instance, he dramatizes the alienated state of modern man by comparing him to the white rat of an experimental psychologist: "All his life he had been confronted by situations which were incapable of being solved, and there was a deliberateness behind all this, behind this changing of the card (or door), because they would always wait till you had learned to jump at the certain card (or door) the one with the circle—and then they would change it on you."[66] William H. Rueckert has characterized "The Door" in Burkean terms as "that representative anecdote for our time."[67] In it, the only comfort that the nameless central character enjoys is the realization that he is "not the only one."[68] A similar moment of identification and extension marks the climax of White's short story "The Second Tree from the Corner." Overwhelmed by "bizarre thoughts," the main character makes ineffective weekly visits to a psychiatrist, who offers him nothing except occasions for sympathetic identifications. "Trexler found that he increasingly tended to identify himself with the doctor, transferring himself into the doctor's seat—probably (he thought) some slick form of escapism. At any rate, it was nothing new for Trexler to identify himself with other people."[69] But what begins as "escapism" serves in the end as a tentative cure: "Poor, scared, overworked bastard, thought Trexler. . . . Trexler knew what he wanted, and what, in general, all men wanted; and he was glad, in a way, that it was both inexpressible and unattainable."[70] As Jesse Bier has said of the White persona, "It is as if the slightly awry or neurotic response is the only human one left in a dehumanizing age."[71] Ultimately, the tonic for conflict, alienation, and disorder in White's writings is this rhetorical union of narrator and subject, the identification, however remote and indeterminate, of the White persona with "all men."

Clearly, that persona is forged, not found. White does not simply unleash a personal identity on the page; like other essayists, he fashions one. Thus, the textual character of E. B. White is literally an "impostor": a sympathetic figure imposing order, rapport, and a sense of community on subjects and readers alike. And in reading White's essays, we, too, are encouraged to assume a role and momentarily overcome estrangement through identification with a fellow sufferer in comic distress. Out of the "mess" of our lives, we may invite such imposture.

Notes

1. Harold Fromm, "Ethical, Rational, Poetical: What the Essay is Doing Now" *Georgia Review* 41 (Summer 1987): 435.

2. *Essays of E. B. White* (New York: Harper, 1983).

3. *Essays*, viii.

4. E. B. White and William Strunk, Jr., *The Elements of Style*, 3rd ed. (New York: Macmillan, 1979), 69.

5. *Elements*, 69–70.

6. Roland Barthes, *Writing Degree Zero*, translated by Annette Lavers and Colin Smith (New York: Hill and Wang, 1977), 58.

7. *Elements*, 69.

8. Monroe C. Beardsley, "Style and Good Style," in Glenn A. Love, ed. *Contemporary Essays on Style: Rhetoric, Linguistics, and Criticism* (New York: Scott, Foresman, and Co., 1969), 5.

9. In his study of John McPhee, George Roundy contends that some of White's contradictory prescriptions in *The Elements of Style* reflect the paradoxical injunctions of *New Yorker* editor Harold Ross: "Ross sought to keep the "information" his writers collected "pure," devoid of his writers' preconceptions, biases, points of view. At the same time, however, he asked for such qualities as wit and gaiety in their prose, qualities of stylistic self-expression that depend upon point of view, bias, self-revelation." To a great extent, White himself resolved this dilemma by imposing his own stylistic traits and textual self on the *New Yorker* as a whole. See "Crafting Fact: The Prose of John McPhee" (Ph.D. diss., University of Iowa, 1984), 65.

10. Roundy, 62.

11. *Letters of E. B. White*, ed. Dorothy Lobrano Guth (New York: Harper, 1976), 655.

12. *Letters*, 582.

13. Although numerous critics have praised White, few have subjected his essays to close examination. By characterizing White as "a natural writer" whose works demand no "expatiation," D. J. Enright typifies those readers who view the essay naively as a transparent, self-explaining genre: "[White] requires no mediator, for he comes complete with sustaining information, his symbols are so curiously close to what they symbolize." See "Laurel—or Brussel Sprouts" *Encounter* 50 (April 1978): 74. Interestingly, the author of a recent dissertation on White, Dale Everett Haskell, reaches a similar conclusion: "The works of Faulkner or Yeats may await critics who would illuminate the dark corner and interpret the artist's voice and vision; the *Essays of E. B. White* speak pretty well for themselves." For the most part, however, Haskell's own thoughtful study belies this observation. See "The Rhetoric of the Familiar Essay: E. B. White and Personal Discourse," (Ph.D. diss., Texas Christian University, 1983), 108.

14. Rhoda Koenig, "Books in Brief" *Harper's* (Feb. 1978): 90. Edward C. Sampson, *E. B. White* (New York: Twayne, 1974), 158. John Wesley Fuller, "Prose Styles in the Essays of E. B. White" (Ph.D. diss., University of Washington, 1959), 48.

15. *Letters*, 402.

16. *Elements*, 70.

17. E. B. White, *Every Day Is Saturday* (New York: Harper, 1934), 225. *Letters*, 261. *The Wild Flag: Editorials from the New Yorker on Federal World Government and Other Matters* (Boston: Houghton, 1946), 53.

18. *Essays*, 158.

19. *One Man's Meat* (New York: Harper, 1944), 78, 18.

20. *Meat*, 234.

21. Norris W. Yates, *The American Humorist: Conscience of the Twentieth Century* (Ames: Iowa State University Press, 1964), 315.

22. Walter Blair and Hamlin Hill, *American Humor from Poor Richard to Doonesbury* (New York: Oxford University Press, 1978), 438.

23. *Essays*, 205.

24. *Essays*, 7.

25. *Essays*, 71. Through the title character of his children's novel *Charlotte's Web*, White expresses similar thoughts about the "mess" of life: "We're born, we live a little while, we die. A spider's life can't help being something of a mess, with all this trapping and eating flies." See *Charlotte's Web* (New York: Harper, 1952), 164.

26. *Essays*, 59.

27. Kenneth Burke, *A Rhetoric of Motives* (Berkeley, University of California Press, 1959), 46.

28. Based on the work of psychotherapist Carl R. Rogers, Rogerian rhetoric seeks to eliminate the sense of threat or opposition in argument. "In using Rogerian strategy," Linda Woodson observes, "a writer would convey to the readers that they are understood, delineate the area where the readers' position is valid, and convince them that they and the writer share moral qualities and aspirations." See Woodson, *A Handbook of Modern Rhetorical Terms* (Urbana: NCTE, 1979), 53. While arguing that "this inclination toward compromise [may be] damaging," Bill Karis acknowledges "the need for collaborators to seek and establish an identification with each other if they are to communicate effectively." See Karis, "Conflict in Collaboration: A Burkean Perspective" *Rhetoric Review* 8 (1989): 114, 115.

29. *Essays*, 241.

30. *Poems and Sketches of E. B. White* (New York: Harper, 1983), 64.

31. *Poems and Sketches*, 64.

32. *One Man's Meat*, 65, 68.

33. *Meat*, 70.

34. *Essays*, 234, 238, 237.

35. *The Second Tree from the Corner* (New York: Harper, 1978), 118.

36. In his comparison of White with Thoreau, Edward L. Galligan contends that while lacking "Thoreau's intellectual brilliance," White "shares [Thoreau's] delight in the microcosmic and in sentences that combine low facts with high feelings while remaining wholly speakable." See Galligan, *The Comic Vision in Literature* (Athens: University of Georgia Press, 1984), 65.

37. *Essays*, 241.

38. *Meat*, 115. White, "One Man's Meat" *Harper's*, April 1940, 553.

39. *Meat*, 6, 7.

40. *Letters*, 515.

41. *Meat*, 8.

42. *Essays*, 67.

43. Koenig, 90.

44. *Essays*, 89.

45. *Essays*, 21, 20.

46. *The Wild Flag*, 134.

47. Terry Eagleton, *Literary Theory: An Introduction* (Minneapolis: University of Minneapolis Press, 1983), 165.

48. Burke, *Rhetoric*, 22.

49. *Meat*, 84.

50. *Meat*, 205.

51. Yates, 312.

52. Wolfgang Iser, *The Implied Reader: Patterns of Communication in Prose Fiction from Bunyan to Beckett* (Baltimore: Johns Hopkins University Press, 1974), 291.

53. Joseph Epstein, *The Middle of My Tether: Familiar Essays* (New York, Norton, 1983), 1983.

54. *Letters*, 402.

55. *Essays*, 224.

56. *Essays*, 195.

57. *Meat*, 9.

58. *Essays*, 161.

59. "The Art of the Essay: E. B. White," interview with George A. Plimpton and Frank H. Crowther, *Paris Review* 48 (Fall 1969): 84.

60. George L. Dillon, *Constructing Texts: Elements of A Theory of Composition and Style* (Bloomington: Indiana University Press, 1981), 163–64.

61. *Meat*, 71–72.

62. *Meat*, 72.

63. Even a simple inventory of White's major themes reveals the extent to which his rhetorical strategies so often coincide with his central beliefs. His resistance to change and the "dim degeneracy" of progress, for example, is based not merely on sentimentality but on a persistent fear that he is being disconnected from his own past (*Meat*, 29). Thus, he mourns the demolition of the Sixth Avenue El and old Grand Central Station, the decline of the Pullman car and of the mansions on Riverside Drive, the loss of the horse-drawn sleigh, the model-T, the iron stove, Moxie, and the one-room schoolhouse. To compensate for this habit of missing (evident even in his earliest writings), White indulges in "the habit of revisitation": seeking out things that apparently have not changed in order to affirm his identification with the past (*Poems and Sketches*, 4). And so, by taking a train journey or revisiting Cornell or (most famously) returning to the Belgrade Lakes in "Once More to the Lake," he can momentarily convince himself that, despite much evidence to the contrary, "beyond any doubt . . . everything was as it always had been, . . . the years were a mirage and there had been no years" (*Meat*, 199).

64. Kenneth Burke, *Attitudes Toward History* (Berkeley: University of California Press, 1959), 144.

65. Paul Fussell has commented disparagingly on "the folksy, coy, over-simplified, self-satisfied sound mastered by E. B. White," while Raymond Sokolov has characterized White as "the Fabergè of prose," whose "world is so ordered, so very much his own, that it leaves out the mess and clatter and pain of the real world." See Fussell, *Wartime: Understanding and Behavior in the Second World War* (New York: Oxford University Press, 1989), 170. See also Sokolov, "Sweet Reason," review of *Essays of E. B. White, Newsweek* (3 Oct. 1977): 42–43.

66. *Second Tree*, 77–78.

67. William Rueckert, *Kenneth Burke and the Drama of Human Relations*, 2nd ed. (Berkeley: University of California Press, 1982), 138.

68. *Second Tree*, 80.

69. *Second Tree*, 98.

70. *Second Tree*, 102.

71. Jesse Bier, *The Rise and Fall of American Humor* (New York: Holt, 1968), 239.

Index

♦